SPORTING FORDS

Other Titles in the Crowood AutoClassics Series

SPORTING FORDS

FORDS

CORTINA TO COSWORTH

The Complete Story

Mike Taylor

First published in 1992 by
The Crowood Press Ltd
Ramsbury, Marlborough
Wiltshire SN8 2HR

British Library Cataloguing in Publication Data

A catalogue record for this book is available from the British
Library.

ISBN   1 85223 601 9

Typeset by Chippendale Type Ltd., Otley, West Yorkshire.
Printed and bound in Great Britian by BPCC Hazells Ltd
Member of BPCC Ltd

Contents

Foreword

As most 'Sporting Ford' enthusiasts will know, Cosworth – the company I founded with my long-standing friend, Mike Costin, way back in 1959 – has enjoyed strong ties with Ford, almost from the day we first opened our doors. Indeed, it is a friendship I am very proud of and one which has stood the test of time.

From the early days, Cosworth set out to be second to none in the field of engine development. The culmination of our considerable hard work was an agreement with Ford in 1965 for us to undertake the DFV racing engine, a unit which I think transformed Grand Prix racing and, of course, the BDA which sprang from it and proved so successful in the Escort.

More recently, we have seen the development of a tohc version of the Ford Pinto engine for the Sierra RS Cosworth and, later still, the Escort, all of which stemmed from a private venture programme we at Cosworth put in hand back in the early 1980s. During a visit arranged by Stuart Turner for Jim Capalongo and Ed Blanch of Ford USA, our guests walked past the prototype 16-valve engine and a whole new chapter in Cosworth/Ford history began.

Mike and I are now both retired, although we find ourselves as busy as ever and keep in close contact. Our work together in setting up Cosworth and seeing it prosper gave us both enormous satisfaction but then we had a great team to help us. Moreover, our relationship with people such as Colin Chapman, Walter Hayes and Stuart Turner in creating a whole line of sporting Fords was invariably demanding but always enormously exciting.

Keith Duckworth
Buckby Folly
Northamptonshire

Introduction

Sporting Fords have always had a special fascination for me from an early age, because they have always represented cars developed for enthusiasts by enthusiasts, yet with the backing of all that a multi-million-pound-turnover company like Ford can contribute.

From the days when Mk I Zephyrs and Zodiacs fought hard-won battles on the snowy Monte Carlo rallies in the 1950s to the current, enormously exciting Cosworth Sierras and Escorts, Ford's competition cars have always attracted strong support from enthusiasts. Then there have been the collectable AV0 cars, SVE following on in the tradition of developing sporting saloons for the performance-minded buyer.

It is because sporting Fords encompass so much of what the enthusiast still demands from his motoring that researching and writing this book has been such fun. The people, the cars, the stories all made it so worthwhile. As for the photographs, The Crowood Press kindly arranged to have the majority of these supplied through the photographic library at the Beaulieu Motor Museum, while the remainder were supplied through the good offices of the Ford Photographic Department.

Finally, I must thank all those who were kind enough to help me in my research:

Jeremy Coulter; Mike Costin; Keith Duckworth; Tony Dron; Dacre Harvey; Walter Hayes; Dave Hibbin; Graham Kent; Tony Llyn-Jones; Jeff Mann; Barry Reynolds and Stuart Turner.

1 Starter's Orders

Sporting Ford enthusiasts have much to be proud of when they look back over the last thirty years. Seemingly without compromise, Ford have achieved continued success in what at first appears to be totally opposing aspects of the motor industry: mass volume sales in the fleet and private sectors of the market and a continued – and what might well be described as an unmatched – career in national and international motor sport. Over the years, Ford have demonstrated their supremacy in designing and building cars which have outstripped the opposition, both on the tracks and in the hard-fought world of rallying. Above all else, this almost unrivalled performance is a story of people (though Ford have long resisted the temptation to expose individuals to the limelight – better that success be associated with the team and the company). Over the next few pages we shall be meeting just a few of the very talented engineers and managers who have made sporting Fords work. They are people who have two things in common: they all love cars and love to see the name of Ford up there among the winners, where it belongs.

Within any large motor manufacturing company there is always controversy over the actual advantage to be had from active involvement in motor sport. Some argue that the rub-off benefit to fleet and volume sales in the dealer's showrooms from advertising race and rally victories is marginal. The counter argument, of course, is that while it *is* difficult to quantify sales through motor sport, it is the company's image that is the all important factor. And it is Ford's image and heritage that we must look at first as we investigate how it all began.

Remarkably, in 1993 the Ford Motor Company will celebrate its 90th birthday, for it was in 1903 that Henry Ford – along with an astonishing 57 other hopefuls all attempting to make their mark in the mushrooming industry of making cars – established his motor business. As it was, the majority of the other tiny firms were not to see the year's end, but Henry, his sights set on

expansion and export, succeeded with a handful of the first generation of Model A cars finding their way to England.

The legendary Model T was announced in 1908. Such was its success that production began in a converted tram factory in Trafford Park, Manchester, in 1911, where the cars were assembled from kits sent over from America. By 1927 over 16 million of these rugged, eccentric machines had been built in factories around the world.

The next car to emerge from Ford's production line was also called the Model A. A big car by European standards, with a 24hp engine, it was as modern in design as the Model T had been fundamental. By this time, Ford had paid some £167,695 for a 310-acre site of marshland east of London where a factory was in the process of being built – reputedly at a cost of £5 million (and that was in 1929/30, remember) – which would eventually become Ford's British headquarters: Dagenham.

Sadly, all too quickly things turned sour, with the boom years of the twenties becoming the depressed years of 1929, 1930 and

'Cortina to Cosworth', marking 23 years between the launch of these two sporting Fords. While early Lotus Cortinas were 'homologation specials' the Sierra RS Cosworth was anything but that.

The Model T of 1913, which was built on assembly line production, established Ford as a volume manufacturer.

1931. No sooner had the Dagenham factory opened its doors than production was limited almost totally to the manufacture of trucks. A desperate signal was sent to Henry Ford in Detroit saying that, if Ford UK were not to experience financial ruin, a new small car should be designed and built.

In December 1931, prototypes of this new model were being developed and in February the following year the car, known as the Model Y, was launched at a Ford exhibition held at the Royal Albert Hall. After considerable redesign work, production began in August setting the pattern for Ford cars which would last until 1959. It was powered by a side valve 933cc engine linked to a three-speed gearbox. Suspension utilized beam axles front and rear with transverse leaf springs and cable operated brakes.

Sales of the Model Y soon began to elevate Ford into the exclusive club of volume British motor manufacturers, the car's strength being its no-nonsense engineering. But sales began to decline as other makers saw the secret of the Y's success. So, determined not to be outdone, Ford slashed its price by an astonishing £100. By 1936 Ford were claiming 41 per cent of the 8hp and under sector of the market.

By the outbreak of war, Ford's factories spanned Europe and they found themselves supplying vehicles to opposing sides. With hostilities at an end, the ageing Henry Ford – he was a spritely 86 years young – handed over the running of the company to his grandson, Henry Ford II, and in September 1946 an International Division was set up to co-ordinate Ford's activities outside America.

Ford Model T production at Highland Park in 1913. Despite the primitive facilities there are clear similarities between this scene and modern flow-line manufacturing techniques.

In Britain, the Anglia appeared in May 1945 and was followed a month later by the larger four-door Prefect. It was powered by the famous 1,172cc side valve engine which, like its smaller sister, was linked to a three-speed gearbox. Suspension was transverse springs front and rear and it had cable operated brakes.

Although there were larger-engined cars in Ford's model line-up it was the Anglia and Prefect which won most friends. These cars were affordable and represented rugged reliability to a sector of the motoring public who had never before owned a car. But they were basic, even by the standards of the day. Consider the Anglia with its 1952 spec: with a compression ratio of 6.3:1, its tiny engine produced just 24.3bhp at 4,000rpm giving a

top speed of around 60mph (100kph). But bravery was a fundamental component in driving an Anglia at that speed. Its suspension produced pronounced roll on corners while the steering was vague and, with the car fully laden and travelling at speed, the cable operated brakes needed a hefty push to produce any reaction. In contrast, while the Morris Minor was certainly more expensive (£582 compared to just £489 for the Ford), the Cowley-built product had a 981cc overhead valve engine which produced 27.5bhp at 4,400rpm giving a top speed of over 60mph (100kph). With its hydraulic brakes, torsion bar front suspension and semi-elliptic leaf springs on the rear, the Minor was an altogether more refined vehicle.

The problem was that until the early post-

*The result of concentrated flow-line production was reached on 27 August 1946
when Ford's Dagenham plant produced its millionth vehicle, a 10hp Prefect.*

war period Ford's design engineering had been handled in Detroit. (Significantly, a young Patrick Hennessey had taken two styling proposals developed in Dagenham over to America for evaluation. Initially discarded, these proposals were eventually incorporated as face-lifts in the Prefect of 1939 while Hennessey himself rose to become Ford's UK Chairman.) A design engineering department was set up at Dagenham which would one day be responsible for designing Ford's UK-built cars. That situation, however, was some way off.

There had been a V8 saloon in Ford's British model line-up since 1932 (the cars being imported from Canada), although initially sales were never strong. Two years later Dagenham began assembly of two types of V8 car, the Model 48 and the smaller 22hp Model 60. In 1936 the 60 was replaced by the 62, which used almost identical coachwork but was powered by what appears to have been a rather unreliable V8 engine. Over a period of four years the crankshaft and cylinder block specifications were reconfigured almost continuously.

With a bold front end face-lift, the pre-war model 62 was launched in 1947 as the Ford Pilot and was fitted with a 30hp 3½-litre side-valve V8 engine. This drove a three-speed gearbox with column gearchange. Brakes were hydraulic on the front and mechanical on the rear. Maximum speed was reckoned to be over 80mph (125kph) with a 0–60mph (0–100kph) time of 21 seconds. It was the company's flagship and featured all the attributes for which Ford had become famous: rugged reliability, no-nonsense engineering and a price people could afford. Surprisingly, 22,000 of these V8s were sold (a 30hp V8 engine was, after all, considered large by European standards) during a period when petrol was still in short supply.

A two-door vehicle of Ford's small car range of 1946, the Anglia, which was powered by a 933cc sv engine producing 24bhp.

A Ford Pilot negotiates the Llandrindod Wells test during a sunny spell on the 1949 RAC Rally. With its sv V8 engine the Pilot often proved a successful rally contender.

A quick reference to any book which covers period international rallying will undoubtedly illustrate a whole host of the most unlikely cars decked out with extra lamps and rally stickers, leaning at impossible angles through Alpine bends. In those days, teams of drivers drove standard specification cars, often achieving the most remarkable results through sheer nerve, courage and driving skill: John Gott, Nancy and Bill Mitchell, Jack and Mary Richmond to name but a few. Ford's basic yet rugged engineering made their cars ideal contenders for this sort of event.

Indeed, Ford cars had been winning rallies for years – a Model 60 managed a first in the 1936 Monte Carlo Rally, while in the late 1940s Ken Wharton and Ken Reece were hired to compete in European events, the team gaining a remarkable victory in the 1949 Tulip Rally driving a SV Anglia. The following year they repeated the triumph in a Pilot and then won again the next year in a newly launched Consul; only the failure to get good marks in a driving test prevented them from making it four in a row!

'Jack Welsh and his partner worked miracles preparing the cars at Lincoln Cars which were based on the Great West Road, London under "Edgy" Fabris who handled both Ford's Competitions and Publications,' said Dacre Harvey who worked for Ford for many years. 'In fact, as an amateur I had a very real reason to be thankful to Jack who was always very supportive, innovative and versatile when I was preparing to compete myself.' (Indeed, rumour has it that when Walter Hayes joined Ford from *The Sunday Dispatch* to take over PR, he asked Fabris to outline his job description. In reply, Fabris said he ran publications and competitions. On enquiring what 'competitions' actually consisted of, Fabris replied, 'finishing publications sufficiently early in the year that it permitted them to take part in the annual Monte Carlo Rally!')

As the 1940s drew to a close it became clear that Ford needed a new top-of-the-range series of models if they were to stand any chance in the quickly expanding international market. Fundamental features such as overhead valve engines, independent front suspension systems, full-width body styling and monocoque body shell structures represented the latest in automotive development trends, all of which were being used to good effect in the newest offerings from major manufacturers such as Austin, Morris and Standard-Triumph. The key was to bring together these latest innovations in a sleek new model at an attractive price.

In 1948 a team from Ford, Dagenham went to the parent company's Detroit headquarters in America for discussions on what form the new cars should take. Ford US were heavily committed to a new model programme, although the size and concept of these cars were clearly directed at the USA market, thereby making them somewhat unsuitable for the British buying public. That said, it seems that the discussions between the British and their American counterparts were cordial and the British team headed back to Dagenham pleased that they had been given the green light to develop a new four-door model range. (Significantly, it was to be the first time the Dagenham Design/Development Department would be allowed a free hand to produce a new car without influence from Ford US.)

Fundamental to the decision to use a monocoque-type body shell structure was the intention to fit a revolutionary new suspension unit designed by American Ford engineer, Earle MacPherson. Known as the 'MacPherson strut', the basis of the unit was a long upright to which the hub carrier was attached, the upright locating with a vertically operating telescopic damper unit, the damper itself being surrounded by a coil spring. The upper locating point was housed in the inner wing panel while the bottom of the unit was held in place by wishbones, aided by an anti-roll bar. Since the downward-acting force of the car's weight was directed at the upper locating point of the strut, the load could be satisfactorily spread across a large area of the body shell, thereby obviating the need for a conventional chassis frame.

The idea for a monocoque body shell, of course, was not new, but from a manufacturing standpoint it made production methods much cheaper since it was no longer necessary to make a separate chassis frame structure of large-section tubing. On the new Fords the subframes and suspension pick-up points could be formed as part of the overall shell and welded up as one integral unit.

Engine-wise, the designers decided upon a short stroke configuration with a dimension of 3.12in × 2.9in (79.37mm × 76.2mm) which in four cylinder form produced a capacity of 1,508cc and in six cylinder form a capacity of 2,262cc. Moreover, the units would be of overhead valve layout, the two engines sharing many common components which, again, helped to keep down manufacturing costs. Both models had three-speed gearboxes operated by one of the better column-mounted gearchanges.

Production of the four cylinder model, known as the Consul, began at Dagenham in January 1951. The six cylinder Zephyr followed on soon after, albeit in limited numbers to start with, since it was felt that the smaller-engined car was more appropriate for the still struggling British economy of the early 1950s. Top speed on the Consul was rated at 75mph (120kph) with a 0–60mph (0–100kph) time of around 27 seconds, while its bigger-engined sister could muster a full 81mph (130kph) in top flight and a 0–60mph (0–100kph) time of 19 seconds. Both these performance profiles were considered most creditable at the time. What these figures do not convey, however, is the general 'unburstability' of the all-new ohv power units, overall handling, and braking, factors which made the new Fords ideal contestants on the hard-fought battle grounds of international rallying, where

reliability rather more than outstanding performance was the key to success. Moreover, the decision to utilize MacPherson strut independent front suspension was also a significant factor in providing the cars with a level of roadholding which far outstripped anything Ford had hitherto produced, while the unitary monocoque construction technique gave the Consul and Zephyr a level of integral strength which was ideally suited to the tremendous body shell stresses imposed under prolonged rallying conditions.

'I don't think that competition featured anywhere in the minds of the designers of the Mk I Zephyr, although the MacPherson front suspension did give the car relatively good handling compared to the competition from other cars of the day,' continued Dacre Harvey. 'But the big fault with the Mk I cars was the weight distribution (59:41) which encouraged many people to carry heavy loads in the boot in an attempt to counterbalance this heavy front-end concentration.'

Proof that Ford's Prefect had a high centre of gravity which made it a handful in competitive motor sport. The scene here is the 1952 Brighton Rally although little harm seems to have been done!

Performance Figures

	Zephyr Zodiac Saloon Mk I (Manual)	Zephyr Zodiac Saloon Mk II (Automatic)	Zephyr Zodiac Saloon Mk III (Manual)
Bore:	79.37mm	82.55mm	82.6mm
Stroke:	76.2mm	79.5mm	79.5mm
Capacity:	2,262cc	2,553cc	2,553cc
Power:	71bhp at 4,200rpm	85bhp at 4,400rpm	109bhp at 4,800rpm
0–30mph	5.4 sec	6.2 sec	4.2 sec
0–40	–	–	6.6 sec
0–50	13.5 sec	14.3 sec	10.0 sec
0–60	20.4 sec	20.9 sec	13.5 sec
0–70	29.4 sec	31.6 sec	18.0 sec
Max speed	Top 84mph	Top 84.6mph	Top 100.3mph
	2nd 54mph	Int. 54mph	3rd 80mph
	1st 31mph	Low 29mph	2nd 51mph
			1st 35mph
	The Autocar 1955	*The Autocar* 1958	*The Autocar* 1962

'The problem was that in the early days when people were beginning to think in terms of setting up a competitions department, those who were in favour could not bang on the table very loudly. There was always a battle in Ford between those who campaigned for a budget to prepare cars for racing and rallying because they said it boosted sales and those who considered that the company sold cars on the strength of its name and the additional competition budget couldn't be justified. The only time I recall when this philosophy was thrown overboard was when Henry Ford, for purely personal reasons, was out to get his own back on Ferrari by winning at Le Mans after he had been shown the door when he tried to buy the Italian-based company. That programme had no financial strings placed on it whatsoever!'

In 1952 a team of Zephyrs was prepared for the tough Monte Carlo Rally. Regulations governing this event precluded modifications to the mechanical specification of the cars and a solitary Zephyr managed to finish in twentieth position overall. It was an unremarkable start to a promising rally career.

However, in 1953 Maurice Gastonsides and Peter Worledge avenged the previous year's performance by gaining an outright victory, the only modifications to the car being the addition of a rather large anti-glare shield attached to the front of the bonnet and the fitting of a comprehensively equipped dashboard and a luxurious, reclining passenger seat to enable the co-driver to relax when the opportunity arose.

From the 1951 introduction of the ohv four cylinder Consul and six cylinder Zephyr engines, Ford were to learn a great deal about engine design and what areas proved weak under the prolonged stresses of competition. The short stroke dimensions produced a strong unit since the crankshaft throw was proportionally small, thereby helping to keep down vibration.

To complement the top-of-the-range Consuls and Zephyrs, Ford introduced, in 1953, a

A smiling Maurice Gastonsides and Peter Worledge on the bonnet of the 1953 Monte Carlo Rally winning Zephyr.

new range of small saloons: the Anglia and Prefect. They were boxy models (almost a Consul in miniature) which used the same unitary body construction as the bigger cars and shared the same suspension arrangement: MacPherson struts on the front and a solid rear axle with semi-elliptic leaf springs. However, unlike the ohv Consuls and Zephyrs, the 100E Anglia and Prefect had the same 1,172cc side valve engine of Ford's previous small cars, updated admittedly, but still driving a three-speed gearbox with floor-mounted gearchange.

To be sure, handling, ride and performance were all a great improvement over their predecessors. Nevertheless, Ford persisted in making small cost savings, an example being the vacuum-operated windscreen wipers which tended to slow almost to a stop under full throttle acceleration! A whole range of cars was offered including two- and four-door saloons as well as cheeky little estate versions. 100Es could also be found locked in battle in many areas of motor sport (a team of cars took part in the

1956 East African Safari Rally winning a class award). Tuning companies began offering conversion kits while Peter Gammon even raced a 100E van!

In 1954 Zephyrs managed a third overall and first in the Saloon Car category in the RAC Rally, while Consuls won the 1301–1600cc Touring Car category of the Dutch International Tulip Rally and the Scottish International Rally. (A Zephyr took the 1601–2600cc Touring Car category in the same events.)

Meanwhile, on the home market front, Ford had signed a contract with Carbodies for the development of a very attractive two-door convertible version of the Consul and Zephyr. However, rather drastic modifications had to be made to the body shells including additional crossbracing welded to the floorpan in order to create the necessary rigidity for the sleek two-door bodies. Then, for the buyer who demanded luxury in his motoring, a top-of-the-range Zephyr Zodiac was introduced in 1953, the new model being instantly recognizable by its two-tone paint finish. Among the items fitted as standard were twin spot and fog lights, a reversing light, whitewall tyres, chrome wing mirrors, woollen cloth headlining, an electric clock and a heater. To overcome the extra weight, the compression ratio had been increased to 7.5:1 which boosted the engine's output to 71bhp at 4,200rpm.

In 1954, a firm of Farnham coachbuilders, E. D. Abbott, exhibited a very practical-looking estate version of the Zephyr on their stand at the London Motor Show. The boot lid had been removed and it had new panels with side windows welded in place. At the rear, a side-opening door provided easy access to the estate platform. The conversion met with Dagenham's approval and customers could order a new car with an Abbott estate body fitted to it. Indeed, Ford's range of Consul, Zephyr and Zodiac vehicles (affectionately known as the 'Five Star Cars' because of the five stars on their body

A Ford Anglia and Zephyr during the 1954 RAC British International Rally.
The Anglia was powered by a 1,172cc sv unit which was tough and reliable,
ideal in rally conditions.

A 1954 top-of-the-range Zodiac competing in one of the driving tests on the 1954
RAC Rally. A Zephyr Six finished first overall.

The Mk I Consul could also be made to perform well in the face of stiff opposition, seen here fighting off a Bristol 403, in the International Trophy Race at Silverstone in May 1955.

badges) was very comprehensive. In addition, a number of tuning companies began to offer equipment for improving performance. One of these companies was Laystall Engineering who offered kits for both the four cylinder and the six cylinder engines; the latter giving a 0–60mph (0–100kph) time of just 13 seconds and a maximum speed of 98mph (158kph)! Another, Raymond Mays, was more adventurous and utilized a six-port alloy cylinder head and twin SU carburettors. This more extreme modification resulted in a true 100mph (160kph) top speed. Hand in glove with these considerable increases in speed capabilities was the suggestion that the car be fitted with a Laycock de Normanville overdrive unit which raised the gearing from 16.1mph to 20.7mph (25.9kph to 33.3kph) per 1,000 revs in top gear, making high-speed cruising much more relaxed.

As for the rally scene, Mk I cars were still hard at it with a Zephyr Six coming fourth overall in the 1955 Monte Carlo Rally.

A Ford Anglia leans heavily into a bend during the B.O.C. hillclimb at Prescott in July 1955.

A 1945 Thames van in action during September 1956 at Silverstone showing how enthusiasts could have great fun at little expense.

A 100E Thames van at Brands Hatch in June 1956. People such as Peter Gammon had many successes in just such a vehicle. Note the additional roll bar at the front.

Zephyrs also finished first, second and third in the 1301–2600cc GT Car category of the RAC International Rally. They also finished first and third in the 1301–3500cc Special Series category, while a Consul came a well-placed second in the same section of the Dutch International Tulip Rally. Finally, a Zephyr Six triumphed overall in the tough East African Safari Rally, also winning the Lady McMillan Trophy Ladies Prize.

A measure of Ford's success in the marketplace with the UK cars can be gauged from the production figures; in 1954 some 49,893 Consuls were built, this number increasing to 55,226 the following year. As for the Zephyrs and Zodiacs, 49,294 cars were built in 1954 and 50,950 in 1955. Without doubt, the new range of post-war, top-of-the-range Fords had done much to revive the company's credibility in the eyes of the British buying public, while the cars' undoubted success on the world's rally stage had created an enviable sporting image. In fact, one magazine (with, perhaps, just a little poetic licence) referred to them as 'an impoverished gentleman's Aston Martin'.

With production of the Mk I Consuls, Zephyrs and Zodiacs in high gear, Ford's stylists and designers immediately got down to the job of working up proposals for the next generation of models. Basically, Ford had 'got it right' with the Mk I cars; their unitary construction, independent front suspension, performance and overall 'style' met with a favourable response from the buying public and motoring press alike. The replacement models had to be even better.

One improvement, though, which could be made would be to give the Mk IIs more interior room so that they would be regarded as true 'six-seater' cars without in any way upsetting their general good handling. To accommodate this the overall width was increased by 5in (12.7cm) and the length by a substantial 7in (17.8cm). Integral to this new body shell design was considerable alteration to the basic sill structure configuration to account for the greater length which, in turn, improved torsional rigidity.

Significantly, while the Mk II cars were considerably bigger all round than their predecessors, the sleek line of the Mk II range carried it off without making the cars look in any way overbearing or bulbous. The man responsible for the Mk II styling was designer Colin Neale, son of Eric Neale who was Chief Engineer of Jensen Motors Limited.

Sales of the Mk I cars had shown that there was a very significant market for both convertible and estate versions, so the Carbodies-made soft-tops and Abbott-built estates were carried over into the new range. Suspension-wise, the Mk II cars retained the same MacPherson strut-type independent front suspension set-up with a beam axle and leaf springs at the rear. As for the brakes, for the time being they

remained drum type all round but were given the benefit of larger shoes. To cater for the larger, heavier bodies the four and six cylinder engines were increased in size to 1,703cc and 2,553cc units which in turn produced 59bhp and 85bhp respectively at 4,400rpm. (No doubt the increase in engine size for the Zephyr and Zodiac units was with at least half an eye on the fact that automatic transmission was to be offered shortly after the Mk IIs were launched.) As for the three-speed gearbox, the original ratios were retained but the final drive gearing was changed so that, in the case of a Zephyr or Zodiac fitted with the optional Borg Warner overdrive, cruising was remarkably long-legged and relaxed at a tall 26.4mph/ 1,000rpm (42.2kph).

That the Mk II was to prove as successful (if not more so) as the Mk I on the international rally scene is shown by the impressive list of wins and placings. In 1956, the very year the Mk II was introduced, two Zephyrs won Coupe des-Alpes in the notorious Alpine Rally with first and second in the 2000–2600cc category. In 1957 they won the team prize and the Ladies prize in the Tulip. However, by the following year the Ford team had really got into their stride with a first in the Over 2-litre Touring Car category of the 'Monte', another first in the Over 2-litre GT Car class of the RAC and a very commendable overall win in the rugged East African. Ford Zephyrs were taking the Team prizes, too! Then came another first in the 1601–2600cc Touring Car class of the Scottish and, to finish off the year, a Coupe des-Alpes and a first and second in the over 1600cc Touring Car category of the Alpine Rally. Phew!

'In the Mk II, Ford had produced a car which was considerably more rigid in its body design and it was possible to increase the engine's power and torque by 50 per cent without it having any detrimental effect on the body shell,' said Dacre Harvey. 'Moreover, with the introduction of disc brakes, here at last was a Ford in which one could take full advantage of the performance. In full rally trim a Mk II Zephyr with three up, four spare wheels and tyres and a complete tool kit would weigh perhaps 30cwt. The front suspension was changed for the up-rated-type struts used on the automatic version and, with bound export rear springs and Koni dampers, the car was capable of out-handling a Citroen DS 19.'

In 1959 Ford introduced a revised body called the 'Low Line', which incorporated a softer styling to the roof section. There were more changes to the brightwork and inside the car the trim was changed to include a square profile housing for the instruments, which were located in a crushable fascia.

That year the Zephyrs really showed the opposition their true metal. In the East African they won second and third position overall and the Team Prize, while they managed a third overall and first and third in the 1601–2600cc Touring Car category, as well as the Team prize in the Tulip Rally. As if this was not enough, Mk IIs took three Coupe des-Alpes, the Team prize and the first three places in the Over 2-litre category for Touring Cars in the Alpine, with outright winner in the RAC International, Jeff Uren taking the Cup in the BRSCC Saloon Car Championship. (Ford's top-of-the-range Zephyrs and Zodiacs were to continue in production through the Mk 3 and Mk 4 series until 1971. On international rallies the Mk 3s proved worthy – if cumbersome – contenders, while the Mk 4's competition career was eclipsed by the world-beating Cortinas and Escorts.)

However, while Ford were notching up an enviable list of rally wins, they realized that if their image and product profile were to remain competitive in the 1960s their small 'economy' saloons would have to be replaced by something which was both more aesthetically pleasing and more mechanically refined; side valve engines were no longer acceptable – nor were three-speed gearboxes, despite the competitive price tags.

The result of this market research and engineering development was the Anglia 105E which was launched in 1959. It was a compact four-seater clothed in a sleek two-door body with an intriguing forward-sloping rear window. Suspension-wise, there were the familiar MacPherson struts at the front while at the rear was a well-controlled solid axle with semi-elliptic leaf springs. Although the 105E engine was an ohv unit like its Consul/Zephyr sisters', it was, in fact, an all-new unit with considerably over-square dimensions of 3.18in × 1.9in (80.97mm × 48.41mm) which gave a capacity of 997cc. Its efficient design made the best use of the cylinder head, camshaft profile and carburation design such that it produced a healthy 39bhp in a fairly tame state of tune. But its specification meant that it was not long before the tuning wizards were extracting quite indecent amounts of power. (Witness the antics of the Broadspeed Anglias which we discuss later.)

Another significant improvement over the earlier 100E models was the use of a smooth-acting four-speed gearbox with synchromesh on the top three ratios. Speeds in the gears were reckoned to be 19mph (30.5kph) in first, 33mph (53kph) in second and 61mph (98kph) in third with a maximum speed of 76mph (122kph).

Moreover, the car's good aerodynamics and efficient engine design meant that the 105E was also a great deal more economical than its predecessors. It was also a much safer-handling car than ever the early Anglias and Prefects had been, both in the hands of the motoring novice and the race expert. It was the start of a new generation of Fords which would develop into the Escort with its exciting Twin Cam and RS derivatives.

Shortly after the introduction of the 105E Anglia with its 997cc engine, Ford launched a 1,340cc version of the same unit, the larger capacity resulting from the use of a longer stroke (increased to 2.56in (65.07mm))

A top-of-the-range Prefect De Luxe. Sometimes thought of as a mini Consul,
rugged engineering and reliable, cheap motoring made Ford's products
attractive to a large section of the motoring public.

accommodated in the same 7.25in (184.15mm) deep cylinder block. The reason for introducing this unit was that it was to power a new mid-range group of cars known as the Consul Classic together with its sporty, two-door, fixed hard top coupé sister called the Capri. Although these models were developed by an in-house styling team at Dagenham, the cars exhibited a marked Detroit influence and it is generally agreed that both the Classic and the Capri were somewhat over-weight for their size. Almost from the day they were launched it seemed that Ford had made a mistake: the Classic/Capri models were expensive to manufacture and the 1,340cc engine was nowhere near as smooth and free-revving as the 997cc unit.

The importance of the new Anglia in the evolution of Ford's model range should not be under-estimated. With its sleek body styling, compact 1-litre ohv engine and four-speed gearbox it was a wholly new Ford-designed car. Significantly, the Anglia's Project Engineer, Fred Hart, was to go on to co-ordinate another very successful car to emerge from Ford – the Cortina.

(Ford Detroit had, indeed, produced a proposal for a medium-sized saloon which would feature front-wheel-drive and a V4 engine. The design was sent to Ford Germany for finalization but was thought by Ford UK's then boss, Sir Patrick Hennessey, to be too complex a vehicle for manufacture in Britain.)

Together with Terrence (later Sir Terrence) Beckett, who acted as Product Planner for the Cortina, Hart pushed the project through in very quick time. In 1962, just 21 months after the green light was given, the car emerged as the Cortina. The shape was produced by the British Ford styling studios under the leadership of Roy Brown. Fundamental to

Silverstone, October 1961, and a 105E Anglia gives an Austin A40 some stiff opposition. The Anglia's short stroke engine made it an ideal unit for race tuning.

the car's design was that it carried no excess weight and used a substantial number of components which were common to other existing Ford cars. Considerable thought, too, had been given to adopting simple technology in order to make servicing particularly easy and cheap.

Such a tight schedule meant that the whole project had to be rushed through at high speed, allowing little time for problem-solving. A total of 20 prototypes were built to ensure that development pitfalls were kept to a minimum. High-speed tests were carried out at Boreham's test track, while pavé and cold condition evaluation analysis was done in Belgium and Finland. The cars were even taken to Africa for testing over rough terrain. (Ironically, they would later return to take part in the gruelling East African Safari Rally where the Cortina truly showed its worth.)

Initially, the power unit for the Cortina was to be a three-bearing 1,198cc unit based on the 997cc Anglia engine but with a 2.29in (58.2mm) stroke. Output was rated at 49bhp which would give the car a maximum speed of around 75mph (120kph). Known as the 'Kent' family of engines, development of these units was in the capable hands of Alan Worters. As mentioned already, tests with the 1,340cc 'Classic' engine had indicated that the unit was not satisfactory at high revs so work began on a larger, 1,498cc unit which featured a five-bearing crankshaft. To

A 1966 Lotus Cortina in 'Special Equipment' trim which meant a more powerful engine (115bhp) using different camshafts and carburettor chokes.

accommodate the 3.18in × 2.86in (80.97mm × 72.75mm) capacity the cylinder block had been increased in depth by 0.66in (16.7mm). Power was rated at 60bhp at 4,600rpm, sufficient to give the Cortina a maximum speed of 80+mph (130kph), reckoned by the motoring magazines to be good for its class.

The faith of Ford's management in the Cortina programme was fully vindicated for in just four years of manufacture the car sold over 1 million units in all its forms against stiff opposition, particularly from the BMC 1100 range. Right from the beginning, sales outstripped the Classic and this model, together with the two-door Capri coupé version, was quietly dropped, along with the 1,340cc engine.

In fact, 1962 was to be a significant year in Ford's history for an entirely different reason

in that it saw the arrival of Walter Hayes, a man whose name is closely linked with all sporting Fords and who will feature significantly in this book.

'When I left the RAF in 1945 I went straight into journalism and was lucky enough to get an editorship when I was 32,' explained Hayes to the author recently. 'But by 1961 I was becoming increasingly disenchanted with Fleet Street, so when Sir Patrick Hennessey invited me to join Ford I was happy to accept.' The job which Hayes accepted was to head up a new function called 'Public Affairs' reporting directly to the Chairman, Hennessey. 'I think the significance of the Cortina has been largely overlooked,' remarked Hayes candidly. 'In the 1950s car ownership was mainly for the rich and well-off. The remainder of the population could not afford cars. The Cortina was the first car which said to the masses, "Here is a car of ample size and adequate interior space, a car which will do the same for you as a big car but you can have it at your price". That was the genius of its success. Also, it more or less pioneered the concept of the sporting derivative.'

It did not take the astute Hayes long to realize that if Ford were going to succeed at all in the mushrooming car market their products had to have extra appeal, and above all appeal to the young for it is they who, in Hayes' opinion, increase car markets.

'When I got to Ford I began talking to people such as rallyist Tommy Wisdom and it soon occurred to me that down nearly every side street there was a Ralph Broad or an Alan Mann trying to get into racing,' continued Hayes. 'When I was Editor of *The*

Sunday Dispatch I looked around for someone who was bright and great and famous to write a column on motorsport. The man I hired was Colin Chapman and while he would never have made a journalist, it sparked off a friendship which was of great value in importance.'

The story of how Hayes contracted Chapman to develop a competition version of the newly launched Cortina is now legendary; it was to be powered by a Ford-based engine featuring a special tohc cylinder head developed around drawings produced by *The Autocar*'s Technical Editor, Harry Mundy. The car was to be very much an 'homologation special' with lightweight alloy body panels and a modified rear suspension arrangement (which, while giving the all-white saloons impressive roadholding on tarmac, produced headaches on rough stage rallies!).

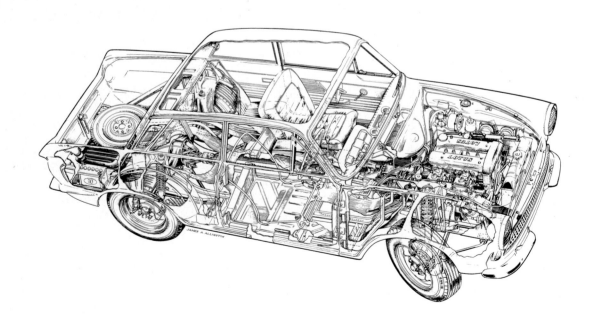

One of James Allington's cut-away drawings showing the layout of the Lotus Cortina. Note the 'A' bracket rear suspension with its coil spring/damper units.

Lotus Cortina Date Profile

January 1963	:	Lotus Cortina launched in two-door body style only available with white coachwork and green side stripe. Alloy bonnet, boot lid and doors. Interior spec. includes new dashboard, Lotus steering wheel, padded central console and new front seats. Powered by 1,558cc 3.25in × 2.86in (82.6mm × 72.75mm) engine producing 105bhp at 5,500rpm. MacPherson strut front suspension with coil spring/damper units at the rear with 'A' bracket and trailing arms. Worm and peg steering.
June 1964	:	Gradual phasing out of alloy panels in favour of steel. Special alloy gearbox and differential casting replaced by 'standard' items. Split prop. shaft introduced and 'Lotus'-type gearbox with high 1st gear replaced by Cortina-type gearbox with uprated 2nd gear.
October 1964	:	Lotus Cortina now available with Cortina 'Aeroflow' ventilation.
June 1965	:	'A' bracket rear suspension set-up replaced by conventional leaf springs and upper radius arms. Special Equipment model available with 115bhp engine, SP41 tyres, safety belts and adjustable dampers.
October 1965	:	Change to 2000E-type gearbox. Special Lotus front seats replaced by standard Cortina GT seats. Modified front disc brakes and self-adjusting rear drum brakes. Fixed front quarter light windows.
September 1966	:	Model phased out.
February 1967	:	Cortina Lotus introduced (assembled entirely by Ford) similar to two-door Cortina GT but with black radiator grille, body side flashes optional, battery relocated in boot. Engine as Mk I SE version (109bhp at 6,000 rpm). Gearbox specification as for Corsair 2000E. 3.78:1 final drive. Full race/rally option pack available from Ford's Competition Department.
October 1967	:	Aeroflow ventilation controls simplified, 'Twin Cam' letters added to boot lid, 'Lotus' badge deleted. Clock moved to centre console.
November 1968	:	'Ford' in caps on boot and bonnet. Revised centre console with floor mounted handbrake.
July 1970	:	Production ceased.

When news of this special car filtered through to Fred Hart and his team in styling they were galvanized into producing their own 'GT' version. While not being the same 'full-house' conversion of the Lotus Cortina, the Cortina GT was fitted with an uprated 1,498cc engine with a high lift camshaft, Weber carburettor and tubular manifold, sufficient to increase power to 78bhp at 5,200rpm and give a top speed of 94mph (151kph). Inside, the car was improved and a rev counter fitted in line with its sporty image. A prototype was demonstrated to Henry Ford at Monthérly airport in September 1962 when the Ford chief was in Europe to attend a marketing conference and the project was given an enthusiastic green light.

In all fields of competition Ford's 'hot' saloons proved worthy contenders. The cheeky little Anglia was raced for the factory by both Superspeed and Broadspeed, Sir John Whitmore winning the hotly contested Saloon Car Championship in a Broadspeed-prepared Anglia in 1966. It also highlighted the value of the 'small car/big engine' philosophy in producing large gains in performance. Some competitors fitted 1,650cc and even 1,800cc twin cam engines, making the Anglia

To fit the Lotus tohc engine into the Cortina engine bay the battery had to be moved to the boot and the twin Weber carburettors were given a special slim air cleaner.

(Opposite) The classic lines of the Lotus Cortina stand up well against the contemporary shape of the Sierra RS Cosworth. How will the Sierra look in twenty years' time?

From the rear, the vestigial fins of the Mk I Cortina body styling clearly reflect a transatlantic influence. The green flash, of course, was the Lotus Cortina's hallmark.

into a very quick car indeed. But it was the Cortina which really chalked up the competition successes. In 1965 Sir John Whitmore won the European Saloon Car Championship in a Lotus Cortina, while the following year a Lotus Cortina won the RAC, Geneva and Acropolis rallies.

The GT Cortina also had its name up in lights gaining, among other victories, first, third and team prizes in the 1964 East African Safari Rally. Whereas the Lotus Cortina was very much the sophisticated – if somewhat temperamental – race machine which bore all the famous Lotus hallmarks, the Cortina GT was a rugged, reliable and overtly simple vehicle making it ideally suited to the roughest of rallies.

By the mid 1960s, Ford UK had established itself in just the way Walter Hayes had envisaged by gaining valuable prestige and publicity in the formidable world of international rallying, while in Britain Ford had earned a well-respected name in saloon car track events. Suddenly, the BMC Minis were not having it all their own way. The engineering integrity of the Cortina was proving correct, making the car easy to maintain on a tough rally while at the same time providing an ideal vehicle for the budget-conscious motorist – contrasting strongly with the sophisticated BMC front-wheel-drive Minis and 1100s. Without doubt, the Cortina had a resounding effect on the British car-buying public, not least because it offered a vast variety of models, trim packages and performance ratings at prices which suited most pockets.

While Ford's efforts in racing and rallying in the UK were reaping huge benefits from large-scale media publicity, so Ford in America were equally anxious to change their image as builders of staid products for

*The Consul Capri GT (along with its saloon sister called the 'Consul Classic')
fitted between the 105E Anglia and the Cortina; the model range proved too
expensive to build.*

middle-of-the-road buyers. Their marketing department was talking earnestly about something called the 'youth market'. Young people now had money to spend on cars, clothes and leisure. You were what you drove and Ford Detroit wanted to ensure that this latest generation of car-buying citizens drove Ford cars.

The Cobra story has been too well documented elsewhere to go into detail here. Briefly and simply, the astutely charming Carroll Shelby first made overtures to AC Cars in the Autumn of 1961. His idea was simple: install an American Ford engine into the AC Ace, thereby transforming it from a spritely sports car into a real road burner. The first prototype was completed by February 1962 and featured a strengthened chassis and suspension, a 221cu.in (3,621.5cu.cm) engine and Borg Warner four-speed gearbox.

Further testing was then carried out in California where the car was fitted with a 260cu.in (4,260cu.cm) unit with a Holley carburettor. The first 75 production Cobras were also fitted with this engine. However, with the later introduction of the larger, stronger and more powerful 289cu.in (4,735cu.cm) unit cars were then fitted with this. For the larger 4.7-litre unit, power was rated at 195bhp at 4,400rpm.

Development of the Cobra was very much an ongoing situation with experience gained on the tracks being reflected through to production cars. From mid-1965 the Cobra could be bought with a monster 7-litre engine, the car being called the Shelby American Cobra.

However, it was on the race tracks where the Cobra (and the sleekly styled coupé version called the Daytona) really proved its worth, winning the GT Championship in 1964 *and* 1965. (Today, some thirty years after Shelby first mooted his idea to Derek Hurlock at AC Cars, the Cobra is the most replicated car of all time.)

In order to evaluate public reaction to

Len Bailey

Born in the picturesque town of Stratford-upon-Avon, Len Bailey's list of contributions as race and sports car designer to the motor industry must rank among the most prolific. Len was educated at Kings Norton Grammar School before taking BSc and MSc courses at Birmingham and Michigan Universities. To comply with his father's wishes he started his career as an articled clerk intending to become a chartered accountant; he stayed just 6 months before leaving to join British Leyland as an engineering apprentice.

Then followed an illustrious career spanning time with BRM, Daimler, Rolls-Royce, Jaguar and Rover as engine designer before leaving to join American Motors in Detroit where he was involved in the design of a V8 engine. But he was never to see the project to completion, leaving to join Ford where he was involved with the fascinating gas turbine Fairlane and Thunderbird cars.

Then it was on to Ford Research and work with advanced suspension design (Len was asked to help develop the suspension for the Cobra 427: he felt insulted, calling it 'back street design') before becoming Chief Designer for Ford Advanced Vehicles and the legendary GT40 programme, at which point he came back to the UK. When John Wyer took over GT40 production he followed. Then, in 1968, Ford moved Bailey to Alan Mann's headquarters in Byfleet where he designed a number of exciting cars including the P68 and P69 cars.

But, it has not all been race/sports car design. Bailey has also been involved with helping to develop Ford's race and rally Escorts including the Cosworth and Twin Cam race Escorts and the BDA rally Escorts as well as the sleek GT70 mid-engined road sports car.

Meanwhile, Bailey has also done work for Renault, Toyota, Panther, Autokraft, Mitsubishi, Aston Martin and Mercedes, an impressive list which includes the design of some 48 complete cars.

John Wyer

The name of John Wyer and the GT40 are synonymous in most enthusiasts' minds. Wyer died in April 1989 at his home in Scottsdale, Arizona and motor racing lost one of its remarkable and capable personalities.

An engineer by profession, it was his analytical approach to team management throughout the years which gained him such success. Wyer also had a knack of surrounding himself with talented people who were only too happy to work under his leadership.

Wyer began his career in 1948 at Monaco Motors, a London-based garage which specialized in the preparation of racing cars for the wealthy, Wyer running Dudley Folland's Aston Martin in the prestigious 24Hrs race at Spa. It was while he was there that he was spotted by entrepreneur David Brown who later invited Wyer to take charge of his Aston Martin DBR2s for the 1950 season. The appointment was contracted to last for 12 months, but Wyer remained for 13 years, during which time he was promoted to Technical Director and later Managing Director of one of the world's best known sports car manufacturers. During that time he had the satisfaction of seeing the team win both Le Mans and the Sports Car World Championship for 1959.

In 1963 he was lured away to join Ford, taking charge of the GT40 – Ford's new weapon with which to beat Ferrari at Le Mans. Based at Slough, Bucks, the operation was called Ford Advanced Vehicles where, with input from such masters as Len Bailey and Eric Broadley, the team designed and built what is arguably the most attractive and legendary of all sports racing cars. The proof of their performance was victory for the GT40s in both the 1966 and 1967 Le Mans events.

By this time Ford felt they had made their point and Wyer took over operations, calling the team JW Automotive Engineering run by himself and friend John Willment. Despite running what some criticized as out-dated cars, the GT40s won again, this time in their orange and blue livery.

Such was his performance that Porsche asked Wyer to take charge of their exciting 917 programme. Again, sponsorship was to come from Gulf Oil and while the cars failed to win at Le Mans they did win 11 out of the 17 events they entered during the 1970 and 1971 season, an impressive achievement.

At 62 John retired. He had had enough of company politics although, as President of Gulf Oil, he was persuaded to take charge of the GT40-based Mirage team cars (again designed by Len Bailey), their Le Mans victory making it five wins in a row for Wyer.

European-styled sports cars, Ford in Detroit set up an Advanced Vehicles Concepts Division which came under the control of Yorkshireman Roy Lunn. One of their first projects to be shown to the public in 1962 was a mid-engined, two-seater sports car powered by a 1.5-litre Taunus engine which, with a bigger carburettor, a high lift camshaft and balanced valve train developed 65bhp. *Small Car* gave the top speed as 112mph (180kph) with a 0–60mph (0–100kph) time of 10.5 seconds. The price? As a prototype it was valued at around £25,000!

To look at, Mustang 1 (as it was named) was a very striking motor car and inevitably, perhaps, was a mix of parts from the Ford parts bin (Cortina front discs, for example). They called it the '100-day project' because that was how long it took the team at Advanced Vehicles Concepts Division to put it together. Only one was ever built. Shame . . .

'When I began to promote the idea of the sporting Ford in this country I was in the happy position that Ford in America had its own 'Total Performance Programme' aimed at the youth market,' recalled Walter Hayes. 'In the post-war baby boom in the States there were something like 70 million babies and in 1963, the year the Mustang production model (not to be confused with Mustang 1) was launched, one in every two Americans was under twenty-four years old.' As a result, this programme was drawn up which would include both stock and racing cars.

Meanwhile, there was the GT40 programme. Walter Hayes again: 'It all began with the story that Ford might be interested in buying Ferrari,' explained Hayes. 'The German Consul in Milan told the General Manager of Ford Germany that he thought Ferrari was up for sale since Ferrari himself was interested in racing cars but not at all interested in production cars and understood that Ferrari was losing money. The proposal was that Ford would take over the production car division and the F1 racing team, which Ferrari would run. (Rumour has it the deal was for £6 million. MT.) The negotiations almost reached the point of agreement but eventually failed through fundamental differences in personality of the companies and countries involved. So Ford decided to embark on the GT40 programme with Ford Advanced

Vehicles being set up under John Wyer with myself as one of the directors.'

Most people agree that it was an enlightened decision that Ford should locate the GT 40 programme in Britain. 'The key to race car building is knowing where to go to get specialist expertise,' said Len Bailey, who became the GT40's Chief Engineer. 'Ford talked to both Colin Chapman and John Cooper about the project but eventually came to an agreement with Eric Broadley.' The foundation upon which the project was based was the development of Broadley's Lola GT since in everyone's opinion this sports/racing car came closest to how they saw the final GT40. Powered by a mid-mounted 4.7-litre Ford V8 engine, the car was unveiled at the Racing Car Show in January 1963. Later in the year the car made its racing debut at Le Mans driven by David Hobbs and Richard Attwood. Despite losing all but top and bottom gears the car still managed to out-accelerate the Ferraris and set the second fastest lap of the race just before coming to an untimely halt. However, its performance turned sufficient heads that Ford Detroit began to take a closer look since the Broadley Lola GT could, they thought, be developed into a Ferrari-beater.

The result was that Broadley signed a contract with Ford for twelve months to co-ordinate the potential 200mph (320kph) Ford GT. Of course, by American standards, the whole project was laughably small, with Broadley, Roy Lunn, Len Bailey and the team moving into Robbie Rushbrook's tiny workshops in Bromley, South London during August 1963. Almost from the beginning the name 'Lola' was quietly dropped and the car quickly became known as the Ford GT.

Sadly, for a project of this nature, there was soon strong conflict between Broadley and Lunn. To overcome these difficulties, John Wyer was brought in from Aston Martin. 'John was a very forceful, strong-willed man who was determined to push the GT40 programme through – which was just what a project like this needed,' continued Bailey to the author recently. At least problems over space limitations had been solved by moving the whole operation to premises on a trading estate in Slough and calling it Ford Advanced Vehicles.

The first engines to come over from America were 255cu.in (4,178cu.cm) push-rod 'Indy' units designed by Bill Gay in Detroit. Based on aluminium cylinder blocks and heads these units produced around 340–350bhp. By March 1964 two cars had been completed. Initial testing began at MIRA and Goodwood and the second prototype was sent – much against John Wyer's wishes – to the New York Motor Show. 'There was much wrong with the car at that stage,' recalled Bailey with feeling. 'The handling was poor and the Colotti gearboxes were very badly made. Then we took the prototypes to the Le Mans test days, which proved to be an unmitigated disaster. Fuel bags were leaking and it rained heavily which did nothing to help the poor roadholding.'

Gradually, after much testing, the Ford GTs began to handle like true super cars. Eventually, six very fast Fords emerged from the Slough workshops. Their first race was the Nurburgring 1000Km in which the Phil Hill/Bruce McLaren car showed its potential until suspension and gearbox problems intervened. It was then on to the Le Mans 24 Hours in which Richie Ginther led the pack for the first hour and a half, reportedly seeing 206mph (331kph) down the Mulsane Straight. But again, unreliability prevented success. Hill set a new lap record in the other car before he, too, had to retire.

By the end of July 1964 Broadley's contract had come to an end. 'It's been an interesting and fruitful experience,' he told *Small Car* magazine, 'but one way and another there has always been a lot of confusion about my actual part in the project. I was given a 12-month contract to build a GT car . . . Lola Cars was never bought or taken over by Ford of America.'

For 1965 Ford arranged for Cobra-man Carroll Shelby to become involved, along with one member of his very talented staff, Phil Remmington. Modifications were soon made to the cars with the earlier 4.2-litre 'Indy' alloy units giving way to iron-blocked 4.7-litre engines and becoming known as GT40 Mk Is. Road-going versions of these cars were also developed and referred to as Mk IIIs since another version of the GT40 had been developed under Roy Lunn at Kar Kraft fitted with the monster 7-litre 427cu.in (6,997cu.cm) unit and called the Mk II. Finally, there was the Mk IV which was based on a honeycomb chassis and powered by a tuned version of an even lustier 7-litre engine.

In 1966 Mk IIs finished at Le Mans in first, second and third places – the cars actually crossing the line three abreast! The following year Mk IVs finished first and fourth. Undoubtedly, not to say dramatically, Ford had achieved what they had set out to do. They had generated enormous publicity which, naturally, was used to promote Ford's products both in Europe and America. In just two years Ford had created a legend (witness the sale prices of GT40s now in the 1990s!).

That should have been the end of the GT 40 story, but in fact it was to last another two years until 1969. With Ford's withdrawal from the GT40 programme, John Wyer bought the proceeds of Ford Advanced Vehicles and, with Gulf Oil sponsorship, set up JW Automotive Engineering Ltd. His team of GT40s were slightly redesigned by Len Bailey and won again in 1968 and 1969.

Ford Dagenham had not been idle, either. To begin with, in 1966 the old Mk I Cortina gave way to the Mk II with its less aerodynamic, more 'square' body shell available, as before, in both two- and four-door forms. For a short time the old 1,498cc engine was carried over into the Mk II cars but was replaced in 1968 by the famous Kent 'crossflow' series of engines in both 1,298cc and 1,598cc form.

Stylists working during 1964 on the full-size clay model which was to form the next generation of Cortina. The Mk II was less aerodynamically efficient and heavier than its predecessor.

A Cortina being crash-tested at the Road Research Laboratory at Crowthorne, Berks. The impact speed of the Cortina was 39.1mph (62.9kph) yet damage was restricted to the engine compartment.

A late model Cortina Lotus. By the introduction of the second generation, this version of Ford's best-selling Cortina had become a most civilized and exciting car. Introduction of the lighter, faster Escort Twin Cam eclipsed a promising competition career.

This was done by increasing the stroke size to 2.48in (62.99mm) on the 1.3-litre unit and 3.05in (77.62mm) on the 1.6-litre version. To accommodate this the cylinder block depth was increased by some 0.47in (11.94mm)

Technically, however, the most interesting thing by far about this new series of Ford engines was the 'crossflow' cylinder head. Of Heron design, the combustion chambers were recessed into the tops of the pistons, thereby creating an almost flat surface to the cylinder head. Moreover, the carburettor and exhaust manifold were on opposite sides of the engine. Without doubt, the result was

better breathing and therefore greater running efficiency. As installed in the 1600GT Cortina this engine was tuned to produce some 88bhp at 5,400rpm giving the car a top speed of around 94mph (151kph) and a 0–60mph (0–100kph) time of 11.8 seconds. Also worth mentioning is the introduction of the highly acclaimed 2000E-type gearbox. A direct descendant of the gearbox first seen in the old 105E Anglia, the 2000E 'box had synchromesh on all forward gears while the ratios were revised to give better spacing between the gears.

Most certainly, the Mk II Cortina was a

The 'Cortina Twin Cam' badge on the rear face of the bootlid indicates Ford's strong marketing direction away from Lotus's name appearing on the Mk II Cortina's exterior. Ford worked hard during the Mk II's development to improve the car's reliability.

The interior of the Cortina Lotus showing semi-bucket-type front seats and re-styled facia which dropped auxiliary instruments from a bulge above the dash to a new location above the heater controls. The cockpit boasted more room than the Escort Twin Cam successor.

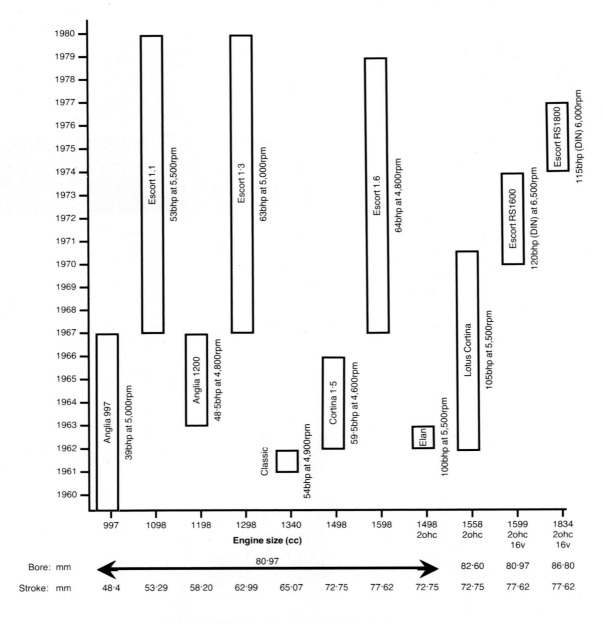

*Graph showing the 80.97mm bore family of Ford engines and the respective cars
into which they were fitted from 1960 to 1980.*

*Not all Lotus Cortinas were raced by the factory. Alan Mann Racing Ltd of
Byfleet also campaigned these exciting cars to good effect.*

far better car – in all its guises – than its
predecessor. In addition to the Cortina GT
another model to emerge with the introduction of the Mk II range was the Cortina
1600E, a car which quickly became a cult
machine even while production was running. With lowered suspension and the GT
Cortina drivetrain, the 1600E's interior was
improved dramatically with wood fillets and
an improved level of trim. A far cry, indeed,
from the austerity models for which Ford
had become so well known in the pre-war
years.

With the introduction of the Cortina Mk
II, 1967 also saw the Lotus Cortina production line move from Lotus's Hethel site near
Norwich to Ford's Boreham factory. (This
also coincided with the subtle name change
to Cortina Lotus!). Standard two-door
1600GT Cortinas were delivered to the Boreham site where the engines were replaced by
the now famous 1,558cc tohc Lotus unit,
tuned to SE specification (involving the use
of 'hotter' Cosworth-type camshafts) which
developed a reputed 115bhp on a compression
ratio of 9.5:1. Underneath, the suspension
was lowered to provide better handling,
while the braking system utilized parts from
the larger Corsair 2000E saloon. Also, after
development testing by the Ford engineers,
the 3.77:1 differential was strengthened
with high tensile bolts and the MacPherson

The Lotus twin cam engine was supplied in SE form to overcome the Mk II's extra weight and less slippery body. Work was also done to make it more reliable.

strut body location points were toughened to withstand the rigours of an international rally. Under the bonnet, a large elliptical air cleaner (which replaced the old 'box' affair) was located on top of the engine, dwarfing the cam. boxes, while the exhaust was replaced by a system made of thicker gauge metal. All this work was done in an attempt to improve on the Mk I Lotus Cortina's reliability, which was far more suspect than most motoring magazines would admit to.

Of course, 1967 is also important in Ford's history because it was the year that Ford amalgamated all of its 15 European companies into one, calling itself 'Ford Europe'. It was a determined attempt on behalf of the company to co-ordinate production facilities and integrate the expanding world of technology.

'By the mid-1960s my own position within Ford was changing,' remarked Hayes. 'With the setting up of Ford Europe, I became one of its first Vice Presidents.'

On both sides of the Atlantic, Ford's aggressive Total Performance Programme had successfully transformed the company's image. In all aspects of production logistics, management and organizational strategy,

One of the immaculate Team Broadspeed Anglias in its familiar maroon and grey livery during 1968. Ralph Broad put his success down to first-class preparation.

Ford had changed out of all recognition during the 1950s and 1960s. Cynics would say that Ford simply threw money at problems but then as a multi-national company all their budgets (advertising, development and so on) represented huge sums of investment.

But, most of all, they could justifiably claim to offer race and rally-bred cars for the enthusiast as part of a broad showroom model base. The time was now right to launch their next all-conquering saloon: the Escort.

2 They're Off

By the mid-1960s, Ford's image as a manufacturer of cars with style, flair and performance was growing, thanks largely to the Lotus Cortina and its competition career which, while not actually works-prepared, managed to thrill the crowd. Driven by the likes of Peter Arundell and Jim Clark, the twin cam Cortinas often outstripped tough opposition. As for international rallies, there were outright wins with Boreham-prepared cars in rallies such as the Geneva, the RAC and the Acropolis – tough, testing events which quickly had the measure of weaker cars and lesser drivers.

When Walter Hayes joined Ford in January 1962 one of the first areas to receive his attention was the Competitions Department. During the 1950s, Ford's competition cars were prepared at the Lincoln Cars depot on the Great West Road. The team were very dedicated and worked miracles but, clearly, if Ford were going to be successful in the increasingly tough world of motor sport they would need bigger and better premises. The site chosen was Boreham, north-east of Chelmsford, Essex.

The first to inhabit the 630-acre site at Boreham airfield were American forces in 1940. They constructed runways for their Martin Marauder bombers and put up accommodation blocks which, at the airfield's peak, housed some 1,700 men. With the war over, like many disused airfields, Boreham's perimeter track was turned into a race circuit. It soon became one of the country's foremost race tracks where many of the great names in motor sport, such as Roy Salvadori, Duncan Hamilton, Reg Parnell and Mike Hawthorn, competed. Another star was Archie Butterworth who,

in addition to being a gifted driver, was also a designer/builder of racing cars. (The car he drove in the April Fools Day event in 1952, for example, featured a 4-litre engine and four-wheel-drive.)

Ford's Motorsport department moved into Boreham airfield in 1963, spending some £60,000 setting up the factory accommodation which was to house one of the world's foremost rally teams. When talking to Walter Hayes on one occasion, Bill Barnett, ex-Ford rally manager, had once referred to the Lincoln Cars depot as 'a bit of a hole in the wall operation'. In characteristic style, Hayes reflected Barnett's comments at high level, the result being the move of Motorsport's whole operation to Boreham. As Barnett later commented, 'The beauty of Boreham was its motor racing circuit. We could bring a car out of the workshops and 100 yards later we were on the test track.'

In the autumn of 1965 Alan Platt, Boreham's Competitions Manager, was replaced by Henry Taylor, an ex-grand prix driver and businessman/farmer. This was, perhaps, an unusual choice, yet his steady stream of inventive ideas was to prove invaluable – if a little wearying – to his boss, Walter Hayes. It was, for example, one of Taylor's 'ideas' which resulted in the Escort Twin Cam!

'I was always very impressed by Henry Taylor,' recalled Walter Hayes candidly. 'He was one of our rally stars who would finish an event and the following Monday morning would be sitting in my office at 8 o'clock to tell me what was wrong with the car. He was a Bedfordshire farmer whom, I do not think, ever saw himself as anything else. But I persuaded him to come and work for us as Competitions Manager. After all, it was one

Escort Twin Cam and RS Range

January 1968 : Model announced utilizing 'Export' version of two-door Escort GT (first 25 cars assembled by hand in Boreham workshops during spring of 1968, remainder built at Halewood). Cortina Lotus 1,558cc engine, gearbox and back axle. Suspension as Lotus Cortina. Rack and pinion steering. Available in white coachwork only with slightly flared wheel arches, black grille and quarter front bumpers. Many competition extras available as homologated items.

September 1968 : Small changes to door and external body trim.

July 1969 : Round QI headlamps replace original rectangular type.

January 1970 : Introduction of RS1600. Similar to Twin Cam but with Cosworth 16-valve BDA 1,601cc engine producing 120bhp (DIN) at 6,500rpm. First cars built at Halewood.

October 1970 : Production changed to Rallye Sport production facility (AVO) at South Ockendon. Specification remains unchanged. Introduction of Rallye Sport dealer network and range of RS after-market extras.

November 1970 : Introduction of Escort Mexico using RS1600 body. 1,599cc Cortina GT/Capri 1600 engine producing 86bhp (DIN) at 5,500rpm. Rubber interior mats and no oil cooler. RS1600 and Mexico available in a choice of colours.

April 1971 : Escort Twin Cam no longer available.

April 1972 : Dellorto carbs replace Weber on RS1600.

October 1972 : Alloy cylinder head replaces cast iron type on RS1600. Spec. now includes hazard warning lights and sports road wheels for both models. Carpets replace rubber mats, battery relocated in boot. Spare wheel mounted upright on Mexico.

July 1973 : RS2000 model launched (initially for export only) with RS1600 body shell, suspension and transmission powered by 1,993cc ohc 'Pinto' engine developing 100bhp (DIN) at 5,750rpm. Full interior spec. including reclining front seats.

November 1974 : RS1600 model discontinued.

January 1975 : Mexico and RS2000 models discontinued.

January 1975 : RS1800 model introduced with 1,845cc version of BDA 16-valve engine but with single dual-choke Weber carburettor producing 115bhp (DIN) at 6,000rpm. RS1600 type transmission and suspension in latest Mk II 'heavy duty' body. First cars built at Halewood. Flared wheel arches. Front and rear spoilers. Optional Custom Pack including high-back seats and centre console.

January 1976 : Production of RS1800 moved to Saarlouis (using Mk II Mexico as basis) with engines and badges fitted in UK. Introduction of Mexico and RS2000 Mk II models. Mexico mechanical spec. as Mk I car but with engine producing 95bhp (DIN) at 5,750rpm. RS2000 engine now producing 110bhp (DIN) at 5,750rpm. Body trim now includes 'shovel' front incorporating twin headlamps, wrap-around rear bumper, cloth seats. Black surrounds to all windows, improved ride, sound deadening, interior trim spec. on all models.

January 1977 : Custom Trim Pack no longer available on RS1800.

September 1977 : RS1800 discontinued.

September 1978 : Mexico model discontinued. 'Standard' RS2000 model uses Mexico interior with reclining seats and steel road wheels. Custom RS2000 features Recaro front seats, remote control door mirror, tinted glass, boot light, centre console, glove box, carpet in boot area, better quality trim and 6J × 13in alloy road wheels.

September 1980 : RS2000 model range discontinued, replaced by FWD vehicles.

of Henry's 8 o'clock ideas to put a cheap Cortina engine into a racing car and call it Formula Ford. I agreed and it was done, just like that.'

Production of the Mk I Lotus Cortina had stopped in mid-1966 with a total of 2,894 units having been sold – a quite remarkable achievement for both Lotus (as a low volume specialist manufacturer) and Ford (for whom the Lotus Cortina meant a complete departure from their normal 'image' products). It also says much for the way sales are influenced by competition successes. Without doubt, it had become a legend in its own lifetime and even today, some twenty-five years later, stands up remarkably well against other, similar machinery (a 0–60mph (0–100kph) time of around 10.5 seconds, maximum speed of 105mph (169kph) with a fuel consumption in the region of 25mpg (11.3l/100km), unless driven with a very determined right foot!)

As we have already seen, the introduction of the Mk II Lotus Cortina (or more properly, Cortina Lotus, as Ford preferred it), saw Ford take over from Lotus the responsibility for the car's development and assembly. The Mk II body shell was somewhat bigger and heavier than its predecessor, although power output from the now reliable tohc engine seemed to have gained a little, thereby restoring the balance, with overall performance hardly impaired.

With the first part of 1967 being taken up with development testing of the Cortina Lotus it was clear that demands on the Boreham team would be light, at least during the early months of that year. Moreover, homologation was not due to start until May, with production coming on-stream in February 1967.

Meanwhile, Team Lotus began running a brace of Cosworth-FVA-engined Group 5 saloons driven by such luminaries as Jacky Ickx, Graham Hill and John Miles. Concentrated development resulted in a gradual rise in tohc power output to the point where it was producing some 200 reliable bhp in racing form and around 165bhp for rallying; where torque rather than revs was the order of the day. These units were assembled at Boreham by engine experts Terry Hoyle and Peter Ashcroft.

It is certainly true that there were production and reliability problems with the Mk I Lotus Cortinas, which even the press in those days were often too polite to point out. But, if Ford wanted a specialist car with which to attract the public it was a price they were going to have to pay. 'It would have been bizarre to have put the Lotus Cortina down the same track as the other Cortinas because it was so much more sophisticated,' explained Walter Hayes. 'So it was necessary not to build them in-house. Lotus were first and foremost a race car company and a plastics company. (Indeed, Chapman's leadership in the car plastics industry has, to my mind, never been fully recognized.) The fact is that the early Lotus Cortinas did run into quality problems which required an enormous amount of re-work, simply because of lessons we were all learning about limited production. Also, Colin himself, through necessity, was devoting a large proportion of his time to racing. But those lessons learnt with the Mk I Lotus Cortina were put to good use with the Mk II, the Escort Twin Cam and the other limited production models.' Mk II Cortina Lotus production was to run from February 1967 until July 1970 during which time some 4,032 cars were built.

Meanwhile, Henry Taylor was looking to the future and possible ways to offset the ever-growing threat from such adversaries as Lancia and Porsche (to say nothing of the home-grown challenge from the likes of BMC). What Taylor needed was an altogether lighter body shell capable of taking the tohc engine. The answer was not far away.

While it is true to say that in the early days the Anglia was very much overshadowed by the spritely Minis when it came to motor sport, by 1962–3 the tuners were working their magic on the little Dagenham saloons to good effect. In went tuned 1,498cc Cortina engines, often with high lift camshafts and performance Weber carburettors, while the front brakes were changed to disc-type in an effort to bring the handling in line with the performance. But it was not just the race cars which were modified. Road Anglias, too, were given the treatment; the Allard Motor Company marketed their Allardette which featured the 1,340cc 'Classic' unit and disc front brakes.

Soon after the launch of the Anglia in 1959 Ford's styling department began getting down to the task of designing the company's next generation of small car. But despite the trend for smaller and smaller cars, it was known from the outset that the Anglia's replacement would be a slightly bigger model all round giving more interior space. The wheelbase was increased from 90.5in (2,298mm) to 94.5in (2,400mm) while the cabin width was increased by 5in (12.7cm). Incredibly, however, the new car was some 2in (5cm) lower yet still managed to give greater headroom, while the overall length was increased by 3in (7.6cm) to give a bigger boot size. In addition, while the frontal area was bigger than the Anglia, work in the wind tunnel had reduced the drag coefficient from 0.46 to 0.43. Moreover, since the Anglia was available with either the familiar 997cc engine or the 1,198cc 'Super' unit, the next model range would be given a 1,098cc base unit and a 1,297cc unit for the 'up-market' models, these engines featuring the latest bowl-in-piston-type 'Kent' engines with crossflow breathing. Also, the Anglia gearbox, which lacked synchromesh on first gear, gave way to an all-new gearbox with synchromesh on all forward gears. Finally, Ford's latest small car would be truly pan-European – the result of Ford's unification of its European factories. The name of the new car: the Escort.

Constructionally, the Escort would be very similar to the Anglia, using a solid rear axle with semi-elliptic leaf springs. However, the front suspension, initially at least, used 'compression-strut' units and track-control arms but without an anti-roll bar. Also, the new model range would be given rack and pinion steering – in sharp contrast to the worm and peg type fitted to the earlier Anglias and Cortinas. Finally, the Escort would ride on 12in (30.5cm) road wheels, an unusual size for any British saloon car. Bodily, of course, the shells would be of unitary construction, assembled on the Halewood production lines on Merseyside, the 346-acre site bought by Ford in 1960.

Production start date for the Escort was planned for late 1967. Halewood would manufacture the bodies and gearboxes while engines, trim packs and axles would arrive by train from Dagenham and Swansea.

Almost certainly it was the tuned racing and road Anglias that influenced Ford's Product Planning people into thinking that a GT version of the Escort would make marketing sense. For this model the 1,297cc engine was tuned to give 71bhp at 6,000rpm while the gearbox ratios were changed slightly to align it with its sporting image. The front brakes, too, were changed to 8.6in (21.8cm)-disc-type. Inside the car the dashboard boasted a neat six dial fascia together with Escort 'super' trim packaging.

One day in 1966, Ford's development engineers were testing a prototype Escort when, reputedly quite by chance Henry Taylor and team foreman Bill Meade caught a sneak glimpse. They immediately realized the car's potential – given that they could shoe-horn a twin cam engine into the bay of the neat and compact Escort. Would it fit?

First, Taylor held a meeting at his house on the morning of 25 January 1967 in order to throw around ideas and put together a proposal to persuade Walter Hayes to let them borrow an Escort prototype. With his support anything was possible.

Testing a prototype Escort at Cobham. It was during these trials that the Escort's body shell was found to be so much stronger than the Mk II Cortina, making it ideal for rallying.

However, in spite of Taylor's enthusiasm for the programme (everything had to be done *now*), Bill Meade was worried that his talented but heavily committed Competition engineers simply would not have the time to build up a prototype. Everyone knew that, despite their ability to improvise and modify as the occasion demanded, what sometimes appeared to be an easy job on the surface could quickly become very greedy in time and effort when unforeseen problems arose.

As for getting the car itself, Taylor persuaded, bullied and cajoled the people at Ford's Engineering headquarters at Dunton. Unfortunately, Taylor's timetable did not mesh with Ford's own plans for bringing the Escort on-stream. (Taylor was anxious to

start as soon as possible, while Ford were not due even to begin pilot production for several months. Prototype Escorts were as rare as hen's teeth.) Eventually, someone in Dunton said 'yes' to Taylor being lent a plastic Escort monocoque; it would be delivered on Friday. 'Oh, and by the way, we will be picking it up again on the following Tuesday!'

Since the Escort was some 12in (30cm) shorter than the Mk II Cortina things would be a tight fit. As enthusiasts, the 'Boreham Boys' had taken a keen interest in the privately prepared racing Twin Cam Anglias so they had a feeling for the sort of difficulties they would encounter. However, just as important as the modifications needed .to

A line-up of Escort Twin Cams outside Ford's Halewood Plant near Liverpool. The first consignment went to international race and rally stars.

make the Lotus engine fit into its new surroundings was the extent of these alterations and whether they could be effected on the production line or needed to be part of a 'special build' programme. After all, this was Ford and volume manufacture could not be upset by the necessity to make small alterations in the process of building a handful of homologation 'specials'.

The plastic-bodied Escort prototype was delivered to the Boreham workshops late on a Friday afternoon in March 1967. It was carefully unloaded from the truck and pushed inside. The doors closed and work began. It was not going to be an 'all-nighter' but the guys worked in 12-hour shifts through Saturday and Sunday to make the best use of time.

Clearly, one of the major snags in the whole transformation was that the Escort's engine bay and transmission tunnel was configured to take the smaller 1,100/1,300cc

Escort drive train. The Lotus Twin Cam was much bulkier, particularly with its bulbous Weber carburettors.

At the first attempt the twin cam engine seemed to be fouling almost everything in sight as it was carefully offered up. Right, all stop to see exactly where things were coming into contact. Mainly, it seemed, around the brake master cylinder and the cable for the clutch. Solution? Simple. Make the clutch hydraulically operated and move the master cylinder inside the cockpit. Next, in order to find room to accommodate the Webers and any sort of air cleaner, the entire engine was twisted anti-clockwise in the engine bay so that the crankshaft nose moved closer to the nearside inner wing. Unfortunately, by so doing the cam covers fouled the battery. So the battery was moved to the boot! That left just two major problem areas: the wheel arches, which were just not designed to take 13in (33cm) wheels with fat competition tyres, and the transmission tunnel itself because its bend radius was designed to take the latest single rail Escort gearbox and not the larger Corsair 2000E-type as fitted to the Lotus Cortina.

By the end of that hard-working weekend, Taylor and Meade had the answers they needed. Yes, the new Escort could be transformed into their next generation of rally car *if* the list of modifications they had drawn up could be made to the car. In this respect, that eventful Saturday and Sunday had proved both satisfying and frustrating; satisfying because they had proved that the Twin Cam engine would fit – if only just – frustrating because they knew that there were certain alterations which had to be made to the basic shell to make the transformation possible. (Taking a hammer to the inner wings in an effort to make more space was *not* a production solution to the question of enlarging the engine bay!).

The next step was to formulate a modification list and present it to the production engineers at Halewood where the Escort was to be built. Clearly, their response would have a bearing on the viability of the project. Halewood's reaction was really quite predictable. Yes, they would fabricate some special panels to include the large wheel arches. But in the case of the other changes, well, despite the fact that they were interested in the *idea* of a Twin Cam version they just did not feel the alterations were something they should be responsible for.

At this stage Executive Board agreement had yet to be given for the project and in order to get the 'green light' Walter Hayes needed a working car. He asked Henry Taylor to build him a running example to convince the Ford executives of its viability.

A 1300GT – one of the very first off-tools models from Halewood – was sent down to Boreham where they quickly set about turning the ten stone weakling into a twelve stone Adonis. Unfortunately, while a driver

In its first season of motor sport the Escort Twin Cam won six major international rallies and took the British Saloon Car Championship for 1968.

Performance Figures

	Mk I Lotus Cortina	Mk II Cortina Lotus	Escort Twin Cam	RS 1600
Bore:	82.55mm	as Mk I	as Mk I	80.97mm
Stroke:	72.75mm	as Mk I	as Mk I	77.6mm
Capacity:	1,558cc	as Mk I	as Mk I	1,601cc
Power:	105bhp at 5,500rpm	109bhp at 6,000rpm	109.5bhp at 6,000rpm	120bhp at 6,500rpm
0–30mph	3.5 sec	3.6 sec	3.8 sec	3.4 sec
0–40mph	5.2 sec	5.6 sec	5.2 sec	4.8 sec
0–50mph	7.4 sec	7.9 sec	7.2 sec	6.8 sec
0–60mph	10.4 sec	11.0 sec	9.9 sec	8.9 sec
0–70mph	13.8 sec	14.9 sec	13.0 sec	12.4 sec
0–80mph	19.4 sec	20.1 sec	16.8 sec	16.1 sec
Max speed	107mph	104mph	113mph	113mph
3rd	81mph	83mph	81mph	85mph
2nd	56mph	58mph	56mph	60mph
1st	38mph	39mph	38mph	40mph
	Motor Sept 1966	*Autocar* Aug 1967	*Autocar* June 1968	*Autocar* April 1970

from the test team was putting the car through its paces a steering bracket sheared, robbing the driver of control. The car rolled spectacularly: exit one prototype Escort Twin Cam!

The project – known as J25, after the date when Taylor had his initial meeting to discuss the programme – had gained momentum by now and a replacement body was sent down to Boreham where the TC parts were transferred. Bill Meade and his team were becoming quite adept at building Escort Twin Cams. Needless to say, the car passed its evaluation by the Ford executives and everyone breathed a sigh of relief.

A programme of tests was then mapped out incorporating a great deal of high speed driving in order to evaluate the car's weaknesses. At least one good thing was emerging from all this work: the Escort body shell was proving to be far more rigid than the larger Mk II Cortina shell which, in Cortina Lotus form, took an instant dislike to continuous rough-house driving on international

rallies by sagging rather sadly about its middle. Moreover, the Halewood specification sheet for Escort Twin Cam bodies involved using strengthening panels normally used for 'export' models.

Just what effect these panels had on increasing torsional rigidity was put to the test in most spectacular fashion by rally exponent Roger Clark. On returning from his victory in the Canadian Shell 4000 Clark was told by Taylor about the Twin Cam's programme. That was during the spring of 1967, although it was not until the autumn of the same year that Clark was to put the car (in fact, the very same rebodied prototype first built by Boreham for Ford executives to evaluate) through its paces at the tough Bagshot proving ground. The session was such that some of the most famous Escort 'action' shots ever were taken during those trials.

Meanwhile, the problem of production still had to be resolved. Clearly, Halewood's timetable for bringing the Escort on-stream

Colin Chapman

Born in 1928, the son of a North London publican, Anthony Colin Bruce Chapman and Lotus – the company he created – matured to become world renowned as manufacturers of sports and racing cars: the Elite, the Seven, the Elan, not to mention a whole list of successful, even controversial, racing cars. The list goes on and on.

Chapman built his first 'kit' car for what might be loosely called production in 1953, its great attributes being that it was light and impressively engineered, a Chapman hallmark. Four years later came the first GRP monocoque-bodied car, the Elite, with its classic lines and Coventry Climax engine. In 1960 Chapman won his first Grand Prix.

Next came his deal with Walter Hayes which resulted in the Ford-based twin cam engine which first appeared in the Elan in 1962, and the Lotus Cortina, a car which gave both Lotus and Ford tremendous publicity. Meanwhile, Lotus themselves were growing and in 1966 they moved to their present location at Hethel, near Norwich and with it Chapman's desire to move his company up-market as manufacturers of prestigious GT cars.

The first stage in this master plan was the design of an all-new, wholly Lotus-based engine – the 16-valve all-alloy 907. But the period 1973 to 1976 saw Chapman struggling to keep his company afloat as the effects of the energy crisis hit home. But, with an almost reckless disregard for the consequences, he launched his new model range: the Elite followed by the Eclat and, later still, the dramatic Esprit.

A key player in Hayes's plan was Colin Chapman whose innovative genius was used to the full in designing and racing cars which were powered by Ford-based and Cosworth-developed engines.

However, it was for his dynamism that Chapman is chiefly remembered, running at first hand his car company *and* his racing team – not to mention having a fundamental effect on designs for both. He also diversified, albeit temporarily, into boat-building and, just before his untimely death in 1982, into light aircraft too. Without doubt, his alter ego was Enzo Ferrari (he always harboured a desire to be the British equivalent). Today, Chapman remains an enigma: sometimes loved; sometimes hated; but almost always admired. Life was never boring when 'ACBC' was around.

could not be overturned by the Twin Cam programme. Some tough talking was needed if the project was to be co-ordinated at all. The solution was to put the Twin Cam versions down the same line as the 'standard' models and take them off at a suitable point where they could be moved away to a section of the plant specially set aside. Here, the power train, trim and minor parts could be fitted by a group of hand-picked 'volunteer' fitters. Then there was the road testing, which, in the case of the Escort Twin Cam,

*The Escort Twin Cam production line at Halewood. At this point in their
assembly they are fully trimmed and wired before being lowered on to their
engine and transmission.*

would involve an actual road test rather
than a brief period on the rolling road normally used for lesser Escorts.

However, all this did not get over the problem that both Boreham and the publicity
department were in urgent need of some cars.
To satisfy demand, the decision was taken to
turn the tiny Boreham workshops into a
production line and the 'Boreham Boys'
turned their capable and willing hands to
putting together the first 25 cars. At last,
Henry Taylor had got his way and the
successor to the Cortina Lotus was now a
reality – a car he was convinced would put
Ford in the lead once more. It takes little
imagination to picture the scene in the Boreham Comps. workshops with cars, parts and
people seemingly everywhere. Moreover,

Dick Boxall (Halewood's Production Manager on temporary secondment) was making
good use of his time at Boreham gaining
experience which would be invaluable at the
Merseyside factory once Twin Cam manufacture got under way there in the spring of
1968.

The decision to build the first 25 cars in
the tiny Boreham workshops was not
exactly ideal since there was still the day-to-
day competition support role which had to
function uninterrupted. There was also the
steady stream of interested visitors – drivers
and so on – who 'just happened to look in
while they were passing'.

The job of juggling who would get one of
those eagerly awaited prototype/production
Escort Twin Cams fell to Barry Gill whose

A late model Escort Twin Cam with its round headlamps. At the time of its launch the Twin Cam was the fastest car Ford UK manufactured.

daily task was to fend off the onslaught of enquiries from all quarters. Meanwhile, Taylor had allocated four of the first 25 Twin Cams to the Alan Mann racing team who would campaign them in the British Saloon Car Championship (all grist to the publicity-machine mill which would promote Ford's new competition vehicle).

The Escort Twin Cam – along with the mainstream Escort models – was announced in January 1968, by which time Escort production at Halewood had already got into high gear. Twin Cam homologation – as every sporting Ford enthusiast knows – was granted for Group 3 (500 units built) in

March and Group 2 approval (for 1,000 units) in May, an impressive achievement in view of the Escort TC's very special completion format which had to be handled away from the main assembly lines.

The specification for the Twin Cam called for a heavy duty body shell (known as Type 49) in 'Super' trim, which included the strange (for a high performance car, at least) choice of rectangular headlamps. From the outset, Boreham had wanted round headlamps but the product planners – who, presumably, were not very enlightened(!) – decided upon round headlamps for the 'basic' Escort versions only. The trim package included carpets, seats and fascia taken from the Escort GT, while the export spec. body shell added stiffening around the suspension location points, floorpan and chassis rails, with minor modifications around the transmission tunnel to accommodate the larger gearbox. Also, provision had to be made to take the rear axle radius arms, since these were not standard on the GT. The wheel arches were flared to take the larger diameter, wider wheels and tyres (although the flaring was only slight). From the beginning the front suspension utilized Lotus Cortina-type MacPherson struts – in contrast to the trailing reaction strut on other Escorts.

Externally, all Escort Twin Cams arrived in white coachwork with 'Twin Cam' badges, a matt black grille, front quarter bumpers (a trend started with the Lotus Cortina) and

From the rear the Escort Twin Cam looks even less like a performance car, the only real giveaway is the lowered ride height and wider-than-standard road wheels.

the standard 5.5in (14cm) road wheels – although some Press cars were shown with optional 1600E Rostyle wheels. Also, the whole car was lowered.

Mechanically, the Escort Twin Cam was almost identical to the Cortina Lotus with the same engine, clutch, gearbox and final drive. The brakes were similar, too, with a remote-acting Girling servo unit mounted on the nearside front of the engine compartment. The battery was relocated in the boot and, with the spare wheel positioned across the boot floor, there was precious little room for luggage!

On the road, Twin Cam performance was impressive enough for its day with a claimed top speed of 115mph (185kph) (at which point the ignition cut-out operated) and a 0–60mph (0–100kph) sprint of around 9.9 seconds. The Twin Cam can best be described as 'fast and furious' since its handling and performance nearly always encouraged its driver to be dramatic, even if the situation did not warrant it! However, if money was spent on a ZF gearbox, a heavy-duty 'Atlas' rear axle and some engine tuning, the potential was there for a very effective rally car.

'I think what was even more important about the Escort (even more than the Cortina) was that it had the great advantage of being the least expensive car in our range,' explained Walter Hayes. 'If you can base your rally car on the cheapest of all your models, it means the youngest of enthusiasts can afford to buy a cheaper version and copy the rally car. In fact, I always felt that the bolt-on 'goodie' market grew from the Escort. I often walked round the car parks at race meetings just to see what the owners were doing with their cars.'

As for publicity, the newly arrived Escort Twin Cam certainly got its fair share. Two of the Boreham-built cars were entered at the Croft rallycross meeting near Darlington, Co. Durham in early February 1968. On this momentous Saturday, in front of a full outside broadcast unit from Independent TV's 'World of Sport', both cars completely outstripped the opposition by winning four races. To an audience of millions the new car demonstrated just how quick it could be.

The Escort Twin Cam's first 'official' rally was the San Remo in Italy during March 1968. By this time, little testing had been done for this type of event and the team (Ove Andersson and John Davenport) even had to carry out their recce in a Cortina Lotus. The lack of preparation was such that they finished only third. A major contributing factor to the car's performance was its handling. There had been so little time for development that it had not become apparent until after the rally had started that the rear damper angles were set so that with the axle on full compression the dampers hardly moved, thereby having little effect on the suspension and causing the car to wallow badly.

Henry Taylor and his team had to wait until Easter and the Circuit of Ireland for their first outright win, Roger Clark managing the feat in glorious style in a specially prepared Group 6 car. With 152bhp under his bonnet, Clark was way out in front by the finish – well ahead of the Coopers and Imps of the BMC and Chrysler teams.

Escorts went on to take the International Rally Championship for 1968 *and* 1969, while the rare and much sought-after Boreham-built Twin Cams allocated to the Alan Mann racing team did well, too, with Frank Gardner winning the 1968 British Saloon Car Championship. Ford were once more back at the very top in competitive motor sport and Ford executives were smiling again. However, as Len Bailey rather laconically put it to the author recently, 'With the Escort we had the best car. The problem was that we (the team engineers and drivers) made it look all too easy and Ford's hierarchy became upset when we did not win.'

A considerable amount of hard work had

Walter Hayes CBE

When it comes to 'fast' Fords most people immediately think of one man, Walter Hayes, for it was he who engineered the company into thinking 'competition' as a very dynamic way of publicizing their products. Born in Harrow, Middlesex in 1924, Hayes was educated at Hampton School before joining the Royal Air Force as a Cadet ·Pilot.

However, it was to be in the media world where Hayes was to make his career, rising to the rank of associate editor of the *Daily Mail* and on to become editor-in-chief of *The Sunday Dispatch* at the age of only 32, making him one of the youngest editors in British newspaper history.

Looking for new fields to conquer he joined the Ford Motor Company in 1962 as Public Relations Manager (soon after that memorable meeting with 'Edgy' Fabris, Publications and Competitions Manager who remarked that hitherto each year they finished publications early so they could compete in the Monte Carlo Rally).

Meanwhile, Ford realized that the future lay in a corporate identity and policy, Hayes being instrumental in helping Henry Ford II to bring together 15 countries, 41 major factories and 135,000 people speaking 14 different languages. By June 1967 all the arrangements had been completed to estab-

Walter Hayes, who left Fleet Street journalism to head up Ford's Public Affairs department and was the major force in putting Ford on to the international motor sport map.

lish Ford of Europe and the following year Hayes was appointed as Vice President, Public Affairs. He was appointed Vice Chairman of Ford Europe and in 1976 he became a member of the Board of Directors, being elected to Vice President of the Parent company the following year. Between 1980 and 1984 he was assigned to the US as Vice President, Public Affairs as well as serving on the boards of Ford Switzerland, Ford Belgium and Ford Germany during his long and impressive career.

However, it was as the man instrumental in setting up the deal with Colin Chapman over the Lotus engine and Lotus Cortina deals, the GT40 programme (which proved so successful during the period Hayes was in charge of Ford's racing programme) and the relations with Cosworth for which Walter Hayes is most readily recognized.

In 1979 Hayes was awarded the CBE for his contribution to Britain's industry and trade. In May 1989 Walter Hayes retired from Ford and is now a director of Aston Martin Lagonda Ltd.

gone on behind the scenes in an effort to make the Lotus engine reliable. As many early owners can testify, reliability of the 1,558cc unit was very much in question.

In mid-1967 Twin Cam engine production was moved to Hethel, where it remained until March 1975. During the time the engine was built there some 25,500 units

A close-up of the rear light cluster of this Mk I Escort Twin Cam. For safety reasons, on the later Mk II Escort the size of the lenses was increased dramatically.

(Opposite) Starting life as an Escort GT, the Twin Cam version used the same trim and fascia pack which included a neat six-dial dash. The seats seen here are non-standard.

To install the Lotus twin cam engine into the Escort's engine bay the unit was angled to the nearside of the car, as can clearly be seen in this view.

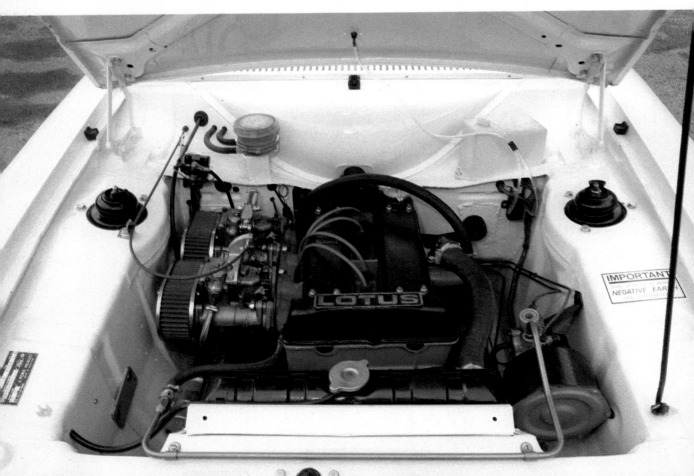

were manufactured and it is said there were no engine failures under warranty – an impressive achievement.

In May 1968, the Twin Cam's rather silly rectangular headlights were replaced by the more powerful circular type, while September saw the introduction of improved trim with a better quality fascia and door panels. Later still, in the autumn of 1970, improvements were made to the face-level ventilators and the wiper and heater controls improved.

At the time of its introduction, the Escort Twin Cam was Ford UK's fastest car. Initial sales had been encouraging but the fickle buying public soon saw through the veneer of high performance to the cramped interior, harsh ride and twitchy handling beneath. Sales began to fall away and something was needed to rejuvenate interest. Also, by the mid-1960s, the 2-valve tohc Lotus engine had almost reached the peak of its development. The answer lay in a new engine: a Cosworth-developed engine.

At Cosworth, the talented Keith Duckworth was now looking to a four valves per cylinder design in an effort to improve gas efficiency and therefore boost power output. What emerged was a new family of engines which has gone into the record books.

The story began in early 1965 when Coventry Climax announced they would not be building any race engines for the new 3-litre Formula One series. Colin Chapman had wild ideas about persuading the SMMT to sponsor a new design of 'national' engine. Not surprisingly, this notion was not taken up so Chapman approached Walter Hayes, the result being a contract between Ford, Keith Duckworth and Cosworth. 'People say I got the bargain of all time by only paying £100,000,' reflected Hayes recently. 'In fact, the exchange rate was different in those days. I actually paid $325,000 which was more than our entire motor racing budget. I went to Detroit to argue the case. Mr Ford said, "What will this new engine do?", to which I replied that I thought it would win some Grands Prix and it stood a good chance of winning the world championship and I also thought it was the seal Ford should be putting on its activities. So Mr Ford said, "Fine, if that's what you think."'

For the following two years Duckworth was deeply involved with the design and development, first with the FVA (Four Valve, Series A) four cylinder engine and then with the DFV (Double Four Valve) V8 unit. Suffice it to say, the record books are full of facts and figures covering the history of these two famous racing engines.

The spin-off from this development work was to be utilized in a road engine designed specifically as a replacement for the Twin Cam which, again, Ford commissioned from Cosworth. However, since Duckworth was still heavily involved with other work, his involvement with this engine (called BDA for Belt Drive Series 'A') was rather more supervisory, the major brunt of development being borne by Mike Hall.

The first time the BDA was shown to the public it was installed in a prototype two-door coupé Capri, and Ford were talking about building about 100 such cars. In fact, the BDA Capris never came to fruition, the unit being put into the Escort and called the RS1600, launched in 1970.

The basis of the 3.18in × 3.05in (80.97mm × 77.62mm) BDA 1600 engine was Ford's slightly taller 1,600cc cylinder block (in direct contrast to the Lotus Ford Twin Cam unit which used the block from the 1,498cc 'Kent' engine with an enlarged cylinder bore of 3.25in (82.55mm) to produce its characteristic 1,558cc capacity). The cylinder head was a light alloy unit with four valves per cylinder set at 40 degrees in a 'pent' roof combustion chamber with two belt-driven overhead camshafts. The Cortina ohv camshaft was retained to drive the distributor and oil pump. Significantly, Ford were able to homologate the engine into the over 1600cc category so it was then possible to enlarge the crossflow cylinder block to

give some 0.39 gallons (1.8 litres).

Like the Lotus–Ford unit, carburation was by twin Webers – the power output being rated at 120bhp at 6,500rpm. Compare this to the 109.5bhp at 6,000rpm rated output of the earlier Lotus twin cam. The bonus, of course, was that the Cosworth-developed engine would run on 2-star fuel and was capable of developing much greater power *reliably*.

Late 1969 saw Ford laying the foundations of what was to become one of the most legendary departments of Ford's contemporary history: Ford Advanced Vehicle Operations, which would be based at South Ockendon. Flying in the face of large-scale, mass-produced vehicles, here was a department which was to be set up solely (as far as possible) to hand-build cars, in some cases to individual customer orders. Hayes again: 'It was purely opportunism which created AV0. The building we used was a big, former parts depot with a design studio alongside. Dunton was built as an engineering research centre while the parts function was moved to Thurrock. I said I wanted the design department as a photographic studio so we could photograph our products properly and the parts area to turn into a small factory where we could build these low volume models. Bill Hayden, who was in charge of production, winked at me and it just seemed to happen. Initially, I put Ray Horrocks in charge and when he left in mid-1972 his place was taken by Stuart Turner.'

Ford Advanced Vehicle Operations opened its doors in January 1970 and quickly blossomed to employ some 200 staff, all eager to be part of something very special within Ford. It also saw the introduction of the hugely successful Rallye Sport programme which was set up to market spares and accessories (as well as the cars themselves) exclusively through Ford's RS dealer network. It was a superb promotional idea which over the years has proved to be a real money-spinner.

The launch of Advanced Vehicle Operations was announced at the 1970 Brussels

*A quick glance and the RS1600 looks very like a late model Escort Twin Cam.
Under the bonnet, though, was Keith Duckworth's splendid BDA unit which
gave the car a sizzling 0–60mph (0–100kph) time of 8.9 secs.*

Motor Show. At the same time Ford proudly proclaimed that the Escort Twin Cam would be gradually phased out in favour of a new model fitted with the Cosworth BDA engine, the car to be called the Escort RS1600. ('RS', incidentally, stood for Rallye Sport, Ford's promotions experts cashing in on the caché of marketing cars, clothing and so on which was closely associated with the company's sporting programme.)

For the time being, however, until South Ockendon (or Averley, as it is sometimes called), came on-stream Escort Twin Cam assembly, which would continue into 1971, and the new RS1600 (code named J26 by Ford) would be built at Halewood alongside the bread-and-butter models. RS1600 began becoming available in the spring of that year and by the beginning of May, 100 units

had been completed. As in the case of the Twin Cam, demand far outstripped production in those early months.

And so Ford began writing the next chapter in the history of their sporting models. The combination of Duckworth's top-flight engineering talent and Stuart Turner's astute mind was to create another winning formula. Yet it wasn't all plain sailing in those very early RS1600 days. 'There were times when Walter Hayes' enthusiasm could result in an untidy aftermath and the adoption of the BDA was an example,' said Dacre Harvey, grimacing at his recollections of running one of the first BDAs. 'The truth was that the durability of the BDA "R" engine was very questionable indeed for the simple reason that there was a consignment of faulty valves. It was also a new and

The four-valves-per-cylinder-head BDA engine which in road trim developed 120bhp at 6,500rpm. Initially based on Ford's Kent cylinder block, later units used the Brian Hart-type alloy block, which increased capacity from 1,598cc to 1,845cc.

unusual engine and at one stage in the very early days there were only a few people in the RS dealer network who could cope with it. The BDA required very great care when maintaining it. A BDA properly set up was a beautiful engine whereas an out-of-tune BDA was a pain in the neck.'

Within a short time, AVO's operations gathered momentum to the point where they were selling their products through some 500 specially appointed agents in countries including Belgium, France, Germany, Norway, Denmark, Switzerland and Austria. Interestingly, for a volume manufacturer like Ford, under the terms of its initial brief, AVO could take any combination of Ford body, engine and transmission and develop it to sell through their RS dealer outlets, production facilities deliberately being made as flexible as possible.

Fundamental to the smooth running of AVO was the talented and enthusiastic workforce. There was always a free exchange of information and experience between the Boreham Boys and the team at Averley. Moreover, the specialist work at AVO always attracted the best names in automotive engineering, development and production. Dick Boxall, whose name was linked with getting the Twin Cam on-stream at Halewood, moved south again (this time permanently) to join men like Rod Dyble, Graham Bridgewater and Ron Owers reporting directly to Stuart Turner. The name of Bill Meade needs no introduction to sporting Ford enthusiasts as the man responsible for the Special Build Section, while Mike Smith, expert in suspension design, joined AVO from Lola Cars where he had worked alongside Tony Southgate. On the turbocharging side, Eric Fuchs was involved with hybrid 3-litre turbo Cortinas. Escorts, Granadas and Capris also benefitted from the master's touch with turbos, while parts and enquiries were handled by two ex-Boreham men: Eric Bristowe and Barry Reynolds.

Another man whose name needs no introduction to fast Ford enthusiasts is Rod Mansfield, a motor racing enthusiast who has always been very much in the forefront of getting out from behind his desk and behind the wheel of a competition car. In 1969 Rod was working in Ford's Truck Production Planning department and came to hear about the plans to set up AVO and the work being done by Horrocks, Taylor and Bob Howe (who went on to develop the RS200 competition car) in getting it established. Rod wasted no time in applying for a job and became the fifth person to join the group. Horrocks placed Rod in charge of the engineering team. Then came promotion to managing AVO's High Performance Programme. The situation was not without irony for his team were responsible for the development of the ventilated disc brakes used on the 2.8i Capri, the first project to be handled later by SVE, under Rod's management.

As Rod recalls, many people were extremely anxious to become a part of AVO and as such it attracted some very talented people who then went on elsewhere: Alan Wilkinson, to Toyota Team Europe and then Mitsubishi-Ralliart; Mike Bennet, to Reliant; and Mike Moreton, to the RS200 and Cosworth RS500 projects before leaving to run Jaguar XJ220 manufacturing.

There were the lighter moments, too. For example, when Horrocks' 3.1 Zodiac was damaged while being manoeuvred off a hoist, the lads had to race round the local dealers trying to get replacement body panels before the boss got back. And the time when an RS1600 was 'borrowed' by someone in Ford who later reported it stolen. The police recovered the stripped body shell and the missing parts in the offender's garage. His days as a Ford employee were numbered!

The Boreham Boys played hard, but they worked very hard, too. Who could have known that AVO's sparkling operation was to be so short-lived?

In the same month that Ford began production of the RS1600 at Averley they also announced their intention to market a smaller-engined version called the Mexico. The name, of course, reflected Ford's victory in the London–Mexico World Cup Rally which had taken place in April/May that year and was entered by pushrod-engined Twin Cams. It was to be another example of Ford's Product Planning Department taking maximum advantage of competition publicity although, behind the scenes, the Mexico's introduction made very good use of the spare assembly capacity at AVO. The plan was simply to broaden the Escort's appeal by fitting a smaller, cheaper and less sophisticated engine into what was, after all, an Escort RS1600.

When Ford opened the new 85,000 sq. ft. (7,900 sq. m.) AVO assembly facility on 14 January 1970 they talked of building some 2,750 units during 1971 and an impressive

Escort Mk I Mexicos and RS1600s in the pre-delivery area at AVO. Production during the early 1970s was mainly Mexicos, with output at around 30 units per day.

6,000 the year after with a workforce of around 300 people. Clearly, the RS1600 was never going to achieve that. The Mexico, then, would go part way to making the whole AVO plan a viable proposition.

Assembly of the Mexico was made that much easier because it shared almost everything with the RS1600: brakes, suspension, steering and final drive, together with almost all the interior trim. In place of the BDA unit there was the 1,599cc 'Kent' engine straight out of the Mk II Cortina GT, with the familiar 2000E gearbox. The alternator specification was changed to a smaller unit and the RS1600 oil cooler was deleted. Producing 86bhp (DIN) at 5,500rpm the Mexico could sprint from 0–60mph (0–100kph) in 10.7 seconds and had a top speed of close on 100mph (160kph).

Inside, the GT seats were replaced by those from the Escort de luxe, while rubber mats were used on the floor instead of carpets. Externally, the Mexico could be easily identified by its side stripes with the word 'MEXICO' on the doors. However, there was a 'delete option' which used more subtle pin stripe side decals and Mexico badges on the front wings.

In July 1971 Ford introduced 'Clubman' packs for the Escort which included a simple roll-over bar, four auxiliary lamps and sport seats and 'Custom' packs, available from October, which included improved interior fittings. The following year came the Special Build facility which offered the customer the chance to buy an RS1600 or a Mexico built to full international rally specification.

During 1971 Brian Hart Racing took the initiative and developed a race version of the BDA engine based on an alloy cylinder block. The bore size for this unit could be increased to some 3.5in (90mm) which gave a 1,975cc capacity, making it a very competitive unit indeed for Formula 2. However, it appears that Ford took no notice until Peter Ashcroft happened across a prototype of this unit while at Hart's Harlow factory. The benefit was obvious – a 40lb (18.1kg) weight saving – and from October 1972 all RS1600s were supplied fitted with an 1,599cc all-alloy version of the BDA.

In the autumn of 1972 the Mexico was given minor improvements in line with the RS1600: the braking system was modified to include a combined master cylinder/servo unit which created sufficient space for the battery to be moved back to the engine compartment; the spare wheel was then mounted vertically; and improved front seats were fitted, together with carpets on the floor.

In many ways, the Mexico was the Mini Cooper of the early 1970s. Rallye Sport dealers could offer the same long list of extras and sporting options that could be had for the RS1600. It also triggered off a series of races and rallies, all of which did even greater things for AVO, the Escort as an image car – and Ford.

Clearly, the shortfall of the RS1600 was its price and complexity which deterred many prospective buyers. Equally, the Mexico, despite its fancy dressing, was a little too slow and a little too 'buzzy' for many people's tastes. What was needed was something which looked sporty, handled well, and was quick and refined. The answer lay in giving the Escort 'Pinto' power.

Launched on 4 July 1973, the RS2000 combined 110+mph (175+kph) top speed with a 0–60mph (0–100kph) time of around 9 seconds. Slotting the large 3.57in × 3.02in (90.82mm × 76.95mm) sohc engine into the Escort 'Type 49' body shell was indeed a squeeze. The space between block and radiator was too small to accommodate a cooling fan so an electric one was mounted in the vulnerable position ahead of the radiator, thereby cutting down marginally on noise levels and saving some 2bhp in power. (Output was quoted as 100bhp at 5,700rpm.)

Another modification which had to be made in order to get the Pinto engine to fit beneath the Escort's bonnet line was the

Bill Meade, who, along with Henry Taylor, conceived the Escort Twin Cam after looking at prototype Escorts being tested at Boreham.

change to a special cast alloy sump which was so shaped that it cleared the front suspension crossmember. The clutch bell-housing, too, was made from alloy which went some way in off-setting the greater weight of the Cortina engine. It also raised an in-built resonance frequency from 5,400rpm to over 6,000rpm which reduced noise levels.

The gearbox, too, was special to this particular Escort, being a German unit which featured a very low first but uprated second and third ratios, while the gear lever movement was different as well insofar that reverse was away to the left and forward, rather than to the driver and back. The final drive was also changed, from 3.77:1 as used in the RS1600/Mexico, to a 3.54:1 which was more in keeping with the torque characteristic of the 1,998cc engine while at the same time giving more relaxed high-speed cruising.

Brakes were 9.6in (243mm) discs on the front and 8.0in × 1.5in (203mm × 38.1mm) drums on the rear (instead of the 9.0in × 1.75in (228mm × 44.4mm) drums fitted to the RS1600) with servo assistance. This change of braking specification was to change the brake bias to offset the increase in weight over the front wheels of the RS2000. Normally, the car was supplied with 5.5 × 13in (14 × 33cm) steel wheels, although a great many owners took advantage of the smart four-spoke alloy wheels available as an option.

Inside the car it was clear that the Product Planning people at Ford had influenced the choice of trim. In fact, many Mexico sales had included the 'Custom' and 'Comfort' option packs, indicating that customers were willing to pay extra for a better standard of trim and seating. As a result, the RS2000 was given a rather better interior package which included very comfortable rally-type reclining seats.

Initially, sale of the RS2000 was limited to Germany where the first 2,000 units were delivered. This meant that British enthusiasts had to wait impatiently until October 1973 before getting their hands on one.

The build process at the South Ockendon plant differed in one major way from all other Ford factories. It was in all respects an assembly centre. Body shells fully wired, trimmed and painted were delivered from Halewood where they were placed on hangers suspended from the ceiling and moved along a circular track. Drive trains, engines, clutches, gearboxes and final drives were then mounted on hydraulic trolleys and manoeuvred into position from beneath, unlike all other Ford production lines where

the units were dropped in from above. Engines for the RS1600 were supplied from Harpers of Letchworth (and not, incidentally, from Cosworth) while the Mexico and RS2000 units came from Ford's engine plant at Dagenham. Back axles were supplied from Swansea, Mexico gearboxes from Ford's transmission plant at Halewood and RS2000 gearboxes from Germany. The Germans were also responsible for manufacturing their own RS2000, with some 1,162 units built at Saarlouis, the factory where the next generation of RS cars would be assembled.

By 1974, the AVO Escort line-up included the Mexico, the RS2000 and the RS1600 – a sporting Escort to suit almost every pocket. In sales terms, however, popularity of the RS1600 dropped dramatically, while the Mexico, too, could not compete with the 2-litre car.

Unfortunately, all was far from well. With the energy crisis beginning to bite, car sales were affected dramatically, especially the sales of performance cars. There was no alternative but to close down the AVO factory. RS1600 production, which had only been limited, stopped completely in November that year while the Mexico and RS2000 continued until January 1975, the last few selling for far more than the book price as news got round that the next generation of RS models would not be available for some months. Meanwhile, many of the staff stayed on while AVO continued to supply RS components.

Despite being short-lived, AVO has already gone down in Ford's history as a remarkable and very successful venture. The old hands still recall with affection the 'behind-the-scenes' projects such as the four-wheel-drive Capri Programme which used V6 engines and Ferguson transmission, as well as a V8 Granada – the list goes on. But then there was the next generation of Escort waiting in the wings . . .

3 Into High Gear

It is hardly surprising that sporting Ford enthusiasts look back on the late 1960s and early 1970s with great affection. Although the Escort Twin Cam was a rather raucous motor car, its top speed, acceleration and handling put it way out in front of almost anything that other British manufacturers could offer. Buyers who demanded its sort of performance (110+ mph (175+ kph) maximum speed) invariably looked to Italy or Germany to find an alternative – and pay considerably more. See how the figures below compare.

In overall terms, the Escort was a very successful car in Ford's model line-up. Less than four years after the Escort had reached production, it set a new assembly record (one million units produced) for a European Ford, leaving the Anglia lagging far behind. (The Anglia did not reach this level until September 1966.) By the end of 1974, some 2,156,519 Escorts (which included prototype and pre-production versions of the Mk II Escort) had been assembled, an impressive achievement.

By the time the second generation of Escort was introduced, Ford's corporate policy to transform its European activities into a slickly organized assembly operation was well into high gear. An assembly facility in Genk, Belgium close to the West German border, was brought on-stream in 1968 to assist with Escort manufacture, hitherto handled solely by Halewood. However, within two years, arrangements were made for Escort production to be moved to Saarlouis, Germany, where Escort manufacture was brought on-stream by 1972. Indeed, by the early 1970s, Ford's European manufacturing strategy took no account of national borders, making communication and transportation a somewhat confusing business!

In line with Ford's product planning, the Escort Mk I was to be replaced with an improved model due for launch in early 1975. In this case, 'improved' meant that the Mk II model range would be specifically designed to attract a broader section of the buying public. Faster, better trimmed and with a greater range from which to choose, Ford's Product Planners and Market Analysis experts were keen to build on the lessons learnt from the first generation of Escorts. What they had not bargained on was an energy crisis, which was to have far-reaching effects on the motor industry – to say nothing of commerce – throughout Europe.

	Ford Escort Twin Cam	Alfa Romeo 2000 GTV	BMW 2002 Tii	Fiat 124 Coupé 1600
Price	£1171	£2491	£2349	£1739
Top Speed	113mph	120mph	116mph	109mph
0–60mph	9.9 sec	9.2 sec	8.3 sec	10.7 sec
Fuel consumption	24mpg	21.1mpg	25.4mpg	23.6mpg

Work on restyling the Mk I Escort was started in 1972. Referred to as 'Brenda' (the Christian name of a Ford director's secretary), the design improvement was given the green light the following year. By the autumn of 1974 pilot panels had been made for a production run of prototypes and the cars finished – an indication of the speed with which Ford wanted the new model range to reach the showrooms. Prototype models were assembled at both Halewood and Saarlouis, the German plant having their cars completed just a few weeks ahead of Halewood. Also as part of the pilot-build programme, 19 fully engineered cars and 9 mechanical prototypes were built.

Under the skin, of course, 'Brenda' shared the same basic dimensions as her earlier sister with identical wheelbase, track and overall length, although the wheel sizes were changed to 13in (33cm) on all but the 1.1-litre version. In tune with the crisper lines which were emerging from the styling houses of the period, the shape of the Mk II did away with the rather bulbous features of the Mk I and was smoother and more angular in design. This allowed for the use of bigger windows and the Mk II had some 23 per cent additional glass area. Inside the car there was 2in (5cm) more legroom for rear passengers. That said, the slab-sided shape was slightly narrower, although in no way

Crash testing a prototype Mk II Escort. Like the Cortina, the Escort body shell, especially in Series 2 form, was very tough which made it ideal as a basis for a rally car.

did this affect internal space. For its size, the Escort continued to provide excellent levels of accommodation. The flip side to all these improvements was that along the way the Mk II body shell had increased its weight by a hefty 200lbs (90.7kg) over the Mk I car and its aerodynamic efficiency had deteriorated to 0.488. (Just how these retrograde 'features' had been allowed to creep in is difficult to understand.) There were also changes to the floorpan design and revised damper locations. (These improvements had, in fact, begun to be introduced on the Mk I cars during the autumn of 1973.)

At the same time as plans were moving ahead for the pilot build of the first Mk II Escort, the team at AVO began thinking of an 'RS' version which could be offered as an option, with a projected sales level of around 100 units p.a. (Only a mere 47 RS1600 Mk Is had been sold during 1974, indicating the very considerable fall-off in the car's demand.) Then, with the announcement of impending changes in homologation which would take effect in 1975, it was decided to take advantage of the design of the alloy cylinder block and enlarge the bore to 3.41in (86.75mm), the resulting capacity falling within the regulations which permitted a 15 per cent increase in engine size. Using a 3.05in (77.62mm) crankshaft from the standard 'Kent' engine family, this produced 1,835cc! To handle the potential increase in power and torque the gearbox was to be changed, too. By using the casing from the RS2000, a selection of gear ratios could be chosen from the Granada range. Initial plans were for the car – which would be called 'RS1800' – to be simply an RS Mexico with an engine/gearbox transplant undertaken at AVO, the car then to be offered with the new body style from May 1975. It was a scheme hatched in order to meet the homologation rules, while at the same time still offering a road car for those who wanted something special.

On 20 December 1974, the last of the Halewood-built Escort Mk Is rolled off the production line, making way for the sleeker Mk II Escort which would be unveiled at the Brussels Motor Show in January 1975.

Judging from the events of late 1974 it is clear that Ford's top management decision to close down the car assembly section at Averley was done in some haste. As one observer commented, 'even the talents of Stuart Turner are not sufficient to keep the wheels rolling'. Staffing levels were drastically cut, although some people were kept on 'just in case'. The parts section, though, remained in business for the ever-present demand from Ford enthusiasts. 'The function of the competition parts service always was to say to the man in the street, "everything we homologate, you can come and buy",' said Walter Hayes. 'I was very anxious that Ford should allow people who raced and rallied privately to have access to the right equipment and we made a conscious effort to encourage such people to come down to Boreham and buy the appropriate parts for whatever event they were entering. There is no point in undertaking all the hard work required to prepare a car, and the vehicle not finish.'

Almost twenty years on, it is, perhaps, a little difficult to appreciate the dramatic effect the energy crisis had on the world at large and the motor industry in particular. Yet who of those caught up in its effect are ever likely to forget it? Prophets of doom were pronouncing the end of the big car (and, indeed, probably all cars), petrol coupons were printed, although never brought into use. Yet, despite this, Ford's plans for the next generation of Escort included a very complex model range, all interlinked with various engine options (driving a new, compact gearbox) and a myriad of trim styles. GT models were renamed 'Sports' with appropriate flashes and low profile tyres.

Although the energy crisis was to affect motor sport considerably, Ford were still

The front nose cone added to the RS2000 Mk II gave the car a very distinctive profile making it look sporty yet not flashy, the polyurethane cone being flexible enough to take small knocks.

committed to their programme for competing in international events. Policy dictated, however, that they could not do so in a car which was no longer in production. Boreham would have to wait until homologation was granted for the Mk II Escort RS1800.

By the time AVO finally closed its doors in the latter part of January 1975, a handful of Mk II RS1800s had been part-built at Halewood and finished off at the Averley factory. However, with the AVO production facility closed, RS1800 series production had to be put on hold.

Meanwhile, the Boreham Boys had somewhat taken things into their own hands by building a non-running RS1800 rally car (using one of the AVO-built RS1800s), complete with Lombard-RAC decals and RS1800 badges, which was put on display at a UK press preview held at London's Dorchester Hotel. However, it was not until May that the first RS1800 went into battle, winning the Welsh International with Roger Clark at the wheel. Homologation had been granted in January 1975, approval being forthcoming based on the number of Mk I RS1600s which had been re-engined and given new body shells. (Boreham's Peter Ashcroft and John Griffiths had argued that many RS1800s would be built using this method.) If the Mk I Escort was reckoned to be one of the world's leading rally cars of its day, with the coming of the Mk II they had seen nothing yet!

It is hard to imagine a car like the RS1800 ever being marketed by a large, volume manufacturer such as Ford. Equally surprising is that no production records exist, although Ford actually marketed (through the Rallye Sport dealer chain) fully trimmed Mk II body shells which were then used as the basis for being built into RS1800s. In his very authoritative work on the Escorts, *The Works Escort* published by Haynes, the knowledgeable Graham Robson suggests that there were less than 500 factory-built RS1800 road cars.

Production-wise, by 1975 it had been established that the RS cars would be built at the Saarlouis factory in Germany, much to the disgust of most British sporting Ford fans. Walter Hayes explained the wisdom for this production decision, 'Until the energy crisis, demand for the Escort "specials" on the home market was growing and in 1968 I went to Germany to set up a motor sport programme. That was when we got Jochen Neerpasch. The following year we won the East African Safari Rally with the Taunus and we began racing Capris. With the introduction of the Mk II Escort we had to consider where the RS versions were to be made. In fact, Bill Hayden was happy for them to go down an otherwise unused production line at Saarlouis. Dagenham was undergoing major redevelopment so I said to Bill, "You could build ten RS cars an hour down the Saarlouis line," to which he replied, "I can build fifteen". So, since we were selling Escorts in Germany, the fact that we had performance Fords coming out of a German factory seemed very good to me.' In reality, this decision upset a large number of British RS enthusiasts.

To satisfy demand, RS1800 assembly began in March 1975 based on the Escort Sport (and later the RS Mexico), although cars did not become generally available through dealers until June. Cars, without engines and gearboxes, were brought over to (of all places) Averley where in a quiet corner of the now disused AVO factory they were fitted out. Under the bonnet, the expensive twin Weber carburettors had been replaced by a single 32/36 DGAV-type Weber mounted on an alloy inlet manifold. As a result, power was restricted to some 115bhp (DIN) at 6,000rpm, although the torque characteristics of the engine made the car hardly temperamental in traffic.

At such low manufacturing levels RS1800 engine assembly was sub-contracted to several firms including Brian Hart Engines in Harlow, Weslake of Rye, East Sussex as well as Harpers of Letchworth, Holbay (who assembled some 50 units using steel crankshafts) and Boreham, too, when the need arose. It was a somewhat *ad hoc* arrangement and very much a low-key production programme.

Under the bonnet this twin cam Escort looked like no previous car. Either side of the radiator were the brake servo and battery. The spare wheel was now strapped to the nearside wall of the boot. Externally, the car could be distinguished by its side 'RS1800' decals, '1.8' badges on the front wings and bumper-level side stripes. Under the front quarter bumpers was a subtle chin spoiler and the boot lid boasted a spoiler, too. The bumpers themselves and the side window surrounds were finished in matt black.

Inside, the car could be ordered as an RS1800 or an RS1800 Custom. The standard car was almost identical with the Escort Sport, whereas the Custom shared much of its trim level with the soon-to-be-launched RS2000 Mk II, and included a centre console with a location for a radio, a clock let into the fascia on the nearside and a pair of rather superior-looking, rally-style front seats.

Despite its limited fifteen month production run, the Mk I Escort RS2000 had been a very successful car for Ford. From the enthusiastic owner's standpoint it made a great deal of sense, being almost as fast as the RS1600 yet much cheaper to run and maintain. Ford's Product Planning people were clearly eager to maximize the reputation which the first generation of RS2000 had established. Moreover, since the mainstream Escort model range already included a 1600 Sport, effectively a Mexico by any other name, every effort was put into developing a new RS2000 which would be even better than the last.

Ford's design team were encouraged to update and improve both the internal and the external profiles of the car, making it as distinctive as possible. The result, of course, was the completely restyled front end which

The 'Sport' models – available in either 1300 or 1600 form – with either 2-door or 4-door body styles which were a direct descendant of the Mexico but were mainstream models built at Halewood and Saarlouis.

included the chin spoiler, a different front bumper and longer bonnet mated with a very sleek, angular nose cone (neatly let into the standard body) which incorporated twin headlamps. Adding an extra 8.6in (218.4mm) to the car's overall length, it was said that the nose cone and rear boot spoiler reduced drag to a very commendable 0.383 Cd, an improvement of some 16 per cent. The front chin spoiler itself reduced lift by some 25 per cent, improving the car's high speed stability. In addition, the reduced drag would be responsible for increasing the car's top speed by some 6–7 per cent.

The first prototype Mk II RS2000 was built at Averley, some sheet metal being attached to the body of a Mk I car to form the unusual beak nose which became the focal point of the production Mk II RS2000. The car was then tested at MIRA and in Italy.

Alan Wilkinson, one of the AVO engineers involved in this work, later went to Saarlouis to help build Mk II RS2000 pre-production cars. In fact, the engineering team still based at AVO went on to undertake the vehicle engineering and product planning of this model, although the production management was handled by Ford's German staff in Cologne.

The Mk II RS2000 was the most dramatic-looking Escort thus far. In addition to the spoilers, all the brightwork was now finished in matt black. The road wheels were 6J × 13in cast alloys with low profile tyres and neat wrap-around bumpers back and front. Gone, however, were the large 'RS' decals on the rear flanks of the RS1800. The RS2000 carried its name on the bootlid only, below the spoiler. 'Neat but not gaudy' might have been an apt description.

Not just a pretty boy-racer addition, the rear spoiler improved the RS2000's aerodynamic efficiency to below 0.4Cd which was only bettered with the introduction of the Mk III Escort range.

Engine-wise, the RS2000 was powered by the familiar 3.57in × 3.02in (90.8mm × 76.95mm) unit producing a respectable 110bhp (DIN) at 5,750rpm, an increase of 10bhp which Ford felt entitled to claim in view of the 'special' free-flow exhaust system. The gearbox was the old favourite from the Cortina 1600E model range linked to a two-piece propshaft. The final drive gearing gave 19mph (30.5kph)/1,000rpm. Braking was provided by 9.6in (243.8mm) discs on the front and 9in (228.6mm) diameter drums on the rear – servo assisted, of course.

Inside, the RS was a delight to Ford enthusiasts who had 'made do' with somewhat spartan fixtures and fittings in earlier models. A tasteful dashboard and well-shaped reclining seats gave the car a real touch of luxury. With a top speed of 110+mph (175+kph) and a 0–60mph (0–100kph) time of 8.6 seconds, the Mk II RS2000 was fast and luxurious.

Production of the RS2000 began at Saarlouis in February 1976 although, in fact, the public's appetite had been whetted some months earlier by the exhibition of a pre-production car at the Geneva Show in 1975. There it had attracted considerable attention;

Stone chips, flies and tar soon make a car look shoddy; the excellent paintwork and black-finish bumper on this RS2000 are a tribute to its owner.

This RS2000 has been fitted with the popular FAVO-type alloy 6J × 13in (33cm) road wheels, which set the car off well. Initially standard wear, later they were offered as an optional extra.

The move away from badges to adhesive graphics-type decals like this began in the 1960s. This RS2000 bootlid badge has been added by the owner.

Originally factory-supplied with matt black mirrors, the owner of this very smart RS2000 has colour-coded his door mirrors like those fitted to second series Escort RS Turbos.

its stylish finish and impressive performance at an affordable price had drawn many admiring glances.

Perhaps the real surprises of the Mk II Escort range was the introduction of the Mexico version, called the RS Mexico, to cash in on the marketing cachet of the name 'RS'. Launched in January 1976, the car had many of the visual traits of the RS1800:

standard grille/nose section, quarter bumpers and front chin and rear boot spoilers. It also had the same matt black brightwork and large rear side decals proclaiming 'Mexico' let into parallel body stripes which ran down the flanks of the car. Inside, the new generation Mexico contained the same dashboard arrangement as the standard RS1800 along with low-backed seats.

Peter Ashcroft

Peter was born in Walton-le-Dale in Lancashire, in 1928. Very much a Ford 'backroom boy', Peter's contribution to Ford's competition successes over the years has been considerable, totally belying his quiet, unassuming manner.

Like many people eager to start in motor sport, Ashcroft began racing in 1950 with a Cooper 500, competing in Formula 3 events. His reputation as a man with considerable expertise in engine tuning began to get round and he soon became in demand as a racing mechanic of some note. Such were his skills that he was able to earn a living from race engine preparation, his knowledge and experience being behind many of the successful cars in the north of England during the mid-1950s.

A man whose career has been shaped working on 'sporting Fords', Peter Ashcroft was the man behind the idea to use the Brian Hart-developed alloy cylinder block for the BDA.

However, it was very much a hand-to-mouth existence and in 1959 Ashcroft joined the Gilby Racing team run by the late Sid Greene, becoming their chief mechanic. During this period he contributed largely to the design and development of the 1,100cc Gilby-Climax sports racing car and later the Gilby Formula 1 car.

In 1962 Peter left the Gilby team to join Ford as a mechanic, although it was to be short-lived for he soon left to take up the post of chief engineer for the Peter Sellars Racing Team. However, only 18 months later Peter rejoined Ford, this time as engines engineer and in May 1972 he was appointed Competitions Manager.

During his career with Ford, Peter's name has been linked with the design and development of the 1,950cc pushrod engines for the London–Mexico World Cup Rally, the development of the 2.9-litre V6 Capri engines and the 1.8-litre thick wall 'Ashcroft Block' version of the legendary Twin Cam engine. Today, Peter Ashcroft heads up Ford's Competition Department.

Under the bonnet, the RS Mexico differed from its predecessor in one major area. While the engine in the earlier car had been the 1,599cc 'Kent' engine lifted directly from the Cortina GT, the new car was powered by a 1,593cc, 3.45in × 2.59in (87.65 × 66mm) single-overhead-camshaft unit very like that fitted in the RS2000 (but with different bore and stroke dimensions), producing some 95bhp at 5,500rpm. In fact, much of the 'plumbing' of the bigger unit had been carried over to the RS Mexico and it was for this reason that the unit produced some 7bhp more than when fitted in the Capri 1600S. Otherwise, the gearbox, brakes and steering were all similar to those fitted to the bigger RS model. Performance-wise, the RS Mexico was a true 100+mph (160+kph) motor car with a claimed 0–60mph (0–100kph) time of 11 seconds.

Ford were granted International Group 4 status for the RS1800 in April 1977. This included the full 2-litre BDA engine, fuel injection or twin Weber carburettors, dry sump lubrication and 5-speed ZF gearbox, the specification which would continue for the remainder of the RS1800's enormously successful rally career.

In September 1977 the production RS1800 slipped quietly away and into the history books with some (so it is reckoned) 109 cars sold in the UK. Four months later the RS Mexico was also dropped.

Had Ford not introduced the Escort Sport version powered by a 1.6-litre engine, the RS Mexico may well have found its own market. As it was, the much faster, more refined RS2000 attracted the bulk of the custom while the cheaper Sport models caught those buyers whose budget was more restricted.

In an effort to bridge something of the gap left by the demise of the RS Mexico, Ford decided to introduce two versions of the RS2000 – a 'base' model and the RS2000 Custom. To reduce the price of the cheaper model the car's interior fittings were less plush, with low-backed seats, while the smart alloy road wheels were replaced by pressed steel ones. In contrast, the RS2000 Custom boasted Recaro-type reclining seats, a remote-operated driver's mirror and bronze tinted glass. Ironically, the base model sold in more numbers than the old RS Mexico ever did, while the Custom version continued the sales success established by the earlier Mk II RS2000. RS2000 production remained in operation until the summer of 1980 when all rear-wheel-drive Escort production ceased.

SPORTING CAPRIS

Like the Escort, the Capri also became very much a 'cult' car, partly due to its overt sporting image and partly due to competition successes across Europe. The Capri model range was introduced in January 1969. The result of a combined programme involving both Ford UK and Ford Germany, the product was a sleek if conventional coupé designed to take advantage of engines from the Dagenham and Cologne model ranges; it would also be further personalized by the availability of three option trim packs known as 'X', 'L' and 'R'.

Suspension-wise, the Capri was similar to other cars in the Ford range with Mac-Pherson strut coil spring/damper units on the front with an anti-roll bar, while a solid rear axle was supported on leaf springs with telescopic dampers; on all versions brakes were disc at the front with drums on the rear, although on the more powerful Capris a servo was fitted.

As for engine options, the potential Capri customer was faced with an almost bewildering choice from the smallest 1,300cc and 1,600cc GT units which were in-line four cylinder units producing from 52bhp to 92bhp, to 2-litre and 3-litre V4 and V6 engines developing 123 and 144bhp respectively. All these engines fitted easily into the Capri's roomy engine compartment.

The RS1800 was available in two forms: standard and Custom. Exact production numbers have proved hard to establish for in classic car circles rarity affects value.

5.5J × 13in (33cm) steel wheels were standard fitment on the RS1800 although many owners opted for RS-type four-spoke alloys available in sizes from 5.5-7in (14-17.8cm) wide.

Compared to the RS2000 this RS1800 hardly looks the top-of-the-range in Ford's Mk II Escort series. Production was based at the old FAVO factory while engines came from a number of suppliers.

Interior trimming on the RS1800 was similar to other models in the Escort range and included the sports six-dial cluster. This car has been fitted with the 'Custom Pack' option.

In road trim the BDA 1,838cc engine was fitted with the Weber 32/36 DGAV carburettor, BDA 1600 valves and a 9:1 compression ratio limiting power to 115bhp at 6,000rpm yet with good flexibility.

The RS1600i was another of Ford's homologation specials conceived by Ford of Germany Motorsport division for Group A and Group N racing. It turned out to be a showroom success. (Inset left) This was one of the reasons the RS1600i sold so well: draylon-type interior trim and top-quality Recaro front seats. There was also a long options list including sun roof and electric windows. (Inset right) Under the bonnet was the familiar 1.6 CVH engine with Bosch K-Jetronic fuel injection (the first Production Escort to be so fitted) producing 115bhp at 6,000rpm.

Largely because of the Escort's success both on rallies and the race track, Ford UK did not put the same emphasis on developing the Capris for competitive motor sport as did Jochen Neerpasch (a former works driver appointed by Walter Hayes), who headed up the German Ford Motorsport Department which had been established just a year before the Capri's launch. In Germany, the performance version of the Capri was available in 2300GT and 2600GT. These engines were based on an OHV V6 format – a format, incidentally, which would run on to spawn the 2.8i engine used in the Capri 2.8 injection and the Granada/Scorpio.

In March 1969 the Capri 2300GT was entered in the Lyon-Charbonnieres rally in prototype form where it managed fourth place overall. Under the bonnet was a tuned unit with triple Solex carburettors and Weslake gas-flowed cylinder heads increasing the output to 170bhp at 6,500rpm. This would later be increased still further to 192bhp at 7,200rpm using Lucas fuel injection. (A rally-prepared 2300 Capri tested by *Cars and Car Conversions* was reckoned to produce around 150bhp at 7,500rpm fitted with triple IDA downdraught Weber carburettors. Maximum speed was measured as 109mph (175.38kph) with a 0–60mph (0–100kph) time of 8.2 seconds.) Then came success with a larger 2600GT which finished third overall in the Corsican Tour de Corse, with a 200bhp engine (compared to 125bhp in street tune).

Capri RS2600 and RS3100

In November 1969 AVO's engineers began work on a prototype RS2600 Capri. Significantly, with Neerpasch already campaigning Capris abroad with the German V6 motor, development work at AVO would involve Ford's Vee family of engines (the British 3-litre Capri unit sharing only the common 60 degree cylinder angle with the German power units).

The V6 engine similar to that fitted to the RS3100 Capri. For the RS3100 the engine was overbored and given a Weber 38 EGAS carburettor, the result being a healthy 148bhp at 5,000rpm.

Initially, two RS Capris, both LHD, were assembled at AVO, one for exhibition at the Geneva Show in March the following year, the second a full race version with an ultra lightweight body and an uprated V6 2,637cc engine. In road tune this engine developed 150bhp at 5,600rpm while the Weslake-prepared race version developed for Group 2 (which was enlarged to 2,995cc with Kugelfischer fuel injection, 11.3:1 compression ratio and dry sump lubrication) put out over 320bhp. The suspension utilized MacPherson coil spring/dampers all round, although small leaf springs were preserved on the rear in an effort to retain something of the car's original design for regulation purposes. The live axle was firmly located by parallel radius arms. Brakes were ventilated discs all round. However, despite such an impressive specification, the RS2600 Capri's performance in the 1970 round of the European Championship indicated that the car

In production form the Capri RS3100 could be spotted by the front quarter bumpers, the four-spoke road wheels and the large rear spoiler. Inside was a three-spoke RS steering wheel.

Capri rarity, the RS2600, which was sold only in LHD European markets. With 150bhp and race-inspired interior trim this was a Capri for the true enthusiast.

required more development work if it was to be really competitive.

Meanwhile, the Cologne plant was speedily gearing up for small-scale assembly of pre-production RS2600 Capris – the first 50 units coming off the line in April 1970 in full lightweight guise. Doors, bonnet and bootlid were glass-fibre panels made by BBS, who subsequently became famous for their alloy road wheels. (The wheels on the RS Capris

There were two versions of RS Capri, the 2600 – based on the German V6 unit – and the more production-based 3100 which utilized an overbored version of the British Essex V6 engine. RS3100s were built in RHD form only.

were Minilite.) The cars could be easily distinguished by their twin headlamps and matt black bonnet, the lack of front and rear bumpers, and perspex side windows which replaced the original glass type.

In August that year approval was given to AVO's specification for the production version of the RS2600. This included modifications to

the front suspension to allow for the alteration of later camber angles, the single-leaf rear springs with coil spring dampers, Bilstein gas dampers for the front struts and the fuel injected power unit. With this in place, the assembly chain was put into high gear for the first 'production' RS Capris to come off the Cologne line in September, destined for the European market.

Like the race car, road-going RS2600 Capris were fitted with a Weslake-prepared engine with Kugelfischer fuel injection system which produced 150bhp. (The addition of alloy cylinder heads was strictly reserved for Group 2 cars.) The gearbox and final drive were a combination of cogs from both the German and British Ford product lines. (Only the race cars boasted a ZF 5-speed gearbox.) A limited slip was available as an option. Suspension was very much like that on the first 50 Capri RSs with Bilstein inserts in the dampers, coil springs all round and miniscule rear leaf springs. Brakes were similar to those used on the standard 2600GT with Ford's usual disc/drum layout. Inside, however, racing austerity had given way to Grand Touring luxury with a set of handsome cord-faced recliners for those in front and a deep, dished steering wheel.

In 1971, Ford Europe decided to rework the car's specification, the modifications centering on improving the Capri's overall 'feel': the suspension height was lifted and the spring and damper settings softened to give a more compliant ride. New AVO-type 6J × 13in (33cm) road wheels were fitted while the brakes were changed to disc all round. Outside, the original bumperless bodies were given chrome protection bars, quarter ones on the front and a full-width bumper bar on the rear. Performance-wise, this up-dated version of Ford's sporting Capri could hit 124mph (199.5kph) flat out and sprint from 0–60mph (0–100kph) in a little over 8 seconds. They were, however, all LHD cars (just a handful were altered to RHD form for British use; Walter Hayes was the proud

Capri RS2600 and 3100 Date Profile

March 1969	:	First appearance of Capri 2300GT on Lyons-Charbonnieres Rally as prototype. Engine producing 170bhp (DIN) at 6,500rpm.
October 1969	:	Approval at FAVO for RS Capri programme.
December 1969	:	Work begins on first LHD Capri RS2600 prototypes at FAVO.
March 1970	:	Capri RS2600 on show at the Geneva Motor Show.
May 1970	:	First 50 pre-production Capri RS2600s built at Cologne.
August 1970	:	FAVO get approval for Capri RS2600 technical specification which includes fuel injection and modified suspension.
September 1970	:	First production Capri RS2600s built at Cologne. Powered by 2,637cc V6 engine with Kugelfischer mechanical fuel injection developing 150bhp at 5,800rpm. MacPherson front suspension with re-drilled Capri crossmember, leaf springs and radius arms on the rear. Bilstein dampers. Richard Grant 6J × 13in (33cm) alloy road wheels. Interior as German Capri 2300GT but with dished steering wheel and reclining cord-covered front seats. Car not for general release in UK.
October 1971	:	Changes to production specification including an increase in ride height, alloy road wheels changed for FAVO four-spoke type, chrome bumpers fitted, later changed to matt black type. Cortina 3-litre ventilated-type front disc brakes.
June 1972	:	Fascia changed to matt black finish. Also, changes to interior trim material including softer cord for seats and modified head restraints. Three-spoke flat steering and opening rear quarter lights.
September 1973	:	Approval given for Capri RS3100 in RHD form to be built at Halewood from November 1973.
October 1973	:	First 6 pre-production Capri RS3100s built at Boreham.
November 1973	:	Introduction of Capri RS3100 available through Rallye Sport dealers only. Based on Capri 3000GT with 3,091cc 'Essex'-based engine with single Weber carburettor and polished ports and inlet tracts producing 148bhp (DIN) at 5,000rpm. Front brakes as Capri RS2600. Rear brakes, servo and final drive, as Capri 3-litre. Lowered ride height with modified front spring rates and cross-member. Rear suspension utilized anti-roll bar from Capri 3-litre Bilstein dampers. Interior trim as Capri 3000GT but with three-spoke RS-type steering wheel. Matt black bumpers (quarter type at front) and boot mounted flick-up rear spoiler.
December 1973	:	Capri RS2600 model discontinued.
February 1974	:	Capri RS3100 model discontinued. Introduction of Capri Mk II model range announced (with three-door coach-work).

owner of one, Stuart Turner another) for sale in many countries throughout Europe. Production ran on until 1973 with some 4,000 of these cars sold.

All of this meant, of course, that British customers had to make do with the standard 3-litre Capri. That was until late in 1973 when plans were hastily drawn up for a RHD Capri RS for the home market. The brief for the AVO team was to produce a

Capri which would share the same suspension, brakes and wheels as the old RS2600 model but use a 3.1-litre *overbored* version of the British V6 engine, which increased its capacity from 2,993cc to 3,091cc.

Assembly of the production Capri RS3100s was planned to start in November 1973 at Ford's Halewood plant. Under the bonnet, power had been increased over the standard 3.0-litre unit to 148bhp at 5,200rpm simply by polishing the ports! Even the EGAS Weber carburettor was the same as that fitted to the 3.0-litre Capri. Externally, the car did at least look the part with matt black bumpers, quarter-width type at the front and a conventional bumper bar at the rear, AVO-type four-spoke alloy wheels, side and bonnet stripe decals and a rather obvious boot spoiler. Inside the car, little was changed from what was standard in the 3.0-litre Capri GT with the exception of the RS steering wheel. Underneath, although the suspension layout was based on the RS2600, component specifications were changed to soften the ride and make the car more attractive for everyday use. Performance, however, was pretty sparkling – with a 0–60mph (0–100kph) time of around 7 seconds and a maximum speed of 124mph (199.5kph). Intended to be sold through Ford's Rallye Sport dealers, the RS3100 build programme was completed during November 1973 in readiness for the Mk II Capri which was scheduled to come on-stream by the beginning of 1974.

But, as we have already seen with the Escort story, by this time AVO operations were being wound up, mainly because the energy crisis was having such a dramatic effect on the sales levels of performance cars. Even so, plans for a 2.8-litre fuel injected Capri Mk II RS were formulated during 1975, although they were to remain just that; producing the RS2000 Escort was taking up valuable resources.

However, as most sporting Ford enthusiasts know, the first job to be handled by

Special Vehicle Engineering (or SVE for short) was the Capri 2.8i which remained in production far longer than Ford ever intended, such was the demand for this sleek Ford coupé. Today, as Ford enters the 1990s, there is no direct replacement. Moreover, it encouraged the development of other quick Capris, notably the Tickford Capri 2.8T with its IHI turbocharged engine (which produced some 205bhp) and the Ford-approved turbo modification for the Capri offered by Turbo Technics.

Meanwhile, a racing version of the RS3100 was developed between Cosworth and Ford's German Motorsport headquarters based in Cologne. The basic 3-litre V6 'Essex' block was increased in bore size to give a capacity of 3,412.5cc. It featured a steel crankshaft and aluminium cylinder heads with belt-driven overhead camshafts operating four valves per cylinder in the usual Cosworth manner. Initial power output was rated at 400bhp, although with special, stiffer blocks supplied from Ford this figure was increased to a very impressive 440bhp at 8,500rpm. Known as the GAA engine, Cosworth were contracted to supply parts for 100 of these units to comply with Group 2 regulations. Sadly, though, the economic climate of the period resulted in few actually being raced. Some were used in Formula 5000 single-seaters while others simply gathered dust. That is not to say that RS3100s were not campaigned to very good effect across Europe and, indeed, as far away as Australia. Their finest hour was, perhaps, in June 1975 in the fourth round of the Championships in Germany when, after a tough battle, an RS3100 driven by Jochen Mass managed to beat the BMW of Hans Stuck. Since then, many talented and experienced people have shown how competitive the Capri can be even against formidable opposition. Today, the RS Capris are highly sought-after collectors' items.

Fitted only to the RS3100, the rear spoiler was a homologation part used on the racing Capris to aid stability and aerodynamics.

A pristine condition Capri RS3100 with added chin spoiler. Sadly, the car's launch clashed with Ford's introduction of the Capri II and the fuel crisis, so sales were poor, despite its price and performance. (Inset) Unlike the RS2600 engine which used Kugelfischer fuel injection and Weslake gas-flow development, the RS3100 – like this one – was simply an overbored V6 3-litre unit with port and manifold polishing; power was increased by some 10 per cent.

One of the very professional Capri conversions which were offered during the early 1970s was the Capri Pirana V8 which was based on the Capri 3-litre GT XLR model, powered by an American Ford V8 engine. (Inset) In case you missed the V8 badge, the real giveaway on this Capri that it is not all it might be is the twin exhaust pipes!

'X' stood for reclining front seats, twin horns and reversing lamps; 'L' meant over-riders, locking petrol cap and dummy side scoops and 'R' included Rostyle road wheels and leather steering wheel. This Capri has the full XLR pack.

The roomy engine bay (designed to take the 3-litre V6) easily accommodates the 302 cu in Ford V8 unit. Producing 250bhp (100bhp more than standard) Capri Pirana performance is very impressive.

ESCORT MK III

Work on developing an all-new Escort began in 1976, the year the Fiesta – Ford's first small, front-wheel-drive car – was launched. Initial plans were that the next generation of Escort (code-named 'Erika') would be a 'World Car' because Ford America were anxious that their financial stake in Mazda (which had brought about a liaison between the two companies) should result in the American and the European Escort being almost identical. In the event, this did not happen although the Mazda 323 did, of course, look very like the European Mk III Escort. Meanwhile, pride prevented the Detroit stylists from being overshadowed by their counterparts in Britain or Germany. The situation was not without irony for, in the end, despite being the products of different stylists, the USA-designed Escort and the European-shaped car looked very similar; so much for influence!

'Erika' was the result of combining the talents of Ford's designers in Cologne under Uwe Bahnsen, Vice President, Design (who were responsible for the car's exterior shape) and Ford's stylists at Dunton (who handled the interior), Bahnsen working closely with Ron Mellor, President of Product Development. Many styling proposals were drawn up, the major factor being to balance out interior room against a practical external shape which had an acceptable coefficient of drag – something which was becoming more important in car design as people became more conscious of efficiency and performance. Wind tunnel tests proved that by extending the hatchback tail to create a mini 'boot', the Cd figure improved. However, just months before the final shape was agreed and 'signed off' for production, this bustle-like extension was increased still further and the bonnet line extended over the headlamps, the result being a most rewarding 0.385 Cd.

The power unit for the latest generation of Ford's mid-range models was to be a new and technically advanced range of engines which would combine high efficiency with low running costs. Known as CVH (short for 'Compound', 'Valve angle', 'Hemispherical

Putting the Mk III Escort through its paces in the wind tunnel. The rear spoiler did much to improve the car's aerodynamic efficiency.

Performance Figures

	Escort RS Mexico	Escort RS2000	Escort RS1800	Escort Mk III XR3
Bore:	87.67m	90.82mm	86.75mm	79.96mm
Stroke:	66.00mm	79.65mm	77.62mm	79.52mm
Capacity:	1,593cc	1,993cc	1,845cc	1,596cc
Power:	95bhp at 5,750rpm	110bhp at 5,500rpm	125.5bhp at 6,500rpm	96bhp at 6,000rpm
0–30mph	3.2 sec	3.0 sec	2.9 sec	3.5 sec
0–40mph	5.5 sec	4.7 sec	4.7 sec	5.1 sec
0–50mph	8.1 sec	6.4 sec	6.6 sec	6.9 sec
0–60mph	11.1 sec	8.6 sec	9.0 sec	9.2 sec
0–70mph	16.2 sec	12.7 sec	12.4 sec	13.0 sec
0–80mph	23.0 sec	16.9 sec	16.6 sec	16.9 sec
Max speed 4th	106mph	112mph	114mph	114mph
3rd	— mph	90mph	96mph	84mph
2nd	— mph	62mph	66mph	56mph
1st	— mph	34mph	36mph	34mph
	Motor Sport Jan 1976	*Autocar* Jan 1976	*Autocar* July 1975	*Autocar* 1978

chamber'), the basis of the unit's design was a centrally mounted, belt-driven camshaft mounted in the cylinder head. Hydraulic tappets activated rocker arms located on both sides of the camshaft which in turn operated valves angled at 45 degrees to each other. Meanwhile, by using a hemispherical-type combustion chamber, volumetric efficiency within the cylinder head was kept to a maximum, which in turn gave the best results in emission control tests, the thermal efficiency being further improved by the use of alloy for the cylinder head.

It seems that initially there were no plans for the model which eventually emerged as the XR3. Executive Designer, Trevor Creed takes up the story. 'This really was almost "the car that never was" because the original programme made no provision for an XR3-type car. There was going to be a GT model in the Mk III range but it was planned to be only a base model. Then Stuart Turner called in our department in Cologne to develop the RS2000, which became a very good "image" car for Ford, and we got a good rub-off on to the Escort name. So much so, that when we in Design saw the product plans for the Mk III range and realized it did not include a high performance version, we became a little concerned.

'So, we took one of the fibreglass models (which are simply shells with no interior trim or running gear and are used for reference while the prototypes are being developed) and fitted it with wide wheels and a tailgate spoiler. In the wind tunnel we found that the higher the rear deck, the lower the Cd factor. Then our senior management saw it, became very excited and began asking questions about what performance it would have with a tuned 1,600cc engine and what the car's potential market might be. Based on sales figures of the Mk II Escort GT projections looked pretty poor. But, gradually, confidence began to grow and the decision was made to develop the XR3 concept.

Competition, notably from the Golf GTi, encouraged Ford into giving the XR3 fuel injection, which increased power output to 105bhp (DIN) at 6,000rpm and resulting in a 0–60mph (0–100kph) time of 8.6 seconds.

Incidentally, the initials "XR" do not mean anything. They were just a conscious effort to get away from the terms "GT" or "XL".'

And so the XR3 became part of the new Escort Mk III model range. Powered by its 1,596cc version of the latest CVH engine, power was rated at 96bhp which gave the car a maximum speed of 113mph (181.8kph) and a 0–60mph (0–100kph) time of 9.2 seconds. Public reaction was enthusiastic and the Press praised its performance and economy, although shortfalls in the car's suspension set-up – and the lack of a five-speed gearbox – were major areas for criticism. It was a job for SVE.

At 9.20am on 1 February 1980, Rod Mansfield (one of the former key men in AVO,

now heavily involved with Automotive Regulations after a brief spell with Public Affairs) answered his telephone. It was Gerhard Hartwig calling to ask if Rod would set up a new development engineering department to be called 'Special Vehicle Engineering' or SVE for short. As Rod was to say later, he thought for about three milliseconds before agreeing. (It took that long to make such a simple decision!)

The brief was that the group had to design cars which would improve the image of Ford's European vehicles. Like AVO, SVE was to fly in the face of almost everything Ford stood for as a volume manufacturer with little time for a small department doing its own thing. But . . . SVE was to have some

Rod Mansfield

Born in Bristol in 1935, Rod Mansfield is the link between almost all the sporting models Ford have produced over the last twenty years.

After attending Battersea Polytechnic and the Chelsea College of Aero and Automobile Engineering, Rod started his career as a young designer working for AC Cars in Thames Ditton. Then followed National Service in the REME, during which time he began racing in, of all things, an Austin A35 van, the only concession to competing being the removal of the hub caps!

National Service completed, Rod applied to over 30 companies, the most attractive reply being from Ford who offered him a post as development engineer. Then followed a period in Noise-Vibration-Harshness before taking on the responsibility for front suspension and steering development. Meanwhile, his interest in motor sport continued; he was 750MC Trials Champion two years running, going on to set up his own racing team with two friends, racing Anglias, Cortinas and Twin Cam Escorts, as well as competing in the Mexico Challenge series.

Promotion followed where Rod was involved with the exciting AVO selling performance parts, building replica rally cars and manufacturing cars like the RS1600 and Capri

Starting as one of the first members of the AVO team, Rod Mansfield rose to head up its successor, SVE, when it was established in 1980.

RS2600. (Rod was also involved with the still-born four-wheel-drive Capri project.) Next, Rod spent a short time working in Public Affairs.

In February 1980 the idea was hatched to set up an all-new department within Ford: SVE. The proposal was for a special department responsible for developing low volume, high performance versions of Ford's mainstream product line. Gerhart Hartwig, Ford Europe's Director of Vehicle Engineering asked Rod if he would set up such a department. Ironically, the first car to receive the SVE treatment was the Capri which, history records, was a tremendous market success.

Then came the Fiesta XR2, the Escort Cabriolet, Escort RS Turbo, Sierra XR4×4, Sierra RS Cosworth and on to the Granada 4×4. All have vindicated the original idea for SVE and the purpose of a specialist group within Ford's empire.

Today, Mansfield has moved away from SVE to work in another low volume section under the Ford umbrella – Aston Martin – taking the post of Engineering Director where, no doubt, his talent and enthusiasm will be well received.

strong supporters: Clive Ennos, now with Jaguar; Mike Dunn, Technical Chief at Rolls-Royce; Ron Mellor, at the time Director of Product Development, and Bob Lutz (a well-known car fanatic with his own private car collection), at that time Chairman of Ford Europe. It pays to have friends in high places!

Together with Harry Worrall, Mick Kelley and Mike Smith, Rod quickly got SVE operations into high gear, their first project being to develop the Capri 2.8i for production at the Cologne-Niehl plant. That this car was to become a sales success (and a personal favourite of Mansfield's) is now common knowledge. Next came the Fiesta XR2, with the XR3i hard on its heels – and all this in the first two years of operations. In fact, within a year of opening its doors, Rod's three-man team had increased to around twelve.

The result of SVE's work on the XR3 resulted in a five-speed version being launched in early 1982. In addition, the final drive ratio was lowered slightly to give the car better acceleration. In October that year the engine was given Bosch fuel injection which increased power output to 106bhp at 6,000rpm. SVE also paid considerable attention to the suspension which had also been criticized on the earlier XR3 model. The result was a car with impressive handling, ride and performance: maximum speed was quoted as being 116mph (186.6kph) with a 0–60 (0–100kph) time of 8.6 seconds. (Compare this with the RS1800 in the list of tables on page 87.)

While the RS1600i was based on the same Erika two-door body shell as the XR3/XR3i, this first RS model in the Mk III Escort model range was developed by Ford's Motorsport Department in Cologne and intended as a 'homologation special'. As early as 1979 the Cologne-based team were finalizing a specification sheet which called for 115bhp in road tune and, perhaps, 150bhp for Group A. By 1981 the first RS1600i was finished and was on display at the Frankfurt Show in September.

Compared to the XR3i, the RS1600i had a higher compression ratio engine (9.9:1 instead of 9.5:1), a different camshaft profile and solid lifters, enlarged exhaust manifold and a different twin coil ignition system with a rev. limiter and Bosch K-Jetronic fuel

injection with different settings from those on the XR3i. (In fact, the RS1600i was the first CVH engine to use fuel injection, although in the UK both cars shared the same stand at the Birmingham Show in October 1982.)

As for gearing, the RS1600i shared the same ratios and final drive with those of the XR3i with the exception that fifth gear was less of an 'overdrive' at 0.88:1. Suspension-wise, the ride height was reduced by 1.5in (38.1mm) and Koni dampers fitted to give a firmer response. At the front, drag links were used to improve wheel location with a specially mounted alloy anti-roll bar. Brakes were similar to those on the XR3i, although the 7in (177.8mm) rear drums were later changed to 8in (203.2mm), a conversion which was offered as an after-market modification through appointed dealers. Oh, and we must not forget those magnificent 6J × 15in (38cm) alloy road wheels with 195/50 tyres. Inside, the RS1600i was the plushest yet of the Mk III Escort range with firm hip-hugging Recaro seats.

Performance figures for the RS1600i were always a contentious point. *The Autocar* reckoned on a 0–60mph (0–100kph) time of 8.7 seconds with a top speed of around 118mph (189.8kph) – not even as good as the figures for the XR3i. In reply, Ford said, 'Ah, your test 1600i must have been down on power'. In truth, the real cachet of RS1600i ownership today is the car's rarity.

Almost a year after its introduction, Ford made changes to the RS1600i's specification to bring it closer to the mainstream models with body and suspension alterations, including a revised front strut tower design while the rear wheels lost their negative camber angle.

Initially, RS1600i production plans had called for some 5,000 units in order to comply with Group A regulations, but demand was such that Ford decided to build a further 2,500.

For sale to British customers, the Boreham

engineers spent some time in perfecting a modification to link the right-hand brake pedal to the left-hand mounted brake servo, thereby overcoming sloppiness in the mechanism. Also, for the British market, the car had a different glovebox, and a four-spoke leather-covered steering wheel replaced the three-spoke Continental one. In competition, the RS1600i showed its true colours with Richard Longman-prepared cars (with over 160bhp on tap) winning their class in both 1983 and 1984.

ESCORT RS TURBO

The Escort RS Turbo was conceived at a product planning meeting held in Stuart Turner's office in April 1983, the very same meeting, in fact, which also gave the green light to the Sierra RS. The initial role for the Escort was seen as being the next generation of works rally car while that of the Sierra was to be the racer. However, these were only perceived guide-lines for development for, when the cars reached production, the Escort was used very successfully in racing at world championship level in Group A and Group N too.

Key issues in the basic Escort RS Turbo format were the addition of add-on wheelarch extensions to cover the 10in (25.4cm) wide tyres on 8in (20.3cm) wide wheels (the largest permissible in Group A), front suspension capable of handling around 200bhp, a Garrett T03-type turbocharger and the highest possible final drive in view of the limited option permissible under Group A regulations. To help improve the 'user friendly' nature of the car when making use of all the power available, Ford proposed to fit a limited slip differential which utilized the unique Ferguson-patented viscous coupling. (Ford had already gained considerable experience with VC

The result of a Ford Product meeting, which also triggered off the Sierra RS: the Escort RS Turbo. It would become Ford's first turbocharged production European car, available only in white.

Fitted with Bosch KE-Jetronic fuel injection and Garrett AiResearch T3 Turbo unit, the engine develops some 132 very docile horsepower at 6,000rpm giving the Escort RS Turbo a maximum speed of 125mph (201kph).

limited slip differentials in the prototype 250bhp Fiesta rally cars and subsequently with the Escort RS 1700T rally development machines.)

The first prototype Escort Turbo was built by Bill Meade (the legendary engineer in Ford's Competition Department at FAVO, whose reputation was linked with the Lotus Cortina and the Escort Twin Cam), ably assisted by Terry Bradley. Based on the XR3, Meade installed a Garrett turbocharger for assessment by Ford's top management. The response was enthusiastic, with thoughts turning to a possible mass production Escort turbo based on the 1.3 CVH engine.

An Escort Turbo Rally Championship was organized by Ford Motorsport during 1983 and 1984, which provided a considerable amount of valuable information. Mark Lovell performed impressively during the first year and Simon Davidson and Rob Stoneman during the second. There was also liaison between the Northamptonshire-based firm of Turbo Technics and former Garrett AiResearch employee Geoff Kershaw and both Ford and Motorsport and Special Vehicle Engineering.

Starting with an XR3, Turbo Technics had perfected the turbo conversion before being lent an XR3i by Ford for similar development.

Kershaw then sold to Ford the jigs and tooling for installing a turbo unit into the fuel injected XR3i engine. (Among other things, this involved a new cast exhaust manifold to take the Garrett T3 turbo unit.) Ford, too, spent some time on further development to create set standards of exhaust emission and engine performance. (Turbo Technics continued to market their own turbo conversions, available either in kit form or factory fitted.)

SVE's Project Manager for the Escort RS Turbo was Mike Smith, with Bill Meade and ex-Weslake engineer John Griffiths also on the team. It was not simply a modified XR3i engine – several basic modifications were made to bring this unit up to Escort RS specification including the use of flat top pistons with special, tapered secondary oil control rings to improve lubrication of the cylinder bores, which reduced the compression ratio from 9.5:1 to 8.3:1 (boost levels were kept low at 7.5psi maximum). Sodium-filled exhaust valves were fitted to handle the enormous, prolonged combustion chamber temperatures, while a camshaft sprocket from the 1.3 Escort suitably retarded the valve timing. Other changes included fuel cut-off and rev. limiting devices (to protect the engine and improve fuel consumption figures) and an oil feed which was fitted between the engine block and the turbocharger unit.

Engine management was looked after by a Bosch-Motorola system which set turbo boost and fuel demand against ignition curve and engine revs. The result was a well-mannered installation with good cold start and running features and with 132bhp at 6,000rpm on tap.

Underneath, the front suspension layout was based on that of the late-lamented RS1600i, although crash tests indicated the need to locate the tie bars in sturdy iron castings mounted on to the body. At the rear, an Orion-type anti-roll bar was fitted (the RS being the first model in the Escort range to boast an anti-roll bar), while front and rear springs were shared with those of the XR3i. However, the specification for the Girling gas-filled dampers was altered to give an improved ride quality. Sadly, for road use, SVE were instructed to retain the disc/drum layout of the XR3i, although additional ventilation and harder pads and linings were used. (RS Turbos prepared for Group A were fitted with AP-type four-wheel disc brakes with a choice of disc sizes.)

To handle this dramatic increase in power over the standard XR3i, feedback of information from the competition cars indicated a need to strengthen the gearbox casing, while SVE's own test programme showed that the size of the final drive gear teeth should be increased. This marginally altered its ratio from 4.29:1 to 4.27:1. Then, of course, there was the use of the viscous coupling in the limited slip final drive.

Inside, the RS Turbo shared the same trim as that found on the slower – and cheaper – XR3i with the exception of the excellent, if a little hard, Recaro front seats. However, while a few RS customers chose to pay the extra cost for a different paint job, the majority were happy to have their cars finished in the only colour the company officially offered: diamond white. Even so, with its body kit, low ride height and impressive-looking alloy wheels the Escort RS Turbo really looked the part. Performance-wise, the car certainly lived up to its appearance with a maximum speed of 125mph (201.1kph) and a 0–60mph (0–100kph) time of 8.2 seconds; not bad for a 1,600cc saloon!

That the first series Escort RS Turbo was a sales success can be measured by the fact that the first 5,000 cars were quickly snapped up as they came off the Saarlouis production line. Group A homologation was granted in the spring of 1985 and by the time production had ceased in the winter of 1985/86, some 9,000 units had been sold – an impressive 4,000 units more than the original production plan; success in any language.

In line with an overall update on all Ford's Escorts, the RS Turbo was given a facelift and was announced as the second series in July 1986. Of course, the major difference between the first and second generations of RS Escorts was the general softening of the body contours in line with the styling trends which were emerging in the mid-1980s. At this point, Ford had decided not to homologate the car and so certain key features of the first series cars (the front suspension tie-bars, the extra-wide wheel arch extensions and the 4.27:1 final drive gearing) were not necessary in the replacement model.

Outside the car there was little to distinguish the second series RS Turbo model from the less potent XR3i version – even down to the apparent similarity between the wheels on the two cars, although the XR3i retained its 6J × 14in (35.6cm) wheel, while the more powerful car used a 6J × 15in (38.1cm) wheel with different off-set. The rear tailgate spoiler was colour coded on the Turbo, and Sierra RS bonnet vents were let into the bonnet panel.

Suspension-wise, Fichtel and Sachs gas-filled dampers were fitted all round (as on the XR3i) while spring rates were changed in an effort to give the car a more 'executive-type' ride quality. At the front, the stabilizer bar mounting points were moved further forward to reduce pronounced see-saw action under acceleration and braking. Also, the brakes were changed to ventilated 10.2in (259mm) discs on the front and 9in (228.6mm) drums on the rear operated by a Lucas-Girling SCS anti-lock system.

Under the bonnet, the Bosch-Motorola engine management system had been re-programmed to make the engine more economic under light throttle opening (as well as allowing the engine to run on unleaded fuel), while Garrett AiResearch had developed a new water-cooled centre bearing for the turbo unit in an effort to overcome the likelihood of damage on switch-off after hard driving. Furthermore,

Ford were gaining considerable promotional mileage from changes made to the 1.6-litre CVH engine which, it was claimed, improved fuel efficiency. Ford coined the phrase 'lean burn' to describe the benefits of these modifications which were adopted on the RS Turbo. Finally, there was a one-piece exhaust manifold and modifications to the air-to-air intercooler to produce greater efficiency.

The final drive gearing was shot-peened for increased hardness and the transaxle casing was now an 8-bolt unit. Attention had also been given to the VC limited slip; more holes were drilled in the plates and manufacturing tolerances were improved to reduce fierceness in the action of the limited slip device under full throttle conditions. In addition, the final drive ratio was reduced to 3.88:1 which, along with the reputed reduced drag factor of the new body shell, was reckoned would increase the car's maximum speed. In fact, tests proved this to be far from true (top speed was said to be around 127mph (204.3kph), with a 0–60mph (0–100kph) time of 8.3 seconds) although there was a distinct reduction in high-speed wind noise; 100mph (160kph) in the Series two model seemed like 80mph (125kph) in the old car. The improved Cd factor also produced better fuel economy with Ford claiming some 34mpg at 75mph (8.32l/100km at 120kph).

For the cockpit, the second series RS Turbo also relied heavily on the XR3i for its interior trim, including the XR3i dashboard arrangement with its easy-to-read dials, yet lacking an all important boost gauge. As with the previous model, the front seats were the Recaro type and a Custom Pack was again available which included electric windows, tilt and slide sun roof and central locking. Moreover, customers could now order the car in colours other than diamond white!

The new facelifted Escorts were launched in January 1986. However, enthusiasts had to wait until July before the latest model of

Last of the line, the Capri 280 before its demise in 1987. Ford had threatened to terminate Capri production many times before but demand kept it in manufacture.

A particular favourite of former SVE manager Rod Mansfield, the last version of the Capri 280 was given this luxury interior with leather-covered Recaro seats. Surely a future classic?

Performance Figures

	Escort XR3i	Escort RS1600i	Escort RS Turbo
Bore:	79.96mm	79.96mm	79.96mm
Stroke:	79.52mm	79.52mm	79.52mm
Capacity:	1,596cc	1,596cc	1,597cc
Power:	105(DIN) at 6,000rpm	115(DIN) at 6,000rpm	132(DIN) at 6,000rpm
0–30mph	2.9 sec	2.9 sec	2.9 sec
0–40mph	4.6 sec	4.4 sec	4.2 sec
0–50mph	6.1 sec	6.2 sec	5.7 sec
0–60mph	8.6 sec	8.7 sec	8.1 sec
0–70mph	11.3 sec	11.8 sec	10.8 sec
0–80mph	15.0 sec	15.0 sec	13.1 sec
Max speed	5th 113mph	118mph	128mph
	4th 104mph	113mph	105mph
	3rd 77mph	87mph	79mph
	2nd 52mph	59mph	53mph
	1st 31mph	34mph	32mph
	Autocar February 1983	*Autocar* February 1983	*Autocar* March 1985

Escort RS Turbo went on sale, Ford taking the opportunity to launch the new top-of-the-range Escort with the Sierra RS Cosworth. Future classics in the making? Only time will tell.

SPORTING ESCORTS FOR THE 1990s

The latest version of Ford's best-selling Escort and Orion range was introduced in August 1990. An important element of the design specification was a smooth body shape that produced 10 per cent less aerodynamic drag than its predecessors (which, in turn, would create less wind noise), while a slightly bigger cabin gave more interior space and improved visibility. The wheelbase dimension was increased by 4.9in (124.4mm) and the track broadened by 1.4in (35.5mm) all round. Ford's technicians had also been busy designing a new suspension system with independent MacPherson struts on the front and a twisted beam axle at the rear. Variable ratio rack-and-pinion steering (with power assistance available as an option) was fitted, with the option of electronic ABS. All power units were said to feature the latest in combustion chamber design with engine management systems developed from Formula 1 racing experience. In fact, despite these apparent improvements, 'motor noters' were less than impressed with these latest Ford offerings, some being highly critical of their looks, handling (despite the new suspension set-up) and ageing 'fast-burn' CVH-type 1.4, 1.6 and 1.6 fuel-injected engines, the basic design of which could be traced back to the late 1970s.

For those who hankered after more performance and extra style there was more than a twelve-month wait before the launch of the first 'Sporting Ford' Escort, the RS2000, introduced in September 1991.

Ford's latest Cosworth-powered sporting saloon. Ford intend offering a
'weekend competition car' which, in addition to featuring full four-wheel-drive
and ABS, will have an extra 40bhp on top of its roadgoing 290bhp, at the touch
of a button.

Powered by a 2.0-litre 150bhp 16-valve version of Ford's latest generation of DOHC family of engines, there is clearly plenty of performance with a 0–60mph (0–100kph) dash of around 8 seconds (Ford's figure) and a top speed of 130mph (209kph). Ford had listened to the critics and suspension modifications included stiffer springs and uprated dampers with a front anti-roll bar. The steering benefits from power assistance and there is ABS on the four-wheel disc brakes.

Externally, the car was fitted with a colour-keyed body kit while inside there is a sports steering wheel and Recaro front seats. 'Subtle but exciting' seemed to be the reaction from the Press. Unveiled at the London Motorfair just a month later came the XR3i model. Similar in outward appearance to the RS2000, this version of Ford's spirited Escorts is powered by a 1.8-litre version of the 16-valve DOHC engine (developed at Dunton and Cologne) which produced a healthy 130bhp. Like the RS2000, the XR3i's interior featured sports seats, sun roof and an up-market stereo system with the option of alloy road wheels.

As for a competition version of the latest Escort, not surprisingly, behind the scenes, the 'Boreham Boys' had been busy developing a Cosworth-engined car, a prototype of which was a winner on its first time out in the Spanish Talavera Rally on 15 September, 1990. Driven by a turbo-charged, fuel-

Latest generation Escort in RS2000 form. Following on in the RS tradition the car gives impressive performance and roadholding yet benefits from the latest in suspension, braking and engine technology. However, enthusiasts may criticize the car's lack of identity.

Plush interior of RS2000 showing simple-to-read auxiliary gauges and well thought out controls. Seats are contoured recliners in draylon-type fabric, and a sports steering wheel, a far cry from the Mk I Lotus Cortina.

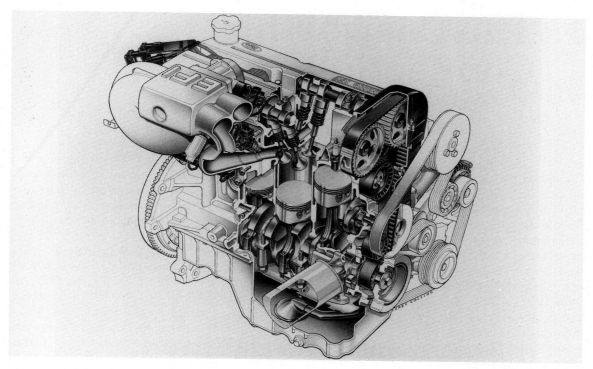

A partial exploded view of the latest four-valves-per-cylinder 1.8-litre tohc engine as fitted to the XR3i. Lean burn technology and high performance efficiency are key features of these latest Ford engines.

injected Cosworth engine the car featured permanent four-wheel-drive linked to a 7-speed MS90 close-ratio gearbox, single dry plate racing clutch and viscous coupling differentials back and front. Power was rated at 295bhp at 6,250rpm with ventilated 4-pot calliper disc brakes all round, uprated suspension and a power-assisted quick rack.

To whet the enthusiast's appetite the car was displayed on Ford's stand at the Birmingham Motor Show in 1990. Meanwhile, a development programme was well in hand for volume production to begin in 1992, in readiness for its international competition debut in the World Rally Championship.

For the club eventer Ford were planning to offer their 'Weekend Racer Concept Car'.

Based on the same Escort RS Cosworth, the car would be powered by a Cosworth engine which in 'road tune' produced 280bhp. At the touch of a switch, however, the unit would unleash a further 40 horsepower, sufficient to give the car a 0–60mph (0–100kph) time of just 4.4 seconds with gearing specifically chosen to give 135mph (217.2kph) in top flight. With its close-ratio, 5-speed gearbox, four-wheel-drive with 34/66 torque split, competition specification springs, gas-filled dampers with anti-roll bars back and front, ventilated front and solid rear disc brakes with full ABS, this ultimate of Monday-to-Friday road cars would be transformed into a race or rally winner. Only time will tell.

4 The Cosworth Connection

As the story of sporting Fords unfolds, so the names of certain people continue to crop up time and again: Walter Hayes (of course), the man who did so much to bring Ford into mainstream motor sport – despite, by his own admission, not having any sort of technical background; Henry Taylor, the man who conceived (among others) the Escort Twin Cam project; and Keith Duckworth, whose association with Ford performance engines stems back more than thirty years. It was Colin Chapman who was to be the bridge between Duckworth, Mike Costin and Ford.

Keith Duckworth joined the fledgling Lotus company in 1957, straight from university, and it was during his short time with Lotus that he struck up his long-standing friendship with fellow engineer Mike Costin. A former De Havilland employee, Costin (like so many others) had gradually become part of the Lotus team; part-time employment working all hours for Colin (as well as having a full-time job) turning into simply working all hours for Lotus! 'By the time Keith arrived at Lotus I was involved with the manufacture of prototype cars and immediately I could see that Keith was brilliant and that his approach to engineering was right,' recalled Mike Costin to the author in a recent interview. 'No matter what he was involved with, it had to work and he was prepared to argue with anyone; sometimes there were strong words between Keith and Colin and I was the one keeping them apart.'

Mike said that it was during one of his emotional 'lows' that he and Keith discussed the idea of setting up an engineering company, the mainstay being their engineering talent which they felt would attract work from many quarters.

'I was working on developing the five-speed gearbox (known as the "queerbox"),' said Duckworth. 'But I could see that its basic concept was wrong. Its motor-cycle gearchange action meant that it was possible to shift gears from top to first in one action – which was potentially disastrous in racing. In 1958 I decided to leave and set up Cosworth. [The amalgamation of the first three letters of COStin's surname and the last five letters of DuckWORTH's.] At that time Colin made Mike an offer whereby he would become Technical Director with a three-year contract. Astutely, Chapman had added a clause which precluded Mike from taking on any outside work which could be construed to be of a competitive nature.' So, since Costin's marital status dictated that he *must* continue in regular employment, he stayed with Lotus while Duckworth began as Cosworth's only employee, establishing the company at the rear of a local North London garage.

'The foundation upon which we based the business was simple,' said Duckworth. 'In those days the general level of work from other tuning companies was so poor that with our background we felt sure we would get work.'

Luckily, one of Duckworth's first customers was Howard Panton, a Ford employee, who commissioned Cosworth to develop a single-

Keith Duckworth

Keith Duckworth was born in Blackburn, Lancashire in 1933. His mother taught domestic science at the local school while his father worked on the Manchester Cotton Exchange before setting up his own mill. Duckworth describes him as a bright, intelligent man who, while not an engineer, became something of a car enthusiast making many mechanical modifications to improve reliability and performance, his favourite car being a pre-war Riley.

Keith was educated at Giggleswick boarding school, taking his 'A' levels before going on to serve his National Service in the RAF. A keen model maker, his interest in things practical matured to motor bikes and assembling a Scott Squirrel from a box of bits.

Next came a degree course in engineering at the Imperial College where he became smitten by the motor racing 'bug'. (A fellow enthusiast was Roger Brockbank, son of cartoonist Russel Brockbank.) Keith managed to persuade his mother to let him spend some of the money he had inherited from his father on a Lotus VI kit, which he built during the summer holidays. The same period the following year saw the young Duckworth working full time for Chapman. It was then that he met his future business partner, Mike Costin.

While still at College, Keith had applied to Napier and Rolls-Royce for a place on their Graduate Apprenticeship courses. But, the likelihood of filing metal blocks for many months did not appeal so, despite having decided to take the Napier job, he contacted Chapman, who offered him the job of Gearbox Development Engineer working on a five-speed gearbox.

However, Keith was far from happy about its design. He had already talked over the idea of setting up an engineering company with Mike Costin so, after just 10 months with Lotus, in 1958 Duckworth left to set up Cosworth (the amalgamation, of course, of COStin and DuckWORTH). Costin joined him in their North London workshops in 1962.

Initially, Cosworth was to offer a composite engineering service designing chassis, suspension and power unit tuning. Very shortly this was dropped in favour of concentrating on engine development alone with the introduction of the legendary 997cc 105E Anglia engine in 1959. Keith soon had this producing very respectable horsepower figures initiating what has proved to be a long-standing liaison with Ford which has included the 105E ohc SCA; the FVA; the DFV; the BDA; the GAA; and, more recently, the tohc turbo unit for the Sierra Cosworth.

In 1980 Cosworth became part of the Unit Engineering Industries Group. Nowadays Keith is retired, allowing him more time for his hobbies such as piloting his own helicopter and water skiing – and keeping in regular touch with his friend, Mike Costin.

seater racer suitable for entry in the Italian-originated Formula Junior Series which had been given international recognition for 1959. The engine Duckworth had intended to use in Panton's car was a Fiat 1100 unit but, try as he might, he could not extract sufficient power to make the car competitive. As a solution, Panton outlined to Duckworth details of the forthcoming 997cc engine which would power the soon-to-be-launched Ford Anglia 105E two-door saloon.

Although the Anglia was not due for its first public appearance until the London Motor Show later in 1959, Ford kindly lent the Brands Hatch organizers an early example as a Course Car for their October meeting. (It seems the race commentator, Anthony Marsh, could not resist the temptation to suggest that it would probably not be long before its 1-litre engine was being developed for FJ!) Within a short time, Duckworth had one of the first production 105E engines in his workshops and a race development programme was hurriedly put into high gear which would have the unit ready for competing in the traditional Boxing Day meeting at Brands Hatch.

The development of this engine was to

Mike Costin

Mike Costin, brother of Frank Costin – who is nine years older and whose name is linked with many of the early sleek Lotus sports racing cars – was born in Harrow, Middlesex where he was educated at a local private school. Mike happily recalls his childhood days saying that because he was lazy and his parents did not push him he did not excel at exams. In the days before the First World War, his father undertook a considerable amount of exploration in Africa, before settling in the UK, where he quickly became established as a marble engraver of some repute. He was, however, something of an inventor and while not an engineer, he did make things like radios.

Mike Costin's interest in engineering emerged gradually as he became fascinated by bikes and motor bikes. Meanwhile, Frank was already working in the aircraft industry so it was hardly surprising that Mike should join De Havilland as an apprentice in 1946. Then came National Service and back to De Havilland developing test equipment, working on the first air conditioning system.

An introduction to Colin Chapman in 1952 (who at the time was a Project Engineer with British Aluminium) resulted in Mike becoming involved with Lotus at a very early stage. The prototype Mk VI had just been completed, Costin's role being to help with the car's development. Gradually, his contribution to Lotus increased and in 1955 he finally left De Havilland to work full time for Chapman.

Soon after, Keith Duckworth joined the team and the idea was hatched to set up Cosworth, Costin joining the company full time in 1962. From there the company grew in stature, becoming the internationally famous firm it is today. However, Mike is quick to point out the immense amount of hard work he put in, both at Lotus and with Cosworth. Like Duckworth, Costin has now retired from the company and is able to enjoy his many pastimes which include skiing and gliding.

mark the beginning of a remarkable success story linking the names of Cosworth and Ford, and underlined Keith Duckworth's undoubted talents for producing engines of marked superiority over their rivals. Moreover, since Mike Costin was still with Lotus, it gave him the chance of selling to Colin Chapman the notion of a contract between Cosworth and Lotus which involved the purchase of 126 Cosworth-prepared FJ units which would be offered with the new Lotus 20 FJ car. 'Although Colin was a marvellous judge of character, I think his one mistake in this area was Keith,' said Costin. 'He should have kept Keith while he had him, paid him the earth and given him the reins rather than let him go and then buy engines from him later.'

During 1960, Keith's work on the 105E engine continued with development being done on camshaft design to improve the engine's breathing, the unit producing some 75bhp at 7,500rpm using Cosworth's A2 camshaft. A Cosworth part-time employee, Bill Brown (who had known Duckworth when they were both at London University) was brought in to introduce an element of business administration. Another early member of the Cosworth team was Benny Rood, whose sub-contract work for Cosworth gradually took him over completely!

A measure of the speed at which the 105E FJ development programme progressed through 1960 can be judged by the increase in power output. By the end of the year the Mk III engine, with an improved A3 camshaft, strengthened bottom end and dry sump lubrication was producing some 85/90bhp at 7,500rpm – a quite outstanding achievement in such a short time. The following year saw even more power. With the 105E cylinder block over-bored to 1,098cc and the use of larger valves, the unit was now giving around 90/95bhp at 7,750rpm.

In 1961, the company also took over the old Lotus racing workshops at Edmonton, recently vacated when Chapman moved his company to bigger premises in Cheshunt, Hertfordshire. This gave Duckworth and his team room to develop still further and in 1962 Cosworth began producing an inexpensive version of the 1,340cc Consul Classic engine (which developed around 80bhp at 5,000rpm) for installation in the Lotus 7. Two other versions of this engine, which were built in limited numbers, were a 105bhp unit for the Lotus Mk V and an overbored 1,475cc engine, which developed 120bhp, for the Lotus Mk VI.

At Cheshunt the Lotus lads were about to embark on an exciting new project. Colin Chapman had burnt his fingers badly in respect of the Coventry Climax FWE engine used in the excitingly innovative monocoquebodied Elite. Chapman had managed to persuade Bernard Lee, Coventry Climax's Chairman, to produce 1,000 units. But, for road use, they proved expensive and unreliable (reputedly needing new bearings every 30–35,000 miles). For his next generation of sports car – the Elan – Chapman's idea was to use a mass-produced cylinder block from Ford but fitted with a high-performance tohc cylinder head. He approached Walter Hayes and discussed Ford's long-term engine development plans. Chapman came away with a deal involving engines and a high performance programme to develop the Cortina saloon!

It was at this point that Colin Chapman called upon the expertise of the then Technical Editor of *The Autocar*, Harry Mundy, his contribution being to design a new cylinder head. An ideal choice (he had once been an employee of Coventry Climax and would later move on to join his old friend Walter Hassan at Jaguar), Mundy calculated the camshaft geometry, the inlet and exhaust tracts and the valve angles. At this stage

there was still much to do before the head could go into production, the job of this falling to another Lotus part-timer, Richard Ansdale, a transmission engineer who worked for Thornycroft. It was Ansdale, incidentally, who also designed the special water-pump arrangement on this engine, which utilized the 105E water-pump bearing amalgamated with a new front cover, back plate, impeller and bearing seal.

The cylinder head drawings were given to a local North London firm who were commissioned to make a casting pattern for the cylinder head. Meanwhile, Lotus engineers Bob Dance, Neil Francis and Steve Sanville were busy preparing an engine test bed. This was the summer of 1961, and Ford had just introduced the 109E 1,340cc 'Classic' engine and Lotus managed to lay their hands on one of the early production units for evaluation. By October the engine had been stripped down and rebuilt as a twin cam unit fitted with an alloy cylinder head (cast by Birmid). The engine was started and while no results were kept it is thought it produced a respectable 85bhp – not bad for a first run.

Throughout the next few months more tests were carried out, SU carburettors were tried and an 1,100cc unit was built using a 105E block fitted with a 109E crankshaft. Power outputs were rated at 85–90bhp although cylinder head gasket failure was proving to be a recurring problem. Weak main bearings caused crankshafts to break and there were camshaft follower problems, too.

In order to evaluate the new cylinder head on the road, a LHD Ford Anglia was bought (from the Belgian Embassy) and a third unit – assembled using a 1,340cc block bored out to give 1,477cc – was installed, the car covering some 400 trouble-free miles (640km). Another cylinder head was taken down to Harry Weslake, the gas-flow specialist in Rye, Sussex, for performance analysis while Steve Sanville trusted his luck in the hard-worked Anglia, driving it down to Bologna in Italy for Weber to fit two twin-choke carburettors for evaluation.

In May 1962 Ford announced their 116E engine which would power the newly launched Cortina. By increasing the cylinder block depth by 0.66in (16.7mm) and increasing the stroke, yet retaining the same bore size as the 105E engine, Ford had produced a unit of 1,498cc, while bottom end rigidity had been increased by using a five main bearing crankshaft. Within a short time one of these engines was being stripped down in Lotus's workshops and fitted with a tohc cylinder head. Despite continued gasket problems, the unit was then installed in a Lotus 23 and taken to Nurburgring for the 1000km race where Jim Clark outstripped the opposition and led the field for 12 laps before leaving the track, overcome by exhaust fumes!

By midsummer, Cosworth were becoming involved with the twin cam programme, building a handful of 1,498cc race engines. To increase power, changes were made to camshaft profiles and cylinder port shapes.

Meanwhile, there was the question of the Lotus Cortina — the other half of the deal which had come out of Chapman's discussion with Walter Hayes. It was intended that the car would be raced in Group 2 (which allowed for engines up to 1.6 litres). Chapman therefore instructed that the tohc engine be increased to 1,558cc which involved increasing the cylinder bore from 3.187in to 3.25in (80.97mm to 82.55mm). This in turn allowed for a 0.020in overbore within the 1.6-litre limit. The job of developing the Lotus Cortina engine for Group 2 racing also fell to Cosworth!

By this time, Costin had left Lotus and joined his friend Duckworth. 'There were several reasons why I left Lotus,' explained Mike. 'It was 1962 and I had come to the end of my three-year contract [as Technical Director]. I was in another of my emotional lows and felt I wanted to leave. Lotus was

getting bigger and in a shambles and I felt I would rather be in a small shambles than a big one. Initially, it was beneficial that my name was linked with Cosworth because at that stage few people had heard of Keith Duckworth. It did not take long for that situation to change. But the situation was not without irony for just before I left Lotus I was working on designing the tohc engine for the production Lotus Cortina, and a few weeks later I was back in Colin's office negotiating with him over the matter of Cosworth taking on redesign work of the same engine for racing.'

Meanwhile, there were still problems with the cylinder heads to resolve. The first batch of heads, supplied by Birmid of Smethwick, were sand-cast units which, when tested, proved to be insufficiently rigid. Under working conditions the heads moved, causing gas seal problems, a situation not helped by cylinder head gaskets which were clearly unsuitable for a high-performance engine. Fortunately, a metal casting company, William Mills of Wednesbury, Staffordshire, submitted a quotation for making die-cast cylinder head patterns, and their offer was too attractive for Chapman to refuse.

Assembly of the Twin Cam engines was to be handled by J. A. Prestwich (JAP) who would machine the heads, fit the valves and so on, and then install them on to the already 'dressed' bottom ends supplied by Ford. In November 1962 the first consignment of 1,558cc cylinder blocks arrived from Dagenham and were sent up to JAP for assembly. By the latter part of February the following year they arrived back for testing.

Unfortunately, the problems persisted and the discard rate of production heads (sometimes as much as 80 per cent) was unacceptably high. Something had to be done. Additional pressure was added to the situation by the announcement of the Lotus Cortina at the Racing Car Show in January 1963, with homologation regulations calling for 1,000 units to be built. As the new year gathered momentum there were long faces in both the Ford and Lotus camps; with reliability problems continuing, neither the Elan nor the Lotus Cortina could be released to customers. And with no cars to sell, Lotus's financial situation began to look bleak.

'I think one must be careful not to try to diminish Chapman by highlighting the things he did not do well,' remarked Hayes, reflecting on the period when relations between Ford and Lotus were becoming strained because of the Lotus Cortina's unreliability. 'Above all else, he was a brilliant man of ideas. Indeed, I think he was the most remarkable engineer I have ever met. That said, he was never given to detail, simply because the next idea was always trying to crowd the details out. He was never going to have the patience to sit down and work on quality control or manufacturing processes because he was always thinking about the next idea. He was marvellously winsome, he could charm the rear wheel off anything.'

Eventually, the cylinder head situation was saved when Steve Sanville finally persuaded Mills to change cylinder head manufacturers from die-cast to sand-cast. At a stroke, all the problems were solved and only a few production modifications were made during the engine's lifetime. William Mills continued manufacture until the engine was phased out in 1975. Lotus Cortina production began in earnest by the middle of 1963 and there were sighs of relief all round.

Engine assembly problems did remain, however. JAP were subsequently taken over by Villiers who later become Norton Villiers, the engines being built at the company's Wolverhampton factory. Unfortunately, union practices sometimes played havoc with good relations. When Lotus moved from Cheshunt to Hethel in November 1966 the opportunity was taken to ensure that Lotus made a greater contribution to the engine's assembly and they eventually took

An intense 33-year-old Keith Duckworth inspects his handiwork as designer of the Ford Formula II during track testing at Silverstone in 1966. Much of the design work on this unit was then carried over to the legendary DFV Formula One unit.

over the entire job in mid-1967 when Norton Villiers could no longer cope with the work.

As has already been mentioned, this change in the Twin Cam engine's assembly programme coincided with Ford's introduction of the Mk II version of the Cortina and the decision that the new car (subtly renamed Cortina Lotus) would be built at Dagenham, not Hethel. However, Lotus continued their build-up of engines; the blocks were specially cast for Lotus by Ford, while crankshafts were modified to take six flywheel bolts and were carefully selected for use in the Lotus engine. More Ford-inspired changes included alterations to valve lift

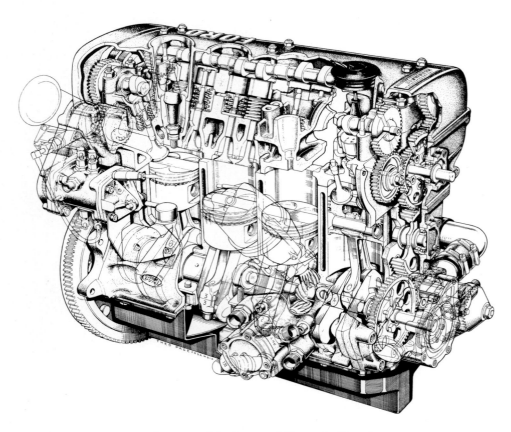

A splendid Theo Page cutaway drawing of the Cosworth Formula II engine.
Based on the 1,500cc 5 main bearing cylinder block, the gear-driven twin
overhead cam unit developed 200+ bhp at 9,000rpm.

and camshaft timing, main bearing caps and the use of better-quality pistons. Modifications to the sump, back plate, rear oil seal and oil pick-up pipe were intended to reduce oil leaks. A large air cleaner located diagonally across the engine replaced the old side-mounted unit used in the Mk I saloon. From then on, under Lotus's direct control, production throughput increased dramatically and this, in turn, improved reliability.

In 1963 Cosworth's work on the Lotus twin cam engine really began to gain momentum. First, a one-off 1,498cc experimental engine was assembled, with chain-driven over-head camshafts and crossflow cylinder head. This would form the basis for the production Lotus Elan unit. Next, a bored out engine of 1,594cc capacity was put together with standard connecting rods but with dry sump lubrication which produced 140bhp at 6,500rpm. However, Duckworth was unhappy about the strength of the standard rods so this was quickly followed by a similar engine but with a better lubrication system and steel crankshaft and connecting rods. Finally, another engine of 1,594cc was assembled with wet sump lubrication. This also produced 140bhp and was for use in the Lotus Cortina in Group 2 racing. These engines underwent Cosworth's critical test procedures to evaluate power and reliability.

Cosworth moved to Northampton in 1964, by which time the staff had increased to some 18 people. 'We decided upon Northampton because it was mid-way between London and the Midlands where most of our suppliers were located – not to mention the proximity to the M1 motorway,' explained Mike Costin. That same year also saw the introduction of the first engine with a layout based extensively on Cosworth design: the 997cc SCA, or Single Camshaft type 'A' unit. It was based on the 116E five bearing cylinder block – the only standard component in the engine – and had a 'bowl-in-crown-type' cylinder head with a gear driven overhead camshaft. It represented a milestone in the company's engine development history and proved a highly successful competitor in Formula 2 events during 1964 and 1965. Power output was rated at a very healthy 115bhp at 8,750rpm.

In the same year a 1,498cc version of the SCA engine was developed which produced 175bhp at 8,000rpm. The following year came a 1,098cc version of the SCA unit – the SCC – which produced 135bhp. Large numbers of all the SC family were sold throughout the world, both in fully built and in kit form, and quickly established Cosworth as a company to be reckoned with in the highly competitive area of motor sport.

By far the most important engine to be developed during this period of Cosworth's career was the FVA (Four Valve type 'A') unit. Based on the legendary 116E Ford cylinder block, the cylinder head featured four valves per combustion chamber with gear driven overhead camshafts. With a capacity of 1,598cc, the unit produced an impressive 218bhp at 9,000rpm, sufficient to make it almost unbeatable in Formula 2, winning all F2 championships between 1967 and 1971. The result of a two-engine development contract between Ford and

Keith Duckworth talks in detail about his new FVA Formula II race engine with Ford's Director of Engineering, Harley Copp. Of the £100,000 fee paid to Cosworth, around £25,000 was apportioned to the FVA project.

Cosworth, the FVA was also to form the basis for the DFV (Double Four Valve, effectively two FVAs in parallel), Cosworth's first Formula 1 engine which went on to become the most successful engine in Grand Prix racing. A lightweight 2,993cc unit, the DFV produced 405bhp at 9,000rpm (this was gradually increased to 480bhp at 1,100rpm by 1980) and was the first Cosworth engine to feature a cylinder head of the company's own design. First fitted in Jim Clark's Lotus 49 in the 1967 Dutch Grand Prix (which it won) the DFV went on to notch up no fewer than 126 Grand Prix victories and 9 World Championships. Mike Costin explained how this engine came about: 'When Coventry Climax gave up making racing engines, Chapman looked around for an alternative. Without doubt, the designer of the new engine had to be Keith Duckworth. Initially,

Cosworth Engine Development History

Year	Engine	CC	Bhp	Rpm	Remarks
1963	Mk X	1498			Purely a one-off experimental engine. Forerunner to the production Lotus Twin Cam engine as fitted to the Elan. The production engines, however, had a capacity of 1,558cc, utilizing twin overhead cam shafts (chain driven) with a crossflow cylinder head.
1963	Mk XI	1098	110	8000	An updated version of the Mk IV Formula Junior engine but with a very much improved specification. A very successful engine and a major development in Cosworth's history.
1963	Mk XII	1594	140	6500	A bored-out racing version of the Lotus Twin Cam engine with dry sump lubrication though using standard cast-iron connecting rods and crankshaft.
1963	Mk XV	1594	140	6500	A wet sump racing Lotus Twin Cam engine fitted to the Lotus Cortina for (then) Group 2 Saloon car racing.
1964	SCA	997	115	8750	SCA=single camshaft type A. The first extensively Cosworth-designed engine, based on the Ford 116E Cortina cylinder block. (The block was the only 'standard' component). Used in Formula 2, it had a gear-driven single overhead camshaft, 5 main bearing crankshaft and a bowl-in-piston combustion chamber. A very successful engine which won the Formula 2 Championship in 1964 and 1965.
1964	SCB	1498	175	8000	A 1,500cc type B version of the SCA made for experimental purposes only.
1965	SCC	1098	135	9500	Same as the SCA but with increased bore. Destined for a North American sports car Formula but only a few were made. Many SCA engines, however, were later sold to the USA and converted to SCC specification.
1965	MAE	997	100		MAE=Modified Anglia Series E (Ford 105E). A very successful Formula 3 engine made in large quantities. A modified cylinder head introduced in 1966 improved the performance slightly but after 1965, few complete engines were made. Many kits and parts, however, were sold to other engine specialists throughout the duration of the 1,000cc Formula 3 regulations.
1967	FVA	1598	218	9000	FVA=Four Valve Type A. An unbeaten Formula 2 engine, winning all Formula 2 Championships from 1967 to 1971 – the duration of the 1,600cc Formula 2 regulations. Based on the Ford 116E Cortina block, the engine featured 4 valves per cylinder with gear-driven twin overhead camshafts.
1966	FVB	1500	200	9000	An experimental 1,500cc version of the FVA made to examine the power output possibilities for the DFV.

Year	Code	cc	bhp	rpm	Description
1967 (1973) (1980)	DFV	2993	405 405 480	9000 10250 11000	DFV=Double Four Valve. Cosworth's first Formula 1 engine and the most successful engine ever used in Grand Prix racing. First fitted to Jim Clark's Lotus 49 at the Dutch Grand Prix in 1967 which it won. Since then it has won 126 Grands Prix and 9 World Championships. A lightweight V8 with 4 valves per cylinder and first Cosworth-designed cylinder block.
1968	DFW	2491	358	9750	A successful short stroke version of the DFV made for the Tasman Series.
1968	BDA	1601	120	6500	BDA=Belt-driven type A. A roadgoing engine designed for Ford for installation in the RS1600 Escort. Using the 1,600cc crossflow Ford block, its design is based on the FVA but with toothed belt drive to the twin overhead camshafts. 4 valves per cylinder.
1969	FVC	1790	235	8750	Long stroke version of the FVA made mainly for the European 2-litre Sportscar Championship which it won twice.
1970	BDB	1700	200	8250	A development engine made for Ford for rallying application Modified BDA with enlarged bore. Only one made by Cosworth but many sold in kit form.
1970	BDC	1700	230	9000	A fuel injected racing version of the BDB developed mainly for Group 2 Saloon Car racing. Only one engine made by Cosworth but many sold in kit form.
1971	BDD	1600	200	8750	Formula Atlantic version of the BDA Only one engine made for development but many sold as kits.
1972	BDE	1790	245	9000	A Formula 2 version of the BDA bored to 85.6mm.
1972	BDF	1927	270	9250	The BDF improved on the BDE by coming closer to the 2,000cc Formula 2 engine limit although its 88.9mm bore was achieved only through brazing liners into the standard block. It won more Formula 2 races than any other engine in 1972.
1972	EAA	1995	275	9000	Based on the Chevrolet Vega block – Cosworth's first non-Ford-based stock-block engine. An all aluminium four cylinder engine which was similar to the BDA in layout and also had belt drive. Designed for Sportscar and Formula 2 racing but was never used in Formula 2.
1973	BDC	1975	275	9250	An improved version of the BDF but with greater reliability. The 1973 Formula 2 engine.
1973	GAA	3412	440	8750	A Ford V6 block based engine under development for use in Group 2 Saloon car racing. (GAA= GA engine type A, GA being merely letters in a new alphabetical code rather than descriptive of the engine.)
1973	BDH	1300	190	10000	A small capacity version of the BDA, based on the Ford 1300 crossflow block. Group 2 Saloon car racing and sportscars.
1975	BDM	1599	225	9250	Large valve fuel injected version of the BDD.
1975	DFX	2645	840	9500	57.30mm stroke turbocharged version of the DFV designed for Indianapolis-type racing in the USA.

it was to have had Esso sponsorship (few people realize just how close this came before Esso pulled out); then Ford stepped in. Although we had received a little help from Ford in the past, the DFV deal – masterminded by Walter Hayes – helped Cosworth enormously.'

To his credit, Duckworth has subsequently stated that, Ford's help notwithstanding, he had every intention of designing and building a four-cylinder, 4-valve racing engine.

In 1966 the first 4-valve engine was completed using the 1,498cc Ford cylinder block and called – surprisingly – FVB! A purely experimental unit, it proved the point of the design and the power potential of the forthcoming DFV engine, the unit producing an impressive 200bhp at 9,000rpm. Duckworth's talent for conceiving a highly efficient engine layout had been proven and the following year saw the launch of the FVA engine which produced just 18bhp more at the same revs. The same year saw the completion of the DFV, the first man to take delivery being Colin Chapman, thereby fulfilling his search for an engine to replace those from Coventry Climax.

'I think the major reason for the success of our engines was their fundamental design,' said Mike Costin. 'However, the more development which is done on an engine, the less its success is down to design and more and more down to luck – luck that the design was right in the first place. In the case of our racing engines, there are two reasons why they are capable of achieving such high revs: the quality of our castings and the quality of the components such as pistons, connecting rods and so on.'

Meanwhile, with the J25 Escort project becoming an open secret at Ford, Hayes began to piece together the wisdom of using the 4-valve science in a suitable engine which would ultimately take over from the Lotus twin cam. 'Although it was an overhead camshaft design, the fact that the Lotus engine was only a 2-valve layout

would eventually limit its development life,' recalled Duckworth recently. So Hayes began talking to Duckworth about just such a project, a road-going 16-valve four-cylinder engine which would power the top performance Escort for the future. Henry Taylor and Walter Hayes outlined their thoughts of a peak power output of 120bhp in road-going tune, the engine being able to take an increase of up to some 240bhp, or equivalent to that of an FVA engine. The result was, of course, the BDA engine. In no way a de-tuned FVA, Duckworth stresses that the only common parts are the valves and springs! Dimensionally everything else was different.

BDA

The responsibility for drawing up the BDA fell to Mike Hall because Keith was too busy with other projects. Quite by chance it was found that the production tolerances of the latest crossflow cylinder block sometimes resulted in an engine of 1,601cc, so the unit was homologated in the larger category. For semi-mass production much of the FVA's valve train and timing gear was redesigned. Thought was given, too, to the engine's accessibility, resulting in the exhaust port face being swept down 30 degrees from the vertical. The thermostat housing was made integral with the cylinder head while the water coolant input and outputs were also different from those of the DFV. Finally, to simplify production and overcome the manufacturing difficulties of maintaining accurate gear centres, the gear-driven camshafts were changed to belt drive.

Under test, the BDA produced a healthy 120bhp in road tune. A prototype high performance version with FVA fuel injection and a race-type BDA cylinder head developed some 238bhp – not far off the 240bhp target outlined by Hayes and Taylor. In 1968 a specification was finalized for a production

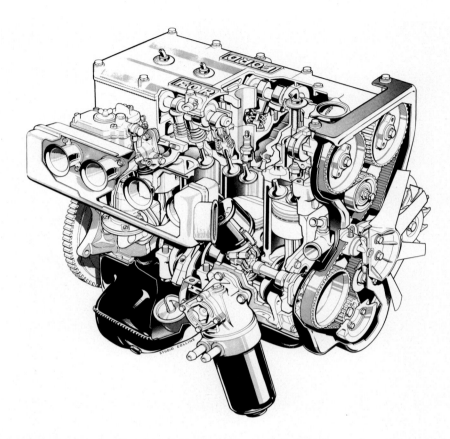

The spin-off of all the Duckworth design work on the FVA and DFV was the 1,599cc Ford Kent-based BDA engine, which in mild tune developed 120bhp at 6,000rpm, and replaced the ageing 1,558cc tohc Lotus unit.

version, and Harpers of Letchworth, Hertfordshire were commissioned to take on the job of assembling the units.

The BDA was first shown publicly in January 1969 when the sleek two-door Capri was launched. Talk was that 100 BDA Capris were to be built, some perhaps raced. History has proved this particular bit of Ford publicity to be inaccurate, although Cosworth were to become involved with another engine for the Capri, a V6 unit – known as the GAA – based on the 3-litre Essex unit. The BDA was fitted to the Escort RS1600 launched in 1970.

Sadly, the first BDAs off the assembly line had their fair share of problems and Keith Duckworth is not blind to their shortfalls. The problems were mainly concerned with lack of accuracy in machining the valve seats. Despite Cosworth's road-tune design, the BDA was, nevertheless, a sophisticated unit and some of the first RS1600 owners found their local RS dealers simply not up to servicing them. But, in their usual quick and thorough fashion, Ford sorted out the trouble and the BDA became a reliable engine much praised by the Press and public alike.

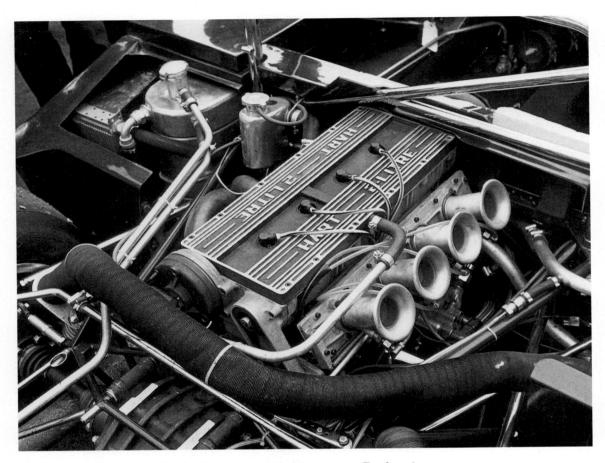

While Cosworth certainly did the lion's share of development on Ford engines during this period, Brian Hart was also involved in instigating an in-house programme to develop a 2-litre alloy cylinder block version of the BDA unit.

In 1970 Cosworth launched a 1,700cc version of the BDA for rallying – the BDB. With its enlarged bore, power was rated at 200bhp at 8,250rpm. While only one prototype was built by the factory, many engines were sold in kit form, as was the BDC, a Group 2 racing version of the same unit, fitted with fuel injection and producing some 230bhp at 9,000rpm. (Perhaps the most famous of the Escort RS1700s to use this unit was built by Broadspeed for John Fitzpatrick.) The following year came the BDD. Again, only one was built by Cosworth although many were sold as kits for the Formula Atlantic single-seater series. In 1,600cc form it produced 200bhp at some 8,750rpm. In 1972, the BDE and BDF appeared, the result of a change in regulations which allowed engines up to 2.0 litres in place of the earlier 1,600cc capacity limit. The BDE was a Formula 2 engine bored out to 1,790cc, producing 245bhp at 9,000rpm. The BDF took even greater advantage of the new capacity legislation by being increased to 1,927cc, achieved by through brazing of special liners into the cylinder block. Producing an impressive

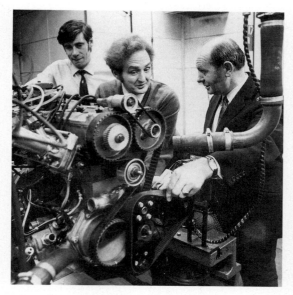

A 2-litre BDA rally Escort engine with alloy cylinder block on test at Boreham. Left to right are: Mick Jones, Workshop Foreman; John Griffiths, Engine Engineer; Bill Barnett, Rally Manager.

270bhp at 9,250rpm, this unit is reckoned to have won more races in Formula 2 during 1972 than any other engine.

Cosworth brought out their BDG unit in 1973. An improved version of the BDF, this 1,975cc engine was initially rated at 275bhp at 9,250rpm for use in Formula 2 events. Continued improvement managed to increase this power further to 280bhp at 7,000rpm. (It was this engine, in overbored form, that powered the Zakspeed Group 5 cars which raced in the German Championship during 1976 and 1977.)

In 1973 the 1,300cc BDH was introduced, for use in Group 2 saloon car racing and sports cars. Based on the Ford crossflow Kent cylinder block, this engine produced 190bhp at a seemingly impossible 10,000rpm. While it had initial teething problems, these were soon rectified and the BDG-powered Escorts proved most effective in both the British and Belgian Saloon Car Championships.

The blue and white racing Capris dominated the European racing scene during 1971 and 1972, taking the European Saloon Car Championship each year. For 1974 it was decided to involve Cosworth in developing a 3.4-litre 24-valve version of the well-known V6 Essex unit with plans to build more than 100 for Group 2 saloon car racing and Formula 5000.

The basis of the engine – called the GAA – was the 2,994cc, 2.85in × 3.68in (72.42mm × 93.66mm) Essex cylinder block, the bore being increased to 3.93in (100mm). The alloy cylinder heads featured four-valves-per-cylinder with belt-driven camshafts and a compression ratio of 12.1:1. Development work on this engine began in May 1972 with considerable influence from Duckworth himself on the design of the cylinder layout and the combustion chamber. Initially, the heads (identical for both cylinder banks) used a single plug per cylinder bore, although the design allowed for triple plugs for future development. Ignition utilized a Lucas transistorized system triggered from the crankshaft.

Taking just 18 months from drawing board to an engine up and being tested on the dynometer, a key factor in its favour was its 'clean' pollution characteristics. Duckworth was to comment, 'It has been encouraging to have such a well-balanced engine. All the way through it has been impressively smooth-running. The current power output (415bhp at 8,500rpm) has been achieved with practically no drama – and there's potential for much further development.'

Sadly, no sooner had the GAA development programme reached this stage than the regulations and a change in Ford's racing policy made the unit obsolete and a pile of unwanted engines began gathering dust in a corner of Boreham's workshops.

From the frantic days of the late 1970s we move on to the more relaxed period of the early 1980s. By this time, Keith Duckworth had orchestrated major changes in the structure

Production RS1600 engines came from a variety of suppliers including Brian Hart and Holbay Ltd. This unit is a 1.6-litre Formula Atlantic unit.

of Cosworth to take account of his (and Mike Costin's) advancing years.

Ford, meanwhile, had introduced their controversial Sierra which some critics claimed looked like an up-turned blancmange mould. It was, despite these disparaging comments, a car whose shape was to have a dramatic influence on the styles which emerged subsequently from other major manufacturers. Like all Ford designs, its basis was to form the backbone for a family of models to suit all markets and pockets.

At a meeting in April 1983 held between Product Planning, SVE and Motorsport staff two new models were commissioned: a Sierra, which would benefit from an engine developed by Cosworth specially for this car,

and a turbo version of the highly popular XR3i (which we have already covered). Both models would prove to be as popular as their performance was impressive.

Ford's first high-performance Sierra was the XR4i. This utilized a two-door version of the Sierra body shell (which, perhaps, tended to accentuate the inverted blancmange appearance) and was equipped with a large aerofoil spoiler fitted to the tailgate. It was powered by the 2.8i V6 Cologne engine (similar to that fitted to the 2.8i Capri). Its performance was best described as quick – as, indeed, it needed to be with its rather unsubtle looks. Top speed was 130mph (209kph) with a 0–60mph (0–100kph) time of 7.9 seconds. The next 'hot' Sierra was the

The foundation upon which the Sierra Cosworth was based: the basic 3-door Sierra saloon which was marketed for only a short time in the UK while RS Cosworth assembly was handled by Ford's Genk plant.

Merkur XR4Ti which was fitted with a smaller, 2.3-litre turbocharged engine, the main market for this car being in America. However, despite not being available in the UK, some were seen performing rather well on European race tracks. Then came the poular XR4×4. Introduced in 1985 and powered by the same lusty, compact 2.8i V6, the XR4×4 was intended to promote the growing trend towards four-wheel-drive on 'domestic' saloons. Its outward appearance was nicely subtle, in sharp contrast to the XR4i.

The story of how the Sierra Cosworth came about could be said to have started when Stuart Turner and Walter Hayes were spectators at a British Grand Prix meeting

at Silverstone in 1983 where they saw Rovers completely outstrip the opposition. Not surprisingly, both men were gripped by the same notion that it would have been nice to have seen Fords rather than Rovers performing for the crowds. The key to making this happen lay, quite by chance, in a visit arranged in mid-1983 for some senior Ford management staff from Detroit (which included Jim Capalongo and Ed Blanch) to view Cosworth and see the latest DFY racing engine. During the tour Turner and the party happened to notice a Sierra engine fitted with a 4-valve overhead camshaft cylinder head which Cosworth had developed privately. Of course! A Cosworth-powered Sierra! Better still, with members

Ford's SVE aerodynamicists spent a considerable amount of time in the wind tunnel finalizing the best position for the rear wing panel; too high and the drag coefficient increased hugely while if the panel was lowered closer to the boot 'lid' its effect on high-speed stability became almost non-existent.

(Opposite) The dramatic front end view of a standard Sierra RS Cosworth with its special nose cone/chin spoiler was designed specifically to improve the car's high speed aerodynamics as well as to give the car its own unique visual identity.

The introduction of the 145mph (233kph) Sierra RS Cosworth at a launch price of under £16,000 attracted many Ferrari and Porsche owners to buying Ford. That the recipe has proved a success can be seen from Ford's decision to continue manufacture of the Sapphire saloon version with four-wheel-drive into the 1990s.

Part of the overall Sierra Cosworth programme was to homologate a more powerful version: 224bhp compared to 204bhp for the first-generation car. An additional 500 cars were assembled and sent to Aston Martin Tickford for conversion to RS500s.

of the Ford hierarchy on hand they, too, could be brought in on the proposals and, hopefully, give their support. 'As part of our usual development programme we had drawn up a package for a 4-valve head to fit the four cylinder "Pinto" engine,' said Keith Duckworth. 'At that stage there were no plans to involve Ford; it was just an in-house prototype.'

Fundamental to the whole programme was the necessity to manufacture some 5,000 units per year to enable the car to be eligible for the international Group A category. Were there sufficient potential customers ready to pay the price of a Cosworth-engined Sierra? The price-tag would, after all, be a huge jump from the XR4i's. However, given that the market was there, it would mean that Ford would once more be back in the front line of competitive motor sport, up against their old adversary, BMW. One hurdle which had to be jumped was to convince Ford's Engineering Department and Product Planning people, who could not see the justification for a Cosworth engine powering one of their saloons. It was Project J25 all over again.

Another fence which had to be cleared was Cosworth's initial reluctance to consider

The transformation to RS500 included an uprated engine and larger turbocharger while external differences included changes to the front spoiler to allow in more air and an extension 'lip' and a secondary bootlid spoiler on the rear.

fitting a turbocharger to their 16-valve engine. The company's experience with multiple valves and camshafts had always worked – and worked well – in the past, giving a good spread of power with instant throttle response. Turbocharging, some might say, is the simple man's easy way to increase an engine's power effectively. But, Ford were adamant and they were the customer. Moreover, it gave the engine another stage of tuning, the only limitations of which would be reliability under competition conditions. Ford Motorsport had already calculated that to be really competitive the engine had to develop at least 300bhp, which in turn dictated a road-tune power output of around 200bhp. (Group A regulations were very strict as to what modifications could be made.)

'When I came back from the States in 1983,' said Walter Hayes, 'I thought the rally scene to be very expensive and difficult to understand. But I thought that an area where we could get back to our competition heritage was on the tracks. The great thing about motor sport between 1960 and 1980 was that it was run from the grass roots up. It was just as acceptable to enter an Escort as a car costing much, much more. In the early 1980s there were various adventures with specialist cars and none with ordinary production cars. I felt that we should be re-establishing ourselves with a production-based competition car and *the* production car at that time was the Sierra. While I helped to make the Sierra Cosworth programme happen, I don't know who invented it because it just seemed such an obvious thing to do.'

A contract was drawn up between Cosworth and Ford for the assembly of 5,000 engines in the first year of production and a subsequent batch of up to 5,000 engines during the next two years. John Griffiths was moved on loan from Motorsport's Boreham headquarters to SVE at Dunton to act as Progress Liaison Manager between Ford and Cosworth. Key Cosworth personnel included John Dickens as Engineering Executive, Mike Hall (who had worked on the GAA unit) and Paul Fricker.

The Cosworth version of the 'T88 Pinto' engine was based on the standard 3.57in × 3.03in (90.82mm × 76.95mm) 1,993cc iron cylinder block. A heat-treated crankshaft and connecting rods were used to give additional strength to cope with the vast increase in stresses. To help reduce piston crown temperatures, oil was sprayed on the undersides of special high-performance Mahle forged pistons. As before, Cosworth utilized their familiar pent roof combustion chamber shape to accommodate the 4-valves-per-cylinder layout, with a centrally located spark plug. Camshaft drive utilized a Uniroyal-supplied glassfibre reinforced rubber belt (the belt pulleys, incidentally, coming from the latest Fiesta/Escort CVH engine). Belt drive was also used for the distributor and oil pump.

To offset the effect of the turbo boost on cylinder pressures, the compression ratio was set at 8.0:1, although this did cause problems initially with maintaining exhaust emission within acceptable limits and poor fuel economy. In order to create the impressive 102bhp/litre power level a Garrett AiResearch TO3 turbocharger was used, giving a pressure of 8psi/0.55 bar. However, crucial to the engine's character had to be good low-speed torque and quick throttle response with little or no turbo lag, the shortfall of many turbocharged engines. This was achieved by using a Weber-Marelli engine management system to control the wastegate mechanism to best advantage. On over-run, fuel supply to the injection system is cut to increase economy and further improve emission control. To help cope with the enormous underbonnet temperatures, the turbocharger was mounted on a nickel-iron casting while an air-to-air intercooler was fitted between the turbo and the inlet manifold. Finally, to help keep oil temperatures within reasonable levels, the oil filter was cooled by an oil/water heat exchanger, the coolant working to a larger radiator.

The choice of gearbox for the RS Cosworth was to be the Borg-Warner 5-speed unit already in the Mustang Turbo which was built in America by Special Vehicle Operations (SVO), SVE's opposite department in Detroit. The only difference to be made for the application in the Sierra was that the fifth gear ratio was to be 0.80:1 (instead of 0.73:1 as used in the Mustang). Under sustained high-speed endurance tests in the pre-production cars a number of gearboxes gave problems, mainly through seizures of the bearings, a problem which had never been highlighted in America due to the limited speed restrictions there. A change to the bearing specification solved the problem with the Cosworth gearboxes being built on a separate Borg-Warner production line, although production start date for the Cosworth RS was delayed by many months as a result.

A major design consideration was a civilised delivery of power at all throttle openings. Indeed, there were some sceptics among Ford's top brass who thought that Rod Mansfield and his engineers in SVE could not overcome this typical turbocharged engine characteristic. That this *was* achieved is a tribute to both the SVE and Cosworth development engineers. With

(Opposite) *Compared to the Sierra RS Cosworth, the Sapphire 4-door version was more subtle in its visual identity. Not only were the body styling panels unique, the rear spoiler was far more refined.*

some 80 per cent of the engine's torque being developed between 2,300 and 6,500rpm, much of the engine's docile power was the result of the engine's electronic management system. Power output was rated at 204bhp (DIN) at 6,000rpm.

Suspension-wise, the set-up for the Cosworth was to be a combination of standard specification Sierra parts and new, purpose-designed items developed in conjunction with the car's competition use. Motorsport had indicated the need to raise the front roll centre by some 3.5in (89mm) and, as a result, new cast-iron hub carriers were manufactured and fitted to the basic Sierra MacPherson struts. Fichell and Sachs gas-filled dampers were fitted all round – twin tube on the front and single tube on the rear. To improve location, uniball joints replaced the more usual rubber bush joints of lesser Sierras. A thick 1.1in (28mm) anti-roll bar was fitted to the front and a 0.5in (14mm) bar to the rear. The result was a compromise (but a very commendable one) between outstanding handling and a rock-hard ride.

The braking system had to be equally impressive to handle the performance of the RS Cosworth. It had 11.4in (289.5mm) ventilated discs and four-pot callipers fitted to the front, with solid 10.75in (273mm) discs on the rear operated by standard Granada Scorpio-type Alfred Teves GmbH electronically operated anti-lock braking with a processor self-check system. Steering was Cam Gears rack-and-pinion type with power assistance giving 2.6 turns from lock to lock. Like the suspension spec., the choice of low-profile tyres was a compromise between those which gave ultra fine grip but with little give, and those which gave good grip characteristics but were quiet and forgiving, too. Eventually, the Dunlop D40 205/50 series were chosen as giving the best results and these were fitted to 15 × 7in (38 × 17.8cm) Rial alloy wheels.

A considerable amount of work was done in the wind tunnel in order to arrive at the most effective position for the tailgate spoiler. This was a compromise between the spoiler creating too much drag (thereby reducing aerodynamic efficiency) and the spoiler having no effect at all on high-speed stability. As many as 92 separate prototype mock-up spoilers were tried at MIRA's wind tunnel test centre before the final shape was agreed. Significantly, Gordon Prout, SVE's aerodynamicist, commented that had it been possible to extend it further rearwards, the test figures would have been even better but the law prevented protrusion beyond the perimeter of the bodywork. The final drag coefficient of 0.345Cd is impressive enough but in no way reflects the equally impressive rear downforce at high speed which gives reassuring stability.

Externally, the RS Cosworth was to be the most distinctive Sierra yet, with its re-modelled nose section and small grille aperture, front bumper/air dam moulding with integral auxiliary lights, brake air scoops and wheel arch extension/sill sections. To release under-bonnet heat, small vents were let into the bonnet panel, which also added to the visual effect. The overall impression hit just the right balance between the XR4i's 'boy-racer' image and the over-restrained impact of the XR4×4. Inside, the RS Cosworth had been equipped as befitted a high performance, top-of-the-range model: electrically-operated front windows with tinted glass all round and a laminated front screen, a leather-rim steering wheel, Ford-finished Recaro hip-hugging front seats and a four-speaker sound system to help while away the hours behind the wheel.

Production of the Sierra RS was programmed into the assembly schedule at Ford's Genk factory in Belgium (shades of the RS2000 manufacture at Saarlouis again) to commence in mid-1986 with a Press launch set for December the previous year. Five LHD and ten RHD pre-production cars were prepared for the Press and shipped to Spain where the world's motor noters tried them for size. Back came the criticism that the steering was too twitchy and over-light for comfort. Mansfield and his team immediately got to work, reducing driver feedback (although the original steering ratio was retained), while the solid nylon-type inner pivot bushes on the track control arms were replaced by more forgiving rubber ones.

The Sierra RS was launched to the public in mid-July 1986. At £15,950 it represented very good value for money and was most competitively priced when compared to the opposition, (such as the Rover Vitesse at £17,029 and almost £22,000 for the Mercedes 2.3 16-valve). It's no wonder that few were left to gather dust in dealers' showrooms.

In an interview which appeared in the March 1991 issue of *Thoroughbred & Classic Cars*, the writer Graham Robson talked to Rod Mansfield shortly after his appointment as Engineering Director of Aston Martin, and Mansfield had this to say about his days with SVE: 'One of SVE's advantages, that of a small team, was that it could push its projects through very quickly. The Capri 2.8i, for instance, was on sale only about 15 months after SVE was set up, and even the Sierra RS Cosworth went from concept to press launch in 30 months.'

RS Cosworth production got under way at Genk in June 1986 at a weekly rate of 96 units, which quickly rose to 300 – the goal being to attain homologation as soon as possible. (Group A and N approval became effective from January 1987.)

With over 100bhp/litre on tap it seems difficult to believe that there should have been a need for even greater power from the Sierra Cosworth. But that was indeed what had been planned almost from the start, the additional horsepower being for the benefit of competition, the result of an on-going homologation programme. It was already known that by simply exchanging the turbocharger for a bigger unit the power could be increased to some 400bhp in race specification. With this

in mind, during 1986 an extra 500 RS Cosworth body shells were stored away with the intention that they would be made into an uprated version, known as the RS500.

Production, or perhaps more correctly, finishing, of the bodies into fully running cars was given to Aston Martin Tickford – a separate company from Aston Martin Cars (who were taken over by Ford in 1984). AMT – part of the CH Industrials Group – had already established a reputation in the motor industry for small-scale specialized automotive production. (Ford had had previous dealings with them regarding the modification of the RS200 rally car, making it suitable for the road.) Aston Martin Tickford were therefore an ideal choice for the specialized work necessary in the RS500 programme and it was to involve AMT in much development work before the assembly line could be established.

The focal point of the engine's increase in power centred around a larger Garrett AiResearch T31/T04 hybrid turbocharger unit. However, this in turn created even greater under-bonnet temperatures. A larger radiator was fitted with a bigger intercooler located directly behind it (as opposed to above the radiator, as on the first generation RS Sierra). An added bonus of the larger intercooler was the reduced temperature of air from the turbocharger. This, in turn, made the air more dense, thereby improving the engine's efficiency. Bigger inlet tracts increased the volume of incoming air to the combustion chambers, although the 1.37in (35mm) inlet and 1.22in (31mm) exhaust valves remained as before.

To comply with the stringent Group A regulations, secondary fuel injectors were fitted with their own supply feed although, in road trim, they were made inoperable. (For road use this extra induction equipment would have given considerable emission control problems, but for racing a different engine management control unit was needed to bring them into operation.)

Detail development work by Ford's SVE under Rod Mansfield and the Cosworth team resulted in improved durability while work was done on low-speed ride quality and roll centre height.

Based on the Sapphire Ghia, the dashboard layout on the Cosworth-engined car boasted Ford's four speaker sound equipment and illuminated car warning display readout although the boost gauge of the Sierra RS was not included in the 4-door version for marketing reasons.

The Cosworth Sapphire 7J × 15in (38cm) road wheels were Ford-designed and unique to this car fitted with 205/50VR × 15in tyres which helped give this model its impressive handling and roadholding.

As with the Sierra RS Cosworth, considerable time was spent on the Sapphire's wind tunnel performance with better cross-wind stability and a lower Cd figure than with the hatchback model.

Ford's product planning was anxious that the Cosworth Sapphire's unusual appearance from all angles was in keeping with its executive image. Moreover, it is a tribute to Rod Mansfield's SVE staff and the Cosworth development team that the Sapphire was turned into a true 150mph (240kph) machine, yet with docile manners for the heaviest traffic.

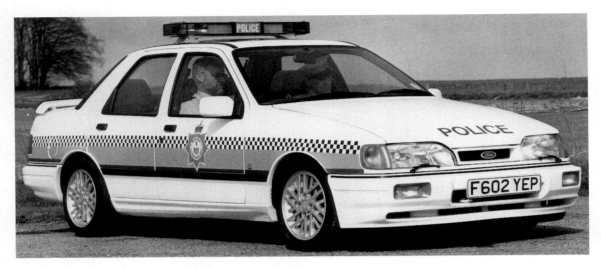

Surely an ideal police vehicle, two members of the Suffolk Constabulary on patrol in their Sierra Sapphire RS Cosworth. 0–60mph (0–100kph) in 6.1 seconds and a maximum speed of 150mph (240kph)!

In order to cope with the considerable stresses of racing, the standard 1,993cc Sierra cylinder block was specially re-inforced, the sand-casting process for RS500 blocks being altered to give stronger top and bottom faces and thicker cylinder walls. With the rigours of racing very much in mind, other significant changes to the engine's specification included different water and oil pumps and pistons. Also, the thermostat housing was given three retaining bolts instead of two. (Brakes and steering were as before.) And the result of these modifications on the road car? Power up from 204bhp to 224bhp at 6,000rpm with an impressive maximum speed of 153mph (246kph) and the all important 0–60mph (0–100kph) time of a neck-snapping 6.2 seconds! Fuel economy returned a creditable (at least for 224bhp) 24.5mpg at a constant 75mph (11.55l/100km at 120kph).

Externally, in an effort to add even greater high-speed stability, the RS500 was given an extra 'bootlid' spoiler to go with the existing mid-window aerofoil, while at the front the aerodynamicists had been at work to increase the much needed air flow into the engine compartment with, inevitably, an increase in the car's coefficient of drag. The price of the RS500? A very competitive £19,950. (Compare this with some £25,540 for the four-door Mercedes-Cosworth 2.3/16.)

In fact, the greatest accolade the Sierra RS and the RS500 could be given came from within Ford itself. The level of sophistication of these top-of-the-range Sierras convinced Ford's high-level management that here, perhaps, was a formula which could be adapted to good effect in the three-box Sapphire, thereby giving the company a very real opportunity to compete on equal terms with their old rival, BMW. But, in stark contrast to the Sierra RS and RS500 programme, the Sapphire Cosworth was to be a road car only and Ford would not impose any production limitations. In 1986, development of the four-door Cosworth began.

'The transition from the Sierra Cosworth to the Sapphire Cosworth was just a natural progression,' explained Walter Hayes. 'One of the snags with the Sierra was that it was a two-door car and there were a lot of people in the fleet market who could not allow their company executives to drive two-door models like the Sierra Cosworth because they are considered to be sports cars. With SVE under Rod Mansfield developing the Sapphire version, the fact that it was a very civilized car is nothing more than one would have expected. It is just an example of how sporting Fords have become more sophisticated with the passage of time.'

Subtle mid-stream production modifications to the Sierra and Sapphire made significant improvements to the integral rigidity of the body shells of both models which, in turn, proved to be a bonus when it came to the Cosworth versions. That, and the inherent smooth delivery of power from the 2-litre, 16-valve, turbocharged Cosworth-developed engine, produced a genuine 150mph (240kph) saloon which even surprised Ford's own Product Planning and Production hierarchy. A tribute, indeed, to the 'Cosworth Connection'.

'Naturally, working with Cosworth in the 1980s on the Sierra was very different to working with Lotus in the 1960s on the Cortina,' recalled Walter Hayes. 'After all, Cosworth by that stage had learnt a great deal and employed people themselves who were experts in business management. What we said to Duckworth was, "You build your own separate Sierra Cosworth engine plant, establish your own financial, supply and delivery schedule and just deliver the engines to us". We then went through costs and were satisfied that it was a profitable programme for them. That was not the way the Lotus Cortina was done. After all, Cosworth today have computer-controlled machines no one had thought of in 1962.'

Mike Costin and Keith Duckworth have now retired, although both remain very active men with an interest in the company they founded. 'I still think Mike was among the best racing mechanics of all time,' said Keith Duckworth to the author recently. 'If there was a problem he could sit down and

Vehicles Developed by SVE
Capri 2.8i
Fiesta XR2
Escort XR3i
Escort Cabriolet
Fiesta XR2 (1984 facelift)
Escort RS Turbo
Escort Cabriolet (1986 facelift)
Sierra XR 4×4
Granada/Scorpio 4×4
Sierra RS Cosworth (two-door)
Escort RS Turbo (1986 facelift)
Sierra RS Cosworth (four-door)
Escort air conditioning and power steering – Venezuela, then Europe
DOHC (four cyl) Sierra XR4×4
Sierra Cosworth 4×4
Fiesta RS Turbo
Escort RS Cosworth

work out what needed doing and have it done in, say, forty minutes before a race while I was still thinking about a reasonable solution. If you want a quick but competent solution, then Mike is your man. But if you want a thoroughly engineered job without any time constraints, then I am the bloke to do it. Mike has an extraordinary intuitive ability to know when something is right or wrong. The strength in our relationship was that we complemented each other perfectly.'

'Keith is the sort of person who can develop something from nothing. He does not need to refer to a book for a formula, he will produce it from first principles,' said Mike Costin. 'I enjoy engineering and nothing else. I have never wanted to be a manager or wanted to be a boss. And what is more, I was never prepared to work at it. I never set myself up to be a top man in industry. I always reckoned to be a good second man. I think I did a good job in supporting Colin Chapman and I have done a good job in supporting Keith.'

5 Racing to Win

'I think there is considerable misunderstanding about what motor sport was like in this country before the Second World War,' remarked Walter Hayes. 'My wife once asked Rob Walker what it was like at Le Mans in those days, to which he replied, "Oh, we had our problems, you know, but the big question was always whether to wear the pinstripe suit by day and the Prince of Wales check at night, or the other way about." And while that is not to diminish the Cobbs and Witney-Straights, it was, nevertheless, a social activity. The lads who began racing after the war were not like the rich young men of the 1930s. Colin Chapman, Keith Duckworth, Ralph Broad: it was an extraordinary flowering of native genius. Down almost every side street there was somebody trying to get into motor sport.'

As we have already seen in Chapter 1, by the end of the 1950s Ford were already beginning to establish an enviable reputation with race and rally successes using the Consul, Zephyr and Zodiac. Even the side valve Anglia had proved its worth, rubbing door handles with the best of them on the tracks as well as taking the dust of the East African Safari Rally in its stride.

But now Ford had new, better weapons with which to confront the opposition: the 105E Anglia, which could be made to go very fast indeed; the Cortina GT, which carried on the trend for the rugged reliability started all those years ago by the Model Y; and the Cortina Lotus, which embodied the fiery, tempestuous spirit of a wanton mistress.

As the table in Chapter 4 shows, the first racing versions of the Lotus Twin Cam engine were developed by Keith Duckworth and Mike Costin at Cosworth. Intended for Group 2 events, these engines were fitted with re-worked cylinder heads, which improved gas flow efficiency (although the valve sizes remained unchanged), and re-jetted 40 DCOE Weber carburettors. However, it was the bottom end which received the most attention since, in Duckworth's opinion, the standard con. rods and pistons were not strong enough for the stresses of racing. So, Cosworth rods, a crankshaft with additional counterbalance weights and steel main bearing caps were substituted, the unit giving 140–145bhp.

Cosworth supplied Lotus with a number of such engines in this form for use in the Lotus Cortina, until the day when Chapman met Tony Rudd of BRM at the Savoy Hotel in London after the Lord Mayor's Show in 1964. Quite why, no one really knows, but Chapman discussed the possibility of BRM supplying race-prepared Twin Cam engines and a deal was quickly agreed upon (in the Gent's cloakroom!).

Initially, BRM, too, experienced problems with head gasket failures as engines on test were run up to full revs. In an effort to overcome the snags, a small number of cylinder heads were specially sand-cast by Aeroplane and Motor. These were reputedly more rigid and, together with a different head gasket specification, it seemed that a solution had been found. Eventually, however, BRM went back to fitting the sand-cast Mills production spec. head, along with the standard Coopers head gasket.

However, it seems that Cosworth and BRM excelled in different areas of race-engine preparation; Cosworth were masters at bottom end development using just the right quality and strength of rods and

The Mk I Cortina was renowned for its rugged strength and reliability (seen here on the tough East African Safari Rally), dominating international motor sport, winning the World Manufacturers' Rally Championship twice and the European Touring Car Championship in racing.

crankshafts whereas BRM, whose bottom ends were reckoned to be grossly over-engineered, were the better company when it came to gas-flowing cylinder heads. Team Lotus found the best compromise by fitting their race Lotus Cortinas with hybrid units, bored out to 1,594cc to keep within the 1.6 litre regulations.

Twin Cam engines fitted to rally Lotus Cortinas were also BRM-prepared, these units, too, being fitted with special rods, pistons and crankshaft. Unfortunately, reliability was a never-ending headache for team engineers Bill Meade and Peter Ashcroft, with oil leakage problems being a constant source of irritation. For a short time, the contract for Boreham's competition Twin Cam engine assembly was moved to Vegantune of Spalding, Lincolnshire, who supplied Ford with Lotus Cortina engines during 1966 and early 1967. But the arrangement was far from a happy one with

Bill Meade finally proclaiming that he could do better! From then on, Twin Cam engines were delivered to Boreham direct from Lotus's headquarters in Hethel and were stripped and rebuilt by the Ford Competition engineers. A few were fitted with Tecalemit-Jackson fuel injection, although the set-up was never a success.

RALLYING

The tough RAC Rally in late 1964 was to be the platform for the Lotus Cortina's rally introduction where, driven with verve and determination by Brian Melia and Henry Taylor, it took sixth place. In fact, it was a triumph for the mechanics, too, for the Cortina's 'A' frame rear suspension location was to prove troublesome. (As, indeed, it did on many tarmac and forest events, causing problems with the differential housing

Henry Taylor in a Cortina GT on the way to winning his class in the 1964 Scottish Rally. The Cortina's straightforward engineering and good power/ weight ratio made it an ideal rally contender.

which, in turn, resulted in loss of lubricant, while the radius arms had a habit of bending or breaking.)

Graham Robson and Roger Clark gave the Cortina Twin Cam its first major win during 1965 in the Welsh International Rally. But there were problems on the Alpine when Vic Elford's efforts were dashed in the final few miles when a distributor fault delayed him. However, Lotus Cortinas won their class with Henry Taylor taking third place. Unreliability dogged the Cortinas' chances again in the RAC. However, by now the cars were homologated with leaf spring rear suspension, so differential and radius arm problems, which had so beleaguered the earlier cars, were a thing of the past.

As for Boreham's performances in 1966, there was both frustration and satisfaction. Clark lost his fourth place in the Monte

Carlo Rally as a result of a dispute over an infringement of lighting regulations and Vic Elford had his fair share of crashes, 'bending' his Cortina during both the Swedish and Circuit of Ireland events. However, it was not all doom and gloom, for Elford managed a second on the Tulip and an outright victory in the San Remo – only to be disqualified for a documentation infringement! On the plus side, Bengt Soderstrom and Gunnar Palm took outright victory in the tough Acropolis, as well as another outright win in the RAC event.

That year (1966), Ford changed the shape of the Cortina with the introduction of the Mk II model, although Mk I cars still continued to give a good account of themselves, with Vic Elford putting up a magnificent performance in the Alpine Rally, only to have his engine fail, and Roger Clark

*Before the Escort took the East African Rally by storm, this toughest of events
was usually won by a local driver. Here, Jack Simonian of Kenya, an engineer
with East African Airways, is lying 8 minutes behind the leader, Bert
Shankland in a Peugeot.*

*While the 'Boreham Boys' concentrated their efforts on rallying, Escort
racing was left in the capable hands of people such as Ralph Broad and Alan
Mann. Here, Chris Craft and Roger Clark share the 1300GT in the Touring
Car GP at Nurburgring.*

finishing a commendable second. A Lotus Cortina won the Geneva Rally, too.

In the forest events Soderstrom won the 1967 Swedish Rally in an 'old' model Twin Cam Cortina although, clearly, Clark's Cortina was just not up to the rigours of the East African Safari, the car leading the field until rear suspension failure put him out. By way of consolation, he managed an outright victory in the Scottish, driving one of the Mk II cars, despite twisting the body shell so much that it looked rather like a banana. Cortina Lotuses also showed their colours in the Gulf London Rally with Ove Anderson at the wheel, while Soderstrom came third in the gruelling, dusty Acropolis.

In Rallycross, too, the Cortina Lotus produced some exciting and spectacular sport with Roger Clark showing his worth. He also gave the Mk II its rally finale, finishing tenth overall in the outrageously tough London-to-Sydney Marathon. (He had led for much of the way in this event until his engine failed.)

History now records that the Escort was probably the most successful rally car of all time. One fact to support this claim is that Ari Vatanen won the 1981 World Rally Championship driving a model which, officially, was four years out of production! Another is that Ford's factory-entered Escorts covered an impressive 12-year period from 1968 to 1979.

But that first year had been a tremendous rush for the 'Boreham Boys'. Homologation into Group 3 came in March 1968 and dictated that 100 similar cars had to be built. X00 355F had the dubious reputation of being the first rally car to emerge from the doors of Ford's competition workshops and was to be entered in the San Remo Rally driven by Ove Andersson and John Davenport. While the car was still being finished the two rally stars had to recce in an old Lotus Cortina. Nothing wrong with that. The difficulty was that lack of time had precluded them from gaining more than a

very limited experience with the Escort before the event began. As it was, they finished third behind Pauli Toivonen in a Porsche 911 and Pat Moss-Carlsson in a Lancia Fulvia HF.

The Escort's first big win came during the first holiday break of 1968, at Easter, in the Circuit of Ireland. The Boreham team built a second Twin Cam to Group 6 regulations, its engine developing a reputed 152bhp. With its skinny Minilite alloy wheels and standard size wheelarches the car looked almost as though it had just come from the local Ford showroom. Yet against the favourite entry of Paddy Hopkirk in a BMC Cooper S and a couple of hot Hillman Imps, the Escort proved unbeatable and an excited Clark returned raving over the car's handling. Clark and the Escort were to be a formidable team, demonstrating in no uncertain terms the wisdom of Henry Taylor's theory of amalgamating the tough yet light Escort body with the powerful Lotus Twin Cam engine. Over the next two months Escorts went on to another five wins. (Four of them – Circuit of Ireland, Tulip, Acropolis and Scottish – were won by Roger Clark while the 1000 Lakes event was won by Hannu Mikkola.) By the end of the year a growing number of parts had been homologated.

As Ford's Competition team began preparing for the next season's events, a quick reference to the results sheet reveals that, after a promising start, the first few months of the year were to be a lean time. It was not until April and the Circuit of Ireland event (that Rally again!) that Clark showed the opposition how it should be done. Meanwhile, it was clear that the standard 1,600cc Twin Cam engine was beginning to show signs of age, despite continuous and enthusiastic development. One of its major drawbacks, at least as a rally unit, was that it lacked torque. In an effort to solve this problem, Peter Ashcroft developed a 'large bore' unit using a thick-wall block, specially cast for the purpose by Ford's Dagenham foundry.

The 1969 Monte Carlo Rally in which Ford entered three Escort Twin Cams; they finished fourth and thirty-second, with the third failing to complete the course.

By using a 3.37in (85.6mm) bore Ashcroft was able to produce a unit which boasted a capacity of 1,791cc. (Dagenham agreed to cast a small quantity, as the demand arose, and christened the castings 'Ashcroft blocks'.) These engines produced a healthy 180bhp.

This led to the need for an alternative – and stronger – gearbox than the Cortina Lotus type already used in the Escort Twin Cam. Ford finally decided upon the rugged – if expensive – ZF gearbox, despite the fact that its ratios were not ideally suited to a race or rally Escort. However, ZF agreed to begin work on developing alternative ratios. To transmit this kind of power to the road the Cologne 'Atlas' rear axle was chosen. This, linked to the ZF gearbox, proved to be

sufficiently rugged to handle the substantial power output from the over-bored 1.8-litre Twin Cam engine.

In stark contrast to the early months of the year, by the summer of 1969 Escorts were beginning to realize some successes, with firsts in the Circuit of Ireland, Tulip, Welsh and Austrian Alpine Rallies, although Clark and Porter had to be content with second place in the Acropolis in May. Then came Escort wins in the 1000 Lakes and the Tour of Belgium. Clark, however, was to finish a disappointing sixth in the RAC later in the year, in November.

Overall, it was a case of 'could do better'. While the Escorts often found themselves up against more expensive, specialized

*The Escort of Mikkola and Palm at the start of the Daily Mirror World Cup
Rally. Ford entered a team of seven cars in this event; only two did not finish.*

machinery, it seemed the car's promising handling and performance was not being reflected in good results on major rallies. Ford badly needed a win – and a *big* win, at that. Luckily, the Daily Mirror World Cup Rally gave them that win with all the promotional bally-hoo which went with it. Moreover, it served to give the 'Boreham Boys' a tremendous fillip. It was also to be the first real taste of Ford rally management for Stuart Turner, who was freshly recruited by Walter Hayes from Castrol.

'Stuart Turner arrived on the Ford stand at the 1966 London Motor Show and I took the opportunity to introduce him to Sir Patrick Hennessey, the Chairman of Ford Europe, saying, "This is Stuart Turner, he is the chap who runs the BMC Mini team who are giving us all the trouble",' said Walter Hayes, remembering with affection his efforts to bring the able and talented Turner into the Ford fold. 'I asked Stuart to come and join us but he wouldn't because he felt that it would be disloyal to BMC, so he went

to work for Castrol. But we continued to keep in touch.'

Ford's entries in the World Cup Rally of 1970 were to be Twin Cam Escorts but with enlarged pushrod Kent engines. The reason for this decision was based on Ford's performance in the 1968 London-to-Sydney Marathon when Twin Cam engines had proved temperamental. Ease of maintenance and poor quality petrol in some of the more remote areas of the route were two other primary considerations. (Thoughts had been turned to using 2.3-litre V6 engines with ZF gearboxes and Taunus rear axles, but engine problems dictated that this idea be dropped.) What finally convinced Peter Ashcroft that he should use the pushrod unit was Holbay's engines fitted to the Lotus Seven. He already had the knowledge to 'stretch' this engine to 1.8-litres and more; these units producing a reliable 140bhp. (The actual size chosen was 1.85 litres.) Drive was then taken through a ZF gearbox to an Atlas 'Capri' rear axle.

Makinen and Staepelaere going well on the World Cup Rally in which they finished fifth overall. Ford considered BDAs and V6s before settling on 1,850cc pushrod units as being the most suitable.

The privately entered Cortina Lotus of I. Harwood, B. Hughes and F. Pierson on its way through Portugal towards Lisbon on the Daily Mirror World Cup Rally of 1970. Note the rather obvious re-routed exhaust system!

Seven Ford Escorts, looking suitably rugged and every inch the part with their 'Rhoo Bars and a multitude of extra lamps, lined up at the start. After dozens of countries and 16,000 miles, five Escorts finished – a commendable performance, the winning car being driven by Hannu Mikkola and Gunnar Palm.

When asked whether it was the cars or the drivers to whom the laurels should be given, Turner replies, 'It is a combination of both. Success depended just as much on man's capacity to endure the strain of high pressure driving for very long periods as it did on the mechanical durability of their cars.' Of the 96 cars which set out from London on 19 April, just 23 survived this roughest, toughest and longest of rallies. Hannu Mikkola had this to say: 'I think all of us who got to Mexico felt the same way: very, very tired but also very elated at having completed the longest rally in the history of modern motoring. I would sum up the event as an absolute copy-book rally which was very tough indeed.' They had beaten 24 other makes of car from 22 different countries; world beaters, indeed. However, as Turner was to say later, had Ford *not* won . . .

With the success of the 1970 World Cup Rally fresh in everyone's mind, enthusiasm for the 1971 season was running high. Bold plans were being made for the East African Safari with six cars being put through the Boreham workshops. Up till then, the rally had been won by East Africans on 18 previous occasions and Turner was anxious to demonstrate that it could be won by a British car with a European driver.

The first major hurdle to overcome was a strike on Ford's production line which lasted nine weeks and which affected both budgets and supplies of parts. But the combined determination of Turner and Hayes ensured that the preparation programme was pushed through. To handle the rigours of the unfriendly East African terrain the cars had been given extra strengthening while the

Zasada and Wachowski in the third of the FTW cars: 48H. The other two were driven by Aaltonen and Liddon, and Malkin and Hudson-Evens. This car came home in eighth position.

1.8-litre Twin Cam engines had been detuned to produce 140bhp to take account of the poor quality petrol.

Sadly, despite the team's considerable efforts, only two cars managed to finish – one in fourth and the other in sixth position. The only consolation was that lessons learnt in gearbox changing resulted in Boreham developing a modification to make the job that much quicker under ordinary conditions. Publicity-wise, it was an expensive disaster, a rally best put down to experience. For the remainder of the year the list of results was equally disappointing with only the RAC in November breaking the pattern with a fourth, fifth, eleventh and thirteenth home.

The finish of the Daily Mirror event in which Ford cars came in first, third, fifth, sixth and eighth. After 160,000 miles (256,000km) both men and machines look extremely tired. Competitions Boss Turner said later he had to contemplate nothing less than a total Ford victory.

For 1972, Ford decided to put the RS1600 in the limelight and engine specialist Brian Hart brought in his talents to help Bore-ham's power unit wizard Peter Ashcroft develop the BDA to give bags of reliable horsepower (despite detuning to take account of the less than superior fuel encountered on the East African Safari). Using cast-iron cylinder blocks with a capacity of 1,800cc the units produced 205bhp on 'cooking' fuel, with an impressive 8,500rpm rev. limit and 7,500rpm possible continuously! As it was, Mikkola finally took the flag, thereby

dispelling the myth that it takes a local driver to take the Safari honours.

Other memorable results during the 1972 season included a first on the Welsh with Clark and Porter; first on the Scottish with Mikkola; first on the Manx with Clark and Porter and another victory for Clark and Porter in the RAC. That year also saw the introduction of the full 2-litre all-alloy BDA rally engine which was used to consid-erable effect by Makinen and Lidden in the 1000 Lakes, held in August that year, where they finished a creditable second overall. In

Smith and Preston's RS1600 having its light guard fitted in readiness for the 1972 Safari Rally in which they finished third. An additional strengthening bar has been added between the suspension turrets.

Mikkola and Palm on their way to a hot and dusty victory in the 1972 Safari Rally in their 1,800cc RS1600. This was the first time that the crew would have two-way radios linked in to a 'spotter' plane with an eagle-eyed Stuart Turner aboard.

Stuart Turner

Born in Stoke-on-Trent, Staffordshire, Turner initially wanted to be a doctor, his boyhood days spent cutting up worms, dissecting them with amateur enthusiasm. Then one day his attitude changed when whatever he was investigating bled red blood and overnight his mind was changed and he decided upon accountancy. Then came National Service and the chance to learn Russian.

Back in 'Civvy Street', Stuart competed in his first rally in a 1937 Rover 14, commanding operations from the back seat. From then on there was no stopping him; 1956 saw him in his first RAC rally competing as navigator (a role he was to become well known for) in – of all things – a VW Beetle. But fame really came when Turner won the Autosport's Navigator's Trophy in 1957, 1958 and 1959. However, the pinnacle of his success in those heady days was his victory in the 1960 RAC Rally with Eric Carlsson.

Stuart Turner.

Also that year Turner joined the team at *Motoring News* although, in the event, it was to prove a short interlude because Marcus Chambers, who headed up BMC's Competitions Department at Abingdon, was looking for someone to replace him. He recommended Stuart Turner, who took up his new post in 1961.

Under Turner's motivation, planning and determination, the Mini Coopers and their drivers became legendary. But it took its toll and in 1967 Turner decided to leave, taking a job with Castrol. However, he had only just settled in when Walter Hayes telephoned again (he had first asked Turner to join Ford while he was still with BMC but Turner had declined) offering him a job heading up Ford's Competitions Department; so in 1969 Turner went to work for Ford.

Just over a year after taking up the job of Competitions Manager, Walter Hayes created the job of Director of Motor Sport for Ford of Europe for Turner, although his time in this job was to be short-lived. His place was taken by Mike Kranefus, allowing Turner to take up the management of the AVO factory, the Competitions Department falling under the control of Peter Ashcroft. Then, in 1975, Turner moved again, this time to head up Ford's Public Relations Department. He retired in late 1991.

the quest for more and more power the Duckworth BDA was proving a worthy successor to the Ford-based Lotus Twin Cam, while the strength of the Escort shell seemed to be capable of withstanding the most appalling thrashing.

With the adrenalin still flowing swiftly, Turner and the Boreham team looked forward to a similar story the following year. A fresh group of cars, decked out with the latest spec. 2-litre BDA engines, was prepared for the season.

Brian Hart recalled his decision to develop the 2-litre all-alloy version of the BDA engine: 'In 1970 we did some crystal-ball gazing, and it seemed obvious there was a capacity for a 2-litre engine. With our knowledge and relationships with the engine and with Ford, we decided to stick with Ford and make an aluminium block, purely for development. We decided early on to use the basic configuration of the Kent engine and the basic BDA components, but this restricted certain aspects of the block.

Looking back, purely from a racing aspect we would have been wiser to design a full 2-litre racing engine off our own bat — despite the cost.' Not only was the Hart all-alloy 2-litre engine some 40lb (18kg) lighter than the iron block BDA, it also proved to be more reliable.

First off in the season, Mikkola and Porter turned in fourth position in the Monte with Makinen and Liddon taking a so-so eleventh spot. All eyes were directed at the Safari to come in April. A five-car team were put through the ever-busy Boreham workshops, kitted out with the latest equipment. This now included radios that gave two-way communication between the cars and the spotter plane carrying Turner and a team of engineers who were capable of being on the scene within minutes to carry out emergency repairs. Yet, like 1971, 1973 was to prove the exception to the rule that says, 'preparation and world-class drivers win rallies'. Clark's car lost its steering *and* its electrics while Makinen and Liddon rolled in a most spectacular fashion. The two other Escorts driven by Mikkola and Shiyukah both retired through mechanical problems. Only the Preston and Smith car managed to complete the circuit, coming home a less-than-impressive fourteenth overall.

By way of compensation, however, there were glories, too. Clark and Porter finished first in the Welsh and the Scottish, while Mikkola and Porter got a first home in the Heatway Rally in July with another Escort in second place. Makinen and Liddon were victorious in the 1000 Lakes the following month. However, the RAC just had to be the most hotly contested of all the events with a full seven-car team which included HRH Prince Michael. Yet, despite this formidable army of contenders, four failed to finish, although Ford were able to claim a 1, 2, 3 result, with Makinen, Clark and Alen taking the first three places; an impressive performance to round off the year.

With the energy crisis of late 1973 beginning to take effect, some areas of the press began calling for wasteful use of fuel, such as rallying, to be stopped. It wasn't, of course, but a tanker driver's strike did take its toll and the Scottish, scheduled for June 1974, was cancelled at the last minute.

Moreover, 1974 was also to be the year of conflict over wheel sizes. Makinen demanded his car be fitted with giant 15in (38cm) alloys (on a car designed to take 12in (30.5cm) wheels, don't forget), which created many headaches for the rally support engineers who had to cater for 13in (33cm) as well as 15in (38cm) wheels and tyres! Mikkola and Makinen finished first and second in the 1000 Lakes, explaining that their performance was the result of the bigger wheels. On the RAC later that year Clark decided on the larger-diameter alloys, too. However, after a nasty moment half way round the course, Clark reverted back to 13in (33cm) to finish seventh. 'Flying Finn' Makinen took the glory, while four out of the seven Ford starters failed to finish. Meanwhile, Preston finished a disappointing ninth on the Safari with Alen and Davenport taking the 'pot' in the Welsh in May.

Following the launch of the Escort Mk II, in January 1975 at a Press reception at the Dorchester Hotel in London, Boreham displayed a rally-prepared RS1800 which boasted a Hart-built 2-litre engine with all the usual goodies including a ZF gearbox.

The RS1800's first international win went to Clark in the Welsh event in May 1975 with a RS1600 in second place and another RS1800 in fifth. For the Scottish in June, Ford entered a team of six cars, four RS1800s and two of the smaller-engined machines. As it was, the Boreham team showed the opposition how it should be done with 1800s finishing first, second, third and fifth with one 1600 coming in tenth (the other failed to complete the course). Constant improvement to engine specification and assembly assured the drivers of more and more power; on the Scottish, Clark was said to have

Roger Clark

Despite a galaxy of foreign rally stars – and in particular those from Scandinavia – in most people's minds it is Roger Clark who stands in the forefront of Works Ford drivers. However, his value to the Ford team was not just as an outstanding driver. It was Clark's ability to undertake test trials – putting cars through their paces at the Bagshot proving ground, getting them into quite extraordinary situations and then recovering from them, only to step out of the car minutes later to discuss, quite dispassionately, suspension settings – which was also of great value.

Roger Clark was born in Leicestershire in 1939. At the time, the Clark family ran a fleet of buses from premises in Narborough. With the war over, Roger's father began to build up a garage business which Roger joined upon leaving school.

Clark's competition career began with an Elva-modified Ford Ten van. This was replaced in 1961 (the year which also saw the start of the legendary Clark/Jim Porter duo) when he bought a Mini Cooper through the family firm. Clark then took second place in the International Scottish Rally in 1963. 1963 also saw Clark's first works drive, for Reliant, in the Alpine. Then came a drive with Triumph in the Liège-Sofia-Liège and then on to Rover in 1964 to pilot their newly launched Rover 2000. He finished sixth overall and first in the Touring Car category in the tough Monte Carlo Rally, enduring quite appalling weather conditions, driving what can hardly be considered to be the most competitive of machines.

Despite his outings in the Rover, Clark resorted to his own transport (the company's Cortina GT demonstrator) when he won the Scottish International in 1964 and 1965. He also won the new London-Gulf Rally in 1965 and came third that year in the Circuit of Ireland.

Meanwhile, not surprisingly, Clark was coming to the attention of the Ford Competition Team and was given a works Lotus Cortina in which he won the 1965 Welsh Rally. His first overseas victory was in the Shell 4000 in 1967. That year he also won the Scottish and took part in arguably one of the world's toughest rallies – the East African Safari.

The following year saw Roger begin his now well-documented career with the Escort. He was involved with much of its initial testing at MIRA, Bagshot and Boreham. Much of Clark's subsequent success can be attributed in part to the fact that his rally cars were prepared by one man, the very talented Norman Masters, who knew *exactly* how Clark wanted his car set up. The result was that Clark was able to match the skilled Scandinavians. Indeed, he is the only British driver to have won a World Championship Rally: the RAC in 1972 and 1976.

A quick glance at Ford's competition entry list is sufficient to prove the point: for 12 years on from 1968, Clark won 20 international rallies driving what was probably the world's most successful rally car ever, the Escort, usually with the loyal Jim Porter as co-driver.

Of Clark, Stuart Turner once remarked, 'It's his awareness and confidence which makes him able to pace himself and only drive just fast enough to win. It must make life very frustrating for the opposition.'

After the Escorts came a couple of seasons driving Triumph TR8s, as well as the occasional drive in a Porsche and a season with a Metro 6R4, 'purely for fun', Clark is said to have remarked. But it was clear that the Escort years could never be repeated and today Roger is busy running his Porsche agency and his latest venture, a power boat business.

backed off when the rev counter pipped 9,000rpm in fifth gear (around 115mph (185kph)) in deference to the engine's longevity and his chances of finishing the rally. The Boreham team was also busy improving the new Escort's suspension set-up by fitting rear anti-roll bars and compression struts on the front. Indeed, a wide range of engine tune, gear ratios, suspension configurations and the latest Dunlop tyres gave the team and their drivers an ideal set-up for any rally situation.

Without doubt, the benefit to Ford from the considerable success of the Escort (and, to a lesser degree, the Lotus Cortina) in international rallies was immeasurable. As Clark was to say, 'The plain fact is that if you don't get factories like Ford spending money on rallying works cars, or supporting semi-works cars, or entering works teams, there would be far less sport, less ambition to get somewhere, less keenness to do well, less competition – and therefore less rallying.' He went on to say, 'Ford have kept motor sport going in England. Without them it would have been a sterile sport.'

Roger Clark and the Escort gave Ford some very good publicity, although there were times when Stuart Turner came in for considerable criticism for signing up Scandinavian drivers in preference to talent closer to home. When asked what a British driver had to do to get into the Ford team, Turner's characteristically caustic reply was simply, 'to beat Roger regularly'.

At the Isle of Man event, Clark demonstrated his supremacy ever the forces of Porsche in the Manx Rally in September by finishing a convincing first with another RS1800 in third place; the other two Ford-entered cars failed to finish. Other less impressive performances were the Tour de France in which Makinen's engine let him down – when he was leading the field – and the 1000 Lakes, when he had to make do with third place. However, an example of things that can happen which no one can plan for was when Dunlop's tyre transporter broke down *en route* for the San Remo Rally. Within hours of starting the event, both Makinen and Clark were out of the rally, their tyres gone and no spares available.

By way of consolation, Dunlop produced a new and very impressive tyre in time for the RAC Rally in November, with a cover which combined all the ruggedness needed for a tough off-road event with the stickiness necessary to give the car traction at all times on all surfaces. The Boreham team

Roger Clark.

produced a formidable six-car team for the often wet and miserable November event: five RS1800s and one RS1600. On its home territory the Escort proved invincible with Makinen coming home first (despite developing a lubrication leak in the last stages), giving the Finn his third win in successive years in that event. Meanwhile, Roger Clark had to make do with second place. Entertainment for the enthusiastic crowds was provided by the rising rally star, Ari Vatanen, when he 'lost it' in a forest stage at over 100mph (160kph). The car rolled over in spectacular style, writing off one expensive – and brand new – rally car. Another Boreham car finished sixth, while the other three failed to finish. It was, in spite of the problems, an impressive first year's outing for the RS1800, giving Ford more press publicity – to say nothing of the sponsors who, in the form of companies such as Calibri, Allied Polymer and Cossack, must have been very satisfied with their investment.

The big news for 1976 was that under revised FIA regulations, Group 2 cars would be eligible for entry into Group 4 events for the next two years, while at a Ford Motorsport press conference held in January, Peter Ashcroft announced that Ari Vatanen would be hired as a works driver (much to the consternation of the purists who were unhappy at a relatively unknown Finn effectively upstaging certain British drivers).

Sadly, 1976 had its fair share of problems for the Boreham team. Early on in the year came the report that, after much consideration and lengthy talks with their sponsors, Boreham would withdraw their entry in the Safari; it was proving too expensive. It was also to be a year when the Ford team had more than their fair share of accidents. Continuous development of cars for certain events had caused a gradual increase in weight while – very surprisingly – the 260bhp Hart-built BDA engines proved to be somewhat unreliable during the year with a total of six engine failures. The cause was eventually identified: cylinder head gaskets were failing through 'head' stud stripping caused by the high compression ratios.

There were other troubles, too. On the Monte in January 1976 Clark's car began suffering with handling problems, despite many changes of dampers. As a result, Clark finished fifth. It was not until the team returned home that they found the calibration of the Bilstein shock absorbers was at fault! In the 1000 Lakes, Timo Makinen's car suffered from poor performance, the problem being – of all things – fuel contamination. It did not affect other entrants. Finally, a huge ten-car team was entered in the RAC, although not all were prepared by the factory. Penti Airikkala, driving a privately prepared RS1800, led the first stages, but fell outside the time limit later in the rally. At the finish it was a highly excited and satisfied Roger Clark who came in first, with newly hired Bjorn Waldegard (fresh from resigning from Lancia) in third spot, Other

Escorts finished sixth and twenty-seventh, although six Escorts failed to finish. This was proof, if proof was needed, that the Escort could outrun the likes of the formidable Lancia Stratos (itself a car developed specifically for rallying). Ford had won for the fifth time in succession; it was a most memorable and emotional occasion.

While 1976 was a year when the team was beset with problems, the following year was one to be spent re-learning many of the old lessons. For Peter Ashcroft, as newly appointed Competitions Manager, it was to be a tough time – especially since the team entered a total of eight international rallies. Ford management had given him the authority to put together a World Championship programme which would involve changes to drivers and cars. Bjorn Waldegard proved Ashcroft was right to bring him into the fold by finishing second in the Portugal Rally and winning the Safari and the Acropolis (which clearly pleased the Ford hierarchy). He also won the Lombard RAC with Russell Brookes and Roger Clark in third and fourth positions. Yet, there were difficulties, too, during the year, perhaps best summed up by mistakes in car preparation, choice of drivers in certain events and lack of budget to allow Ford to field a larger number of cars against their main adversary: Fiat. Even so, Ford must have been reasonably pleased for they gave Ashcroft a larger purse for 1978 which allowed him sufficient cash to sign up Hannu Mikkola and bring him back into the 'club' for Fords works drivers.

A quick reference to the results sheet shows that the team had their fair share of successes: Waldegard, first in the Swedish (as one might expect); Brookes and Clark, first and fourth respectively in the Circuit of Ireland; Mikkola, second in the Portugal; Brookes, first in the Tulip; Mikkola and Clark, first and second in the Welsh; Mikkola and Clark, first and third in the Scottish. For the RAC in November, a strike at Ford put paid to an official Boreham entry,

Looking far less aggressive than the Mk I Safari Escorts, Bjorn Waldegard leaps on to an outright victory in the 1977 East African.

Russell Brookes aviates the RS1800 in the 1978 Mintex Dales Rally in which he finished second; a little over 12 months later Ford retired from running works Escorts, marking the end of a memorable period in international motor sport.

so a 'mini-dealer team' was arranged with Mikkola, Waldegard and Brookes finishing first, second and third. Unfortunately, as for the World Rally Championship, Ford were out of the running by the start of the RAC because by this time Fiat had won five times; Ford had won just once!

1979 was to be altogether different. While enthusiasts will probably agree that during the previous years Ford had deserved to take the Rally Championship, they had also experienced their fair share of bad luck. Strikes, bad planning and unreliability had taken their toll, too. The 1979 season was kicked off in fine style with the Boreham team fielding an entry of 'tarmac terrors' in the Monte. Half way round, Mikkola's driving came in for criticism from the French Police. Then, to cap it all, not long afterwards he rounded a bend to find the road littered with boulders! So that was it; the Escort lost a vital six seconds.

On the Swedish the following month, Waldegard came in second, despite going off the road in an early stage, with Mikkola coming in fifth. In the Portugal held in March, the placings were reversed with Mikkola cruising home to victory closely followed by Waldegard. Mikkola then won the Welsh and Waldegard the Acropolis in May, although the Scottish was a bit of a disappointment with Mikkola only managing a miserable sixth place and Brookes way back in tenth position. By way of consolation, Mikkola won the Motorgard event in New Zealand. Then came the 1000 Lakes. Again, Lady Luck was conspicuous by her absence: Hannu Mikkola's engine blew a head gasket. Vatanen came in second with Waldegard in third place. In the Quebec event in September, Waldegard took the victor's podium with Vatanen third. Days after, Mike Kranefus, Ford's European Director of Motor Sport, announced Ford's decision to withdraw from international rallying at the year's end in order to concentrate their efforts on developing more economic engines

and more aerodynamically efficient body shapes – words which shocked the world of rally enthusiasts.

For the 1979 Lombard-RAC at the end of the year, Boreham prepared a team of seven 'rough-road' toughies. It was to be a grand finale in fine style. Of the 175 starters, only 74 entrants managed to finish. Six of these were Ford's Escorts. They came in first, second, fourth, sixth, ninth and tenth. Only Clark, with another of those head gasket failures, was not able to stay the course. It was a magnificent performance which gave Ford the World Rally Championship.

With the official closure of Boreham's campaign programme for the Mk II Escort, an arrangement was drawn up between Peter Ashcroft and a Ford dealer, David Sutton (who had already established a very close relationship with Ford). With world-class drivers such as Hannu Mikkola and Ari Vatanen, together with sponsorship from Rothmans and Eaton's Yale, Sutton's team (which involved six cars, four new and two rebuilt 'has-beens') continued to prove the supremacy of the Ford Escort: a first and second in the Mintex in February with Mikkola and Vatanen; Vatanen in second place in the Circuit of Ireland; a first and second for Vatanen and Mikkola in the Welsh, with the placings reversed in the Scottish in June. Vatanen managed a second spot in the 1000 Lakes, too, and another second in the San Remo with Mikkola just behind. The year finished with Mikkola gaining second place in the RAC, with Timo Makinen and Vatanen failing to finish. By the end of the year, Sutton's team had accomplished three firsts and five seconds in the British Championship and one win, three seconds and one third in the World Championship – a truly spectacular achievement.

Although the Mk II Escort was dropped from production in July 1980 (to be replaced by the FWD version), it is to Boreham's considerable credit that they continued to give David Sutton and his team enormous support with parts, help and enthusiasm. However, at the end of the year, Eaton's Yale decided to withdraw their support for Sutton's team while Castrol and Dunlop pulled out of *all* major rally sponsorship for the 1981 programme.

Rothmans then decided to take over almost total sponsorship of Sutton's very professionally-run team, with additional help from Pirelli and Duckhams. Indeed, a quick glance at the record books shows just how well the team was run and the results it achieved, the pinnacle being Ari Vatanen's win in the Driver's World Championship. Penti Airikkala won the Mintex in February while Vatanen won the Welsh and the Acropolis in May, not to mention the Brazil and the 1000 Lakes in August. In the Driver's Championship table the positions were very close. After the San Remo, in October, Ari was lying two points behind

Guy Frequelin and a huge eight points behind after the Ivory Coast event later in the month. Nothing less than a very good placing in the Lombard-RAC would ensure him the crown.

The Lombard-RAC in November was to be the clincher and very much a cliff-hanger since there was little chance of Vatanen outpacing Hannu Mikkola, now driving for Audi in the all-conquering four-wheel-drive Quattro. Even so, David Sutton's team built up an all-new car for Ari to contest the event. As it was, Mikkola took the winner's place while Vatanen finished second. *But,* since Frequelin failed to finish, Ari was assured of his Driver's Championship jackpot. A fitting end to the season for a great driver and a car which had truly earned its position among the ranks of international rally-winning cars.

In an interview with Graham Robson in

British Open Rally Champions Jimmy McRae and Ian Grindrod on the Manx Rally in 1987 with their Sierra RS Cosworth. Initially intended as a race car, the RS Cosworth has proved a worthy contender on the world's rallies, too.

Penti Airikkala testing the new Ford-developed seven-speed gearbox on the Scottish Rally in a four-wheel-drive Sierra RS Sapphire.

the December 1989 issue of *Thoroughbred and Classic Cars*, Roger Clark recalled his exciting and very productive period with the Escort: 'I did a lot of the original development work, to sort out the competition suspension . . . I worked closely with Bill Meade and Mick Jones; it was a very personal business – we did a lot of running at Boreham, Bagshot, and at MIRA. You could say the early Escorts were designed around my likes and dislikes . . . . In my day we had a situation where one mechanic – Norman Masters – built all my rally cars. He knew exactly what I wanted and how I wanted it. It was a very good relationship because I never even needed to sit in the car before I saw it at scrutineering.'

RACING

In 1963 the Lotus Cortina was homologated into Group 2 which dictated that, in order to qualify, 1,000 cars had to be built. The engines were bored out to 1,595cc (using specially chosen cylinder blocks, since not all blocks had sufficient metal to take this drastic machining) with re-worked cylinder heads, race profile camshafts and re-jetted Weber carburettors. To survive the stresses of racing, the standard connecting rods and crankshafts were replaced by steel ones. At the rear, the differential was changed to a limited slip type while the suspension was lowered all round with up-rated dampers and the brakes fitted with harder pads and linings. With its already modified 'A' bracket rear end, in the gifted hands of people such as Jim Clark and Sir John Whitmore, the Lotus Cortina could be seen drifting through

*Gerry Marshall holding a tight line through Bottom Bend during the 1971
Mexico Championships at Brands Hatch. This series was keenly contested and
gave Ford immense publicity for the Escort, and the Mexico in particular.*

corners at impossible angles in spectacular
fashion. What the Minis had started in the
early 1960s, the Lotus Cortina continued.
Against stiff opposition, often with much
larger engines, the Cortinas proved almost
unbeatable.

The Lotus Cortina's race debut was at
Oulton Park in September 1963 when Jack
Sears and Trevor Taylor in pre-production
cars finished third and fourth against tough
competition from larger, more powerful (7
litre!) Ford Galaxies, two of which came in
first and second driven by Dan Gurney and
Graham Hill. Suddenly, the favourite stars
of the tracks – the Mk II Jaguars – were not
having things all their own way. Setting
new records, the Lotus Cortinas gave the
crowds a foretaste of things to come. In fact,
Sears went on to win the British Saloon Car
Championship that year. It was a situation
which was to be perpetuated as, with Lotus
Cortina production getting into high gear in

January 1964, they began to dominate
saloon car racing. Despite torrential rain, in
the opening round of the British Saloon Car
Championship at Snetterton in March, Jim
Clark finished second in a works car behind
Jack Brabham in a Galaxie, with Peter
Arundell (also in a works Lotus Cortina)
setting the fastest lap time in the 2-litre
class. Clark won his class, too, with Bob
Althoff in a Willment-prepared Lotus Cortina coming second.

Next, came the Easter Monday meeting at
Goodwood, where Clark out-accelerated
Jack Sear's Galaxie off the line in the Touring Car event. It then went on to become a
tussle between the mighty Ford V8 and the
brilliant white Cortinas. Across the line it
was Sears, with Clark hot on his tail (having
lapped at 90.19mph (145.11kph) – second
fastest time ever) with Peter Arundell in the
other works car and Frank Gardner in the
Willment Lotus saloon.

Two months later, the Lotus Cortinas were at it again, this time taking on the Galaxies and the Brown's Lane 3.8-litre Mk IIs. Clark, who was to set the fastest time in practice, finished ahead of the field with Peter Arundell third in the other works Cortina. It was the same at Brands Hatch in the Touring Car race run of the Guards International Trophy event in August. Clark's 1 minute 53 seconds lap time during practice was 1.2 seconds quicker than Sears could manage in his Galaxie and while Sears took the cup, it was Clark's performance that thrilled the crowds. Bob Althoff, driving the Willment Lotus, came in third. Overall, Clark had a memorable year gaining maximum points in each of the eight rounds of the British Saloon Car Championship series to take the prize.

Abroad, Alan Mann Racing entered the European Touring Car events with drivers such as Peter Proctor, Peter Harper, Sir John Whitmore and Henry Taylor (Whitmore winning on five occasions to Taylor's one). Wherever there was a Ford agency it seemed one could see Lotus Cortinas being raced, South Africa and Australia especially, with resulting good publicity for Ford and Lotus. In 1964 came the introduction of a Special Equipment (SE) version of the Lotus Cortina with a 126bhp specification engine.

During the winter of 1964/65 Team Lotus's engineers beavered away to rectify the rear suspension reliability snags. While these had not proved to be that much of a problem on the tracks (where cars could be rebuilt after a short race), it was less easy on the roadside during an international rally! Finally, they compromised, using leaf springs firmly located with radius arms. By so doing, there were no more stresses imposed on the differential casing and handling was, arguably, just as good as the arrangement being fitted to production Lotus Cortinas from September that year. (Many older 'A' bracket cars were then modified, making it difficult nowadays to find an original early car.)

Meanwhile, the tuning wizards were extracting more and more power from the Twin Cam engines (Willment were regularly getting over 150bhp). For reasons never really made clear, Lotus contracted BRM to supply them with racing engines which developed 160–165bhp. The heavier Galaxies, meantime, had given way to the more agile Mustangs which, with their Ford V8s, could invariably out-perform the Lotus Cortinas in the dry. However, 'Gentleman' Jack Sears took the British Saloon Car Championship for 2-litre cars that year in a Willment-prepared car, while Sir John Whitmore took the European Touring Car Championship driving one of the red and bronze Ford-sponsored Alan Mann Cortinas.

For 1966 it was decided to compete the Cortinas in Group 5 rather than Group 2, to allow the cars to be developed even more. The Twin Cam engines were given fuel injection (which was to prove troublesome, at least in the early days), these units producing some 180bhp in dry sump form. Bodywork had to remain virtually standard but the steel road wheels were replaced by cast magnesium ones. Driving for Alan Mann, Sir John Whitmore made a very concerted effort in the European Saloon Car Championship but was finally beaten to the title by Alfa Romeos. Team Lotus won the Entrant's Title in the British Saloon Car Championship as a result of the efforts of Whitmore, Ickx and Peter Arundell. (Jim Clark's busy diary had prevented him from getting behind the wheel of a Lotus Cortina as much as he would have liked.)

In an article by Philip Turner in the October 1985 issue of *Classic Cars*, Sir John Whitmore recalled, 'My best race at Brands Hatch was when I drove Jim Clark's Lotus Cortina in the saloon car race before the Grand Prix in 1964. I won the race and Jackie Stewart was second with Jack Sears third. Very satisfying to have beaten Jackie Stewart.'

For many people, the most exciting aspect

of watching the masters driving Lotus Cortinas was when they lifted an inner front wheel when cornering hard. Sir John Whitmore again: 'It always felt odd because on left-hand bends it would come up much more as the driver was sitting on the right side of the car. It felt weird, as though the whole car was balanced somewhat precariously.'

1966 was also to be a significant year for another sporting Ford: the Broadspeed-prepared Anglia. Mini enthusiasts everywhere will remember the dicing between John Cooper's works-backed Mini Coopers and Ralph Broad's Minis driven by the likes of John Fitzpatrick – duels which were to cause major embarrassment since Broad's Minis often won! After a disagreement with BMC, Broad turned his attention to the Anglia with Ford announcing in November 1965 that John Young's Superspeed team would compete in the 1,300cc class and Broad with the 997cc engine in the 1-litre series. The key to Broad's thinking was that, within Group 5 regulations, the Anglia could benefit from major surgery to its suspension, brakes and drive train. In the first race of the season at Snetterton in April 1966, Fitzpatrick won the 1,000cc class – just six weeks after Broadspeed had started preparing the car – and went on to win six more classes and the BRSCC Saloon Car Championship.

Initial power output from the FVA-based engine supplied by Cosworth was rated at 112bhp at 9,200rpm although, come mid-season, this was replaced by a Holbay-tuned engine angled over at 30 degrees with a heavily modified head which developed some 115bhp at 9,200rpm. Power was transmitted through to a Hewland gearbox driving a deliberately low 6.1:1 final drive.

Underneath, there were Lotus Cortina front struts and disc brakes with torque tubes and a panhard rod to locate the rear axle. Later in the year this set-up was changed to coil spring/damper units with a panhard rod and trailing arms.

To the race enthusiast the Broadspeed Anglia looked the part with its lowered suspension, wide 7in (17.8cm) alloy road wheels and deep red coachwork set off by a silver-coloured roof. (Better still, Ralph Broad had signed up Anita Taylor to co-star with John Fitzpatrick as team driver.)

That year the Anglias firmly trounced the opposition in the form of the Fraser Imps. (Superspeed's 1.3 Anglias also outstripped Cooper' Minis.) But, despite 124bhp at 9,200rpm from Tecalemit-Jackson fuel injection, the Broadspeed cars did not find the following year such easy work; the Fraser Imps now had more power and better handling. Even so, Broad's cars managed a convincing seven class wins to three for Alan Fraser's Imps. However, as we shall see, the end of 1967 saw a reshuffle with Superspeed losing their 'works' backing and Broadspeed being asked to campaign a team of 1300GT Escorts.

With the introduction of the next generation of Cortina in February 1967, Ford took the opportunity to take over Lotus Cortina production, calling it the Cortina Lotus. It was an altogether more refined vehicle although, aerodynamically, its more angular shape and increase in weight (2,027lb (919.4kg) kerb weight compared to 1,820lb (825.5kg) for the Mk I Lotus Cortina) produced a slight drop in maximum speed.

For racing, Mk IIs were fitted with full-house Formula Two FVA engines which produced in excess of 200bhp, giving the cars very impressive performance. In the hands of Jackie Ickx and Graham Hill (when their busy diaries allowed) they could be seen well up among the leaders. At Oulton Park in September 1967, Hill and Ickx thrilled the crowds. Hill, lying fifth overall behind a gaggle of Ford Falcons and Mustangs, led the 2-litre class until his brakes failed and he detoured into the lake. Ickx also lost stopping power, leaving the circuit over a bank. That year, 1967, was the last year

Ford and Lotus co-operated over racing Cortina saloons, this co-operation ensuring a variety of well-known names getting behind the wheels. Unfortunately, pressure from other commitments meant that Team Lotus had to withdraw from managing their race Lotus Cortinas (the cars being sold off to Brian Robinson), although Alan Mann continued development of their FVA-engined cars. The Cortina Lotus competition programme was, therefore, severely telescoped for, waiting in the wings, was another Twin Cam-engined Ford saloon which was about to make motoring history: the Ford Escort.

While work on building the first Escort rally cars was to be handled by Henry Taylor and his talented team at Boreham, lack of accommodation, time and staff prevented the programme from including any race cars.

A team of 1300GT Escorts was very successfully campaigned in the UK by Broadspeed with drivers Chris Craft and John Fitzpatrick, although the team's first outing at Brands Hatch for the Race of Champions in mid-March 1968 ended in disappointment when the Fitzpatrick car retired with an overheated engine; 145bhp from just 1.3-litres was, after all, asking a lot – even if most of the internals were supplied by Cosworth!

However, these very fast 'screamers' went on to win their class in the 1000km at the Nurburgring as well as six rounds of the RAC Series, although even this was not enough to take the British Class Championship; this went to a works Mini Cooper.

Alan Mann, whose headquarters were on the Slough Trading Estate next door to where the legendary Ford GT40s were built, had taken delivery of four of the Boreham-built prototype Escort Twin Cams during the winter of 1967/68. Suspension development was immediately put into the very capable hands of Len Bailey (whose work was fundamental to the success of the GT40s during their short-lived works-entered years)

who took away the rear leaf springs and replaced them with coils located by Watts linkage and radius arms. Engines were nothing less than 1.6-litre FVA units which produced 210bhp. With Frank Gardner at the wheel, an Alan Mann Escort finished first at the Zolder European Trophy Challenge event as well as first in the saloon car race at the British GP at Brands Hatch in July, and again at the same venue in October. At the close of play that year, Mann and his team had won the British Championship, with the successful X00 349F being put on display at the October Motor Show.

In 1969 Fitzpatrick really made the Escort 1300GT go: first in class in the European Trophy Challenge at Brands; second in class at the British GP at Silverstone; second in class again at the Guards meeting at Brands and first in class at the Show 200 meeting, also at Brands. It was to be a memorable year, with Broadspeed cars dominating their class. Gardner was less successful with a number of placings throughout the season culminating in a win at the Brands Hatch Show 200 meeting, taking third in class overall. However, to be fair, the reason was simple enough. The FVA engine was banned under the new 1969 regulations so Gardner had to make do with a 185bhp Twin Cam engine.

Reflecting on his race at Zolder, Gardner remarked, 'It wasn't any problem because the opposition wasn't very strong. We were able to win pretty well as we pleased with a very conservative sort of lap time. Practice had already shown the potential of the car, because I was able to set fastest time by over 2 seconds.' He went on to compare the Escort with the Cortina, saying, 'On a race circuit the Escort strikes me as being rather like a refined Cortina to drive. It's a little lower in ride height and a little shorter in wheelbase, which gives it a nicer feeling than a racing Cortina. We are running a larger tyre area than on the Cortina which gives it a nice stable feeling. It is very quick right up to the apex of a corner, and then there's no wasted time. There's none of that period when you are trying to anticipate what the car is going to do. As soon as you've finished with the brakes you're polishing the floor with the throttle pedal. Yes, I think all in all it's a jolly good dicer. And I'd think the Escort with the FVA should be quite interesting.'

In 1970 Alan Mann dropped out of Escort racing. The cars were sold off and Frank Gardner went on to race other cars, thereby leaving the entire Ford works-supported effort to Ralph Broad. Entry was now under stricter Group 2 regulations, the 1,300cc engines being fitted with Tecalemit-Jackson fuel injection. With Broadspeed's specially designed downdraught cylinder head, power output was rated at around 150bhp. Broad was also now competing with an Escort Twin Cam (the last year the Twin Cam would be raced, in fact). Engine power was rated at about 180bhp and with the Bailey-type rear suspension layout, albeit with the leaf springs retained, the car proved very competitive.

In the International Tourist event at Silverstone, World Champion Jackie Stewart (who had not driven in a saloon race since getting behind the wheel of a Lotus Cortina in 1966) finished the first part of the race in fourth position behind much bigger machinery – notably Frank Gardner's 5 litre Mustang and Brian Muir's Camaro. Unluckily, when Chris Craft took over for the second part it was found that a valve spring had broken and he had to retire; nevertheless, it was an impressive performance. For Craft, however, he won his class six times driving the Twin Cam, while Fitzpatrick won seven classes in the 1300GT.

In performance terms, the BDA engine was a worthy successor to the legendary Twin Cam. Moreover, while no one had actually managed to develop even an 1,800cc Twin Cam to produce the magic 200bhp with any degree of reliability, an over-sized BDA produced this figure only shortly after production had started. Torque, bhp and rev-range were all improved. The engine fitted in Broadspeed's RS1600 developed 245bhp, around 25 per cent more than the rally-prepared engines. Most significant, of course, was that the BDA was homologated in the 1,601cc class which meant that engines *could* be increased up to full 2 litres, whereas the old Twin Cam homologation restricted it to the 1,600cc class.

As soon as the potential for the BDA was realized, the need to increase its capacity became of primary importance. We have already looked at the way Peter Ashcroft developed his very successful Ashcroft block in association with Dagenham's foundry. However, the real answer emerged – quite by chance it seems – when Ashcroft happened to stumble over what appeared to be a spare cylinder block laying on the floor covered in rags in Brian Hart's Harlow workshops! The old rags were kicked aside to reveal a full 2-litre prototype alloy cylinder block. Hart, who was contracted to build engines for Boreham, had developed the block as a private venture for a proposed lightweight 2-litre unit for Formula Two. The block utilized a 3.5in (90mm) bore (compared to 3.18in (80.97mm) in the 1,601cc production BDA) which would give a weight saving of some 40lb (18kg), while the increase in both power and torque – even over the 1.8-litre version – was considerable.

During 1971 Dave Matthews dominated the 1,300cc class in the works-supported Broadspeed 1300GT Escort, while Fitzpatrick, who was perhaps the busiest Ford driver of the year, finished first at Brands in the Race of Champions, third in the International Trophy meeting at Silverstone and a lowly seventh at the Grand Prix meeting, again at Silverstone. Abroad, it was the same picture with Fitzpatrick finishing first in class at Salzburgring and first overall at Jarama, although other outings proved less successful with punctures and axle failures preventing 'Fitz' from finishing.

In 1972 Ford redirected a great deal of their effort into preparing and entering the Capri. In Cologne, the Ford team under Jochen Neerpasch were getting around 320bhp from their 2.9-litre engines (although that year Neerpasch was to be lured over to work for Ford's main opponents, BMW). Nevertheless, an astute piece of planning by Stuart Turner produced some enviable sponsorship with Escorts winning the 2-litre class in the European Touring Car Championships. The talented Gerry Birrell in the 260bhp Hart-tuned RS1600 managed third overall at Monza followed by a seventh placing at Salzburgring and a class win at Brno. Surprisingly for Broadspeed, Woodman's efforts in the 1300GT Escort were hampered by mechanical breakdowns and a very nasty crunch towards the end of the season at Oulton Park, which

terminated activities for the remainder of the year.

In the background, Cosworth were also developing the Capri engine, although in this case, of course, it was the 3.0-litre Essex V6 unit which, in the hands of engine wizard Keith Duckworth, was made to produce in excess of 400bhp. In 1973 a 2-litre RS1600 Escort was loaned out for Dave Brodie to drive and, although he managed second place in the Race of Champions at Brands and fourth in the Daily Express meeting at Silverstone, his activities were rudely curtailed by what could have been a very nasty accident at the Grand Prix meeting at Silverstone where Brodie's car was involved with Dave Matthew's Capri. Luckily they, and the third driver involved, survived. However, with Boreham's only race Escort now a write-off, so too was their 1973 race programme.

Erich Zakowski's Zakspeed team had

A Capri RS2600 taking on the BMWs during the 24 Hrs at Spa in 1972. The Ford Cologne-built RS2600 Capris realized their first European Championship success with a 1–2 placing at the Saltzburgring in 1971.

An under-bonnet shot of a Cologne-built Group 2 RS2600 Capri. The over-bored 2,993cc Weslake-developed unit is fitted with Kugelfischer mechanical fuel injection and alloy cylinder heads producing around 320bhp. Suspension is coil spring/dampers all round with ventilated disc brakes on all wheels.

already won the German Championship with an RS1600 in 1973 so, astutely, Mike Kranefus (Ford's European Director of Motor Sport) contracted Zakspeed to enter RS1600s in the European Touring Car Championship. With consistently good performances, the Zakspeed Escorts took the cup in the German Championships. The German Escorts were among the first to use 15in (38cm) road wheels – freshly listed in the homologation specs – and fuel injected Cosworth BDG

engines which developed an impressive 275bhp. They won every one of the six European Championship races. A Zakspeed car also won the prestigious Six Hour Championship race at the Nurburgring against the formidable BMWs and Capris.

In contrast to a spectacular season in 1974, the following year was to prove less successful, mainly because many of the Touring Car Championship rounds were cancelled through lack of support. However,

The racing RS2600 Capri in 1972 form with its squared-off wheelarch extensions, bigger front spoiler and an air induction system for the fuel injected V6 engine. In the Spa 24 Hrs Capris finished 1–2–3, eighth in the Nurburgring 1,000km and tenth and eleventh at the Le Mans; an impressive and memorable year.

Wind tunnel testing the Zakspeed Capri for the 1978 series of the German Touring Car Championship. The 1.4-litre engines were turbocharged producing almost 400bhp and with special body styling (allowed under Group 5) would exceed 160mph (250kph).

A Sierra RS Cosworth being cornered very hard indeed, lifting a wheel during the 1988 European Touring Car Championships at Silverstone.

in one particular race – the non-championship Kyalami 1000km even in October – a single 2-litre RS1800 Zakspeed Escort outstripped the opposition (again, consisting of no mean contenders such as Capris and BMWs). The Zakspeed team also won the local German Championship for the third year running.

For 1976 the rules were changed. Cars entered in the European Touring Car Championship would have to be prepared to Group 2 specification. Significantly, this meant wet sump lubrication unless dry sump lubrication was a standard production feature. Despite considerable development, it was simply not possible to overcome the effects of

considerable sideways forces while cornering with the latest type of tyres. Even with careful sump baffling, oil surge resulted in the oil pump sucking in little more than oil mist! With not one race finished – let alone won – to their credit, Zakspeed retired, looking elsewhere to expend their efforts. It was a sad end to an impressive record.

RALLY CROSS

Finally, we must not forget the European Rallycross Championship, which was won by John Taylor in an Escort Twin Cam in

1973 – EUROPEAN TOURING CAR CHAMPIONSHIP

1971 – 4WD RALLYCROSS CAPRI

1979 – BRITISH SALOON CAR CHAMPIONSHIP

1980 – GERMAN CHAMPIONSHIP

A self-explanatory historic profile of the Capri in European motor sport. No wonder sporting Ford enthusiasts were sad to see the demise of the Capri, its performances are legendary.

1973 and Martin Schanche in conventional Escorts in 1978, 1979 and 1981.

Without doubt, all these results – in rallying, racing and rallycross – demonstrate the extreme strength of the Escort body shell, to say nothing of its versatility. Even this, however, would have meant nothing had there not been the original Twin Cam and BDA engines and the likes of Keith Duckworth, Peter Ashcroft and Brian Hart to hone them into world beaters.

6 Behind the Wheel

Nowadays, buying a sporting Ford, such as a Lotus Cortina, an RS Escort or Capri, can be a minefield of potential pitfalls even though, arguably, the average enthusiast is probably far better informed than ever before. The vast numbers of knowledgeable periodicals – to say nothing of books – have provided classic car buffs with a wealth of learning at the flick of a page. In addition, there is the new wave of video cassettes now flooding the market.

Yet, despite all this information, it is still possible to buy a car which – in spite of its gleaming exterior – proves to be nothing better than 'a bit of a nail'. Rocketing prices of cars such as the Mk I Lotus Cortina have resulted in a growth industry in manufacturing fakes, the profit to be had from doing so making the whole business very worth while indeed.

'There are normally two categories of buyer for the "runner" sector of the market for a car like the Mk I Lotus Cortina,' explained Graham Kent, who has been the proud owner of a very smart Lotus Cortina SE for the last 10 years, sometimes using it for the odd track event – despite its immaculate condition. 'The first category may well be referred to as the "uninitiated" because they buy a car which looks right superficially and *seems* to have the proper engine and interior trim. I know of one car local to my home in Sussex which has the right coachwork, the right mechanics and interior furnishings. Even the right headlining. The giveaway is the handbrake, which is mounted between the front seats! It is *not* an original Mk I Lotus Cortina. Then there is the second category, those who will only buy the genuine article.'

'When being asked to part with £12–15,000 for a car in this condition, I think it is important to try to establish some form of previous history,' commented Tony Llyn-Jones, who is himself a previous Lotus Cortina owner and knowledgeable expert within the AVO Club. 'I'm sure that the Lotus Cortina Register must know of the majority of Lotus Cortinas which exist and if one were to surface that is not already recorded, it would be regarded as pretty unusual. There is also a club "grape-vine" and once a car comes on the market, it is often sold within days. That sort of car would probably never even be advertised because the prospective buyer would get to know about it through club contacts.'

'I am convinced of the need for ensuring a car's identity,' said Jeff Mann, also a club expert whose daily job in a Ford Main Dealership Parts Department keeps him up-to-date with the latest spares situation. 'Only rarely do genuine Mk I Lotus Cortinas get on to the general market, which means that any car advertised in the national motoring press should initially be treated with suspicion.'

How, then, can the discerning buyer tell if the car is a genuine article? One way, of course, is to buy through the Ford-based clubs. 'That said,' continued Graham, 'there is one area of the car which can be checked to ascertain the car's authenticity. All the Dagenham-built body shells destined for Cheshunt had '3 A LOTUS' or '3 A LOT' written in felt-tip pen behind the back parcel shelf.' (Just to what extent a prospective buyer will try to establish a car's authenticity must be up to the individual, and the person selling the car! MT)

Buyer's Spot Check

1. Ascertain vehicle's history and whether any options were legitimate Ford parts. Check originality of Vehicle Identification Plate and details against model type.

2. Check for rust in: front valance; tops of inner wing panels; around front headlights; wheelarches and rear of wing section; sills and door bottoms; rear wheelarches and wing panels; rear valance; and cockpit floor and boot floor.

3. Test for weakness in front suspension, and wear in steering and wheel bearings (uneven wear on tyre pattern). Look for scoring on brake discs.

4. Test for weakness in rear suspension and rust in spring hangers. Look for oil leaks from differential.

5. Check overall condition of engine and look for traces of fluid leaks. Test water pump bearing and listen for timing chain rattle on start-up. (Twin Cam engine).

6. Thoroughly road test vehicle in both low speed and open-road conditions. Check for excessive smoking on over-run and variations in oil pressure under constant engine revs. Check free play in clutch take-up and synchromesh action on gearbox. Listen for undue noise from drive train, including differential.

7. Look again at drive train for fluid leaks after road test.

8. Evaluate overall condition of interior taking particular note of wear/rips in seats and carpets.

9. Make final analysis. Consider condition of paintwork, alloy wheels (if fitted) and tyres, spare wheel and tools, interior trim, drive train and any cost incurred in making good.

Before looking in more detail at some of the ground rules involved in what to look for when buying a sporting Ford, let's begin by mentioning a few basics. First, most experts agree that it is far better to invest in the most expensive car you can afford, leaving a little money over for the essentials such as insurance and road fund tax. (If you are under 25 years old and contemplating something like a Lotus Cortina or RS Escort, it might be worth while telephoning for an insurance quotation *before* you buy the car; better to know the worst in advance!)

As we have already said, before you begin scanning the columns of the motoring press, a good starting point is to join one of the Ford-based clubs. Attending a few meetings will help to give you a grasp of the types of problem other members have encountered and at the same time you can pick up a few tips on what to look for when buying. A friendly word of advice should not be ignored and, who knows, you may be lucky enough to find a local member willing to accompany you when you go to look at a possible buy.

Of course, some enthusiasts simply want to buy a car which will make a sound basis for a restoration programme – something which will keep them fully occupied for several years. Clearly, in this case, a different set of ground rules apply. For example, a major consideration – despite the fact that you intend to dismantle the car in preparation for refurbishing it – is always to buy a

Start by looking at the car's overall condition, try to judge how it has been cared for. Then look at the condition of the body. Next, with the car safely up on ramps, start at the front and look closely at the suspension, steering and brakes.

When road-testing a sporting Ford like this Escort Twin Cam resist the temptation to use all the performance; better to concentrate on listening for wear in the drive train and suspension, looking for smoke and feeling for handling peculiarities.

Having satisfied yourself that all is well, raise the rear of the car and go through the same procedure checking the condition of the rear suspension and spring hangers, brake pipes and chassis rails. Any areas freshly painted with underseal should be treated with suspicion!

car which is complete (that way you know you have all the bits) rather than a car which someone else has already stripped down and arrives as a large number of unidentified boxes!

Naturally, you will need a garage in which to work (yes, people have undertaken road-side restoration programmes, resprayed body panels on the kitchen table and so on, but . . .) with electricity and, perhaps, even some form of heating. You will also need a comprehensive set of tools and the skills to use them. However, two other – perhaps often forgotten – ingredients are the cost and the time which a restoration project undoubtedly takes. Are you prepared to give up hundreds of hours of your time and not get bored or bad tempered when things go wrong? And consider the fact that a project which runs out of money – if only temporarily – may well become disheartening. Think about it.

'Cars like the Lotus Cortina, the Escort Mexico and the RSs were considered to be little more than bangers during the early 1970s,' explained Tony, 'so many people tended to repair them using cheap materials and without taking any care over their workmanship. This means there is just a chance that if you do happen across an original car you may have a certain amount of putting-right to do. The favourite places on the Escort and Cortina were the tops of the inner wing panels which rotted through and were simply plated over or, in the case of an accident, body damage was filled in with glass fibre and quickly rubbed down. Nowadays, of course, the value of these cars has risen to the point where it makes sense to do the job properly. Moreover, the numbers of specialist companies who now undertake body panel re-manufacture, high-quality resprays, re-trims and even full restoration programmes were simply not around in the 1970s.'

Another factor to be borne in mind when considering a sporting Ford is the availability

of spares. Here again, the individual Ford-based clubs are a major source of information and may even be able to locate the more difficult-to-get parts for their members. Even body panels for cars such as the Cortina and Escort present problems while the alloy doors, boots and bonnets used on the early Mk I Lotus Cortina are a major problem to find. However, engine parts for the mainstream Kent engines are still readily obtainable, and spares for the Twin Cam units can still be bought from the firms who specialize in these engines. The rarer BDA unit, though, is a different story and parts – when they are available – can be very expensive.

Clearly, any sort of buyer's 'spot check' of this nature has to be somewhat abbreviated, although the very nature of Ford's build philosophy – unitary body construction with mix-'n-match components from the parts bin – means that it is quite reasonable to make bald statements which apply equally to a number of models. The cars we will be considering here will be: Lotus Cortina Mk I; Cortina Lotus Mk II; Escort Mk I (Twin Cam; RS1600; Mexico and RS2000); and Escort Mk II (RS1800; RS Mexico and RS2000).

For the purpose of our guide, we will assume that the car *is* to be bought through the 'For Sale' columns listed in the motoring press. If you do not feel confident of making a detailed survey of the car yourself, as, already mentioned, and you cannot persuade someone from the club to accompany you, then alternatively a few garages operate an evaluation service. The bonus of this route is that (one hopes) the report will be unbiased and written by people who themselves have a reputation to uphold. This is particularly appropriate if you are thinking of a Lotus Twin Cam-driven car, or even an RS1600 or 1800. Also, they should have more experience when it comes to measuring fair wear and tear against age and

The interior of a late 1964 Mk I Cortina GT. When looking at a prospective purchase, especially a Lotus Cortina or rare AVO car, make sure that it is not a cleverly disguised fake by checking documentation, body plates and club information. It could save you money, to say nothing of embarrassment, later!

mileage. If it is not practical to subject the car to this kind of test, or you prefer the idea of scrutinizing the car yourself, go along prepared to get just a little bit dirty. (Some of the checks will mean lying under the car.) You will need some ramps, or a stout jack (preferably a trolley jack), together with a pair of overalls and a couple of rags for wiping oily hands. Make the appointment to view the car for mid-morning or early afternoon. People have bought cars in the dark — and lived to regret it later.

At the outset, establish what history of the car is available. If it is a Lotus Cortina or RS Escort model, check that the chassis number prefix is correct for the model. (This can be found on the Vehicle Identification Plate.) 'That said,' remarked Dave Hibbin, another well-respected member of the AVO Club, 'it is still possible for someone to buy a set of chassis plates and fit them to a car. However, on AVO cars the chassis number was stamped on the offside inner wing suspension reinforcing plate during manufacture and this is very hard to fake, although we in the club are aware of some cars which were not stamped in this way.'

'Another thing to bear in mind,' added Tony, 'is that all the AVO-built cars were very much hand-built and anomalies crept in. In fact, when someone says, "define a standard Mexico", it is almost impossible.'

Generally, a car which is being sold with

factory-approved options by someone who can establish many years of ownership – and with a service record to back it up – is a better proposition than a car with a career which has involved a multitude of owners, little or no history and umpteen modifications. Here, the most notorious offender, perhaps, is the Escort Mexico. In addition to having a variety of brake and suspension parts actually fitted by Ford themselves over the years, this model of sporting Escort is often subjected to any number of go-faster bits from the vast array of performance parts manufacturers. The basic rule is: AVO-approved modifications can add value while non-approved components devalue the car.

An initial appraisal of the car should give you a 'gut' reaction as to whether it has led a hard life (scars to the paintwork, sagging or ripped seats) and, indeed, whether the vendor has made any effort at all in preparing the car for sale. However, do not be swayed into making a snap decision just because the car looks superficially clean and tidy.

Bodily, the Mk I and II Cortina and the Mk I and II Escort were all sturdy shells, although Ford's continued rust prevention programme means that not only will Mk II models be that much younger, they will also have benefitted from better rust prevention protection applied during manufacture. Tony Llyn-Jones again, 'It is interesting to reflect on just how far the motor industry has come over the years when considering rust protection techniques. The Mk I Lotus Cortina was not even undersealed when new, the underside being finished in normal cellulose paint. If a customer wanted the car underseal-protected, this had to be arranged through the dealer before the client took delivery.'

Beginning at the front of the car, look for rust which may have attacked the front valance beneath the bumper, the result, perhaps, of a stone chip which has not been properly treated or rust penetrating from the inside out. Also, on all models, rust can take hold on the areas around the head-lights, again the rot attacking from the inside (where wet road dirt can become lodged), the tell-tale sign being bubbles in the paintwork.

Road dirt can also cause the same reaction at the wheelarch crowns, the rear of the front wings and the inner wing panels themselves.

Next, lift the bonnet and start by checking the leading edge of the bonnet itself. Look at the crucial area surrounding the tops of the inner wing suspension mounting points. As we have already said, cheap repairs are sometimes made by welding plates over already rotten metal. Pay attention, too, to the bonnet hinge locating points and the seam where the inner and outer wing panels overlap and the inner wing/bulkhead joins. All these areas are structurally important to the body shell itself. Finally, look for signs of trouble around the windscreen pillars and scuttle area (the panel directly behind the bonnet, beneath the windscreen).

Moving back to the sills and doors, pay particular attention to the condition of the sill sections since, like the bulkhead/inner wing area, they are fundamental to the strength of the body shell. Rust in these areas almost always acts from the inside out, so by the time a hole appears the condition beneath the surface is serious and could mean new inner *and* outer sills, which can be an expensive job! Rusty door-bottoms are less of a problem since door panels can be replaced with new skins. It is also worth opening the doors and lifting the carpets to see whether rust has begun to attack the floorpan. Damp carpets are often a giveaway here!

The rear wheelarch area, rear valance and boot sections can also harbour their own set of problems. Rust can begin around the rear wheelarches themselves, where moisture and road dirt can attack the inner/outer wheelarch seam. In bad cases the inner wheelarch can rot through into the boot area, so it is worth checking whether rust

Optional extras are always nice but it's as well to ensure that they are true RS parts; a car which has the wrong set of alloy road wheels may look the part but its value is reduced as a result. Also, check to see that the tyre size and speed rating are correct; fat 'boots' are all very well but could impair handling.

has taken a hold here. Meanwhile, the rear valance, under the rear number plate, can rot from the inside out so rust bubbles can indicate trouble lurking behind. Finally, look inside the boot itself, lifting the mat to see if rust is beginning to attack the boot floor. While you are there, look also at the condition of the spare tyre and see what tools – if any – come with the car.

The next part of the check is where you will begin to get a bit dirty! Jack up the front of the car, one side at a time and, with the wheel clear of the ground, gently rock it,

first vertically to see whether there is any wear in the swivel joints, and then from side to side, looking for wear in the steering joints. Remember that the steering on Mk I and II Cortinas was worm-and-peg type, the ratio being peculiar to the Lotus variant, while the Escort was rack-and-pinion type and should therefore have no free play in its movement. 'So long as the lubricant level is maintained to its correct level, the Lotus steering box is a pretty robust unit,' remarked Jeff Mann.

Then it is as well to remove each front

Maintenance Details – Lotus Cortina

Sump: 5.75 pints, SAE 20W/30 (Plus 0.75 pint in filter)
Gearbox: 1.5 pints SAE 80
Rear axle: 2 pints SAE 90
Steering gear lubricant: SAE 90 EP
Cooling system capacity: 10.25 pints (2 drain taps) plus 2 pints in heater
Chassis lubrication: By grease gun to 5 points after 500 miles and then every 2,500 miles
Ignition timing: 14 BTDC
Contact breaker gap: 0.014 to 0.016in
Spark plugs: Lodge 2HLN
Valve timing: Inlet open 22 BTDC and close 62 ATDC
Exhaust opens 62 BTDC and closes 22 ATDC
Tappet clearances (cold): Inlet 0.005in–0.006in
Exhaust 0.006–0.007in
Front wheel toe-in: 0.0625–0.125in
Camber angle: 0 degrees 40 minutes
Castor angle: 0 degrees 36 minutes negative
Steering swivel pin inclination: 5 54'
Tyre pressures: (front) 20lb
(rear) 20lb
Brake fluid: Castor oil/polyglycolether mixture
Battery type and capacity: 12 volt 38 amp/hour

---

wheel and check for score marks on the disc and the general condition of the brake pipes, especially the flexible hose feeding the slave cylinder. (However, do not at this point, be tempted to get under the car with it only supported on a jack.)

Satisfied that the front suspension area is satisfactory, run the front of the car up on to the ramps, switch off the engine and place blocks behind the rear wheels. Then, lie under the car to see the condition of the monocoque chassis box sections and the bumper mounting points and check for any serious signs of oil leaks. You will also be able to see the general condition of the suspension and steering rubbers. If these look cracked or are soaked in oil, when it comes to the road test, the car's handling will feel soggy and imprecise. Finally, ensure that the brake and fuel pipes are in good shape.

Next, remove the blocks and run the rear of the car up on to the ramps, putting the blocks under the front wheels. You will now be able to see the condition of the spring 'hangers' and the area of the monocoque chassis box section where it passes over the axle. At this point there are reinforcing plates which carry the rubber bump stops, the plates themselves being vulnerable to rot through harbouring moisture. Again, check the condition of the brake and fuel pipes for rot as well as damage. Look to see if there is any sign of oil weeping from the differential nose, and check the overall condition of the exhaust system. Both Graham and Tony agreed that while earlier Lotus Cortinas might well be considered to be the more collectable, the later cars – with their leaf rear springs and better ventilation – are reckoned to be the more practical.

'The irony is that perhaps 80–90 per cent of the earlier 'A' bracket rear suspension cars which have been changed to leaf springs are now being reconverted back for originality,' laughed Graham. If the car has

Production Milestones and Chassis Identification Details (Lotus Cortina)

Model			Series	Chassis No.
January 1963	:	Introduction of Lotus Cortina	125E	74C041109
January 1964	:	Introduction of Aeroflow ventilation	125E	74D424314
January 1965	:	New numbering scheme	125E	74EJ.....
September 1965	:	Leaf springs replace coils on rear	125E	74EC.....
September 1966	:	Model ceased	125E	74F......
February 1967	:	Introduction of Cortina Lotus	3020E	91GD07068
October 1967	:	Detail changes to trim	3020E	..GU22262
July 1970	:	Model ceased	3020E	91K.19612

been fitted with a modified system, look to see that it has been properly fitted. 'Also, check to see that the self-adjusting rear brakes are functioning correctly,' said Tony. 'They were introduced in 1965 and were never the most reliable.' Finally, some Lotus Cortinas were fitted with a two-piece propshaft which utilized a centre bearing. 'This type are more than up to the job so long as the car is not abused,' remarked Jeff. 'The main thing prone to failure is the rubber insulator which protects the bearing itself, although this part is special on the Lotus Cortina so if it needs replacing you will probably need the services of a transmission specialist.'

Having finished with the underside you can now take the car off the ramps and begin to look in some detail at the engine. To simplify matters we will look at the power units in two separate categories: the Twin Cam type and the standard Ford ohv/ohc units. As already mentioned, the BDA really is for the enthusiast who can afford to have his/her car serviced by a specialist. Moreover, with almost twice as many moving parts as the Mexico engine, each part sometimes costing twice the price, a BDA engine can be very expensive to overhaul. Also, reliability (or should we say longevity) is not their strong suit. In contrast, the lusty Lotus

Twin Cam unit is more robust than many give it credit for and once properly adjusted should give many miles of trouble-free service. However, the Twin Cam does seem to attract the 'twiddlers' who, with misplaced confidence, attempt all manner of adjustments; they do need a little more knowledge than that necessary for servicing the engine of a Healey Sprite, say, or a Triumph Spitfire.

Run the engine until it is warm and the moving parts have reached their normal operating tolerances. Lotus engines do have a reputation for leaking oil, although sometimes this is simply the cam box cover gaskets in need of replacement. If oil is escaping from elsewhere, an engine strip-down may be the only cure.

Another reputation associated with Twin Cam engines is the unit's thirst for water pump bearings. The complexity of the work involved in replacing it can often take an amateur around two days, so it is best to check its condition. By grasping the pump pulley, assess the degree of side-to-side free play. Moreover, when the engine was started there should have been no detectable screech or rumble. The key to long bearing life is never to over-tighten the fan belt.

Those lovely-looking dual twin choke carburettors are the focus of attention for many

Equally, body badges, such as this fitted to the front wings and boot lid of the Escort Mk I Twin Cam, will no longer be a Ford stock item although badges for specialist cars are just the sort of thing that clubs are having re-manufactured.

Steel road wheels, like the ones fitted to this RS1800, can be made to look smart once more by giving them a coat of paint from an aerosol can. However, alloy wheels, like the four-spoke RS-type, become pitted and should be professionally cleaned and re-stove enamelled to bring them back to 'as-new' condition.

The Lotus tohc engine is a tight fit in the Escort engine bay. However, it is a reliable unit needing only regular servicing if it is overhauled properly. Unfortunately, the twin Weber carburettors are a twiddler's paradise.

Good for 100,000 miles and more, Ford's ohv and ohc units (like the one fitted to this pristine RS2000) are reliable if treated with respect. Parts are cheap and while the 2-litre unit gives almost BDA-like performance, running costs are nothing like as expensive.

Body graphics and black-finished bumpers can easily get scratched, making the car look tired. Bumpers can be re-treated but body decal graphics, like this originally for the RS2000 bootlid, may be more difficult to replace.

A good yardstick to judge how a car has been cared for is the condition of the interior. This is the inside of a Mk II Escort RS2000 with the very comfortable rally-type front seats. If the seats in the car you are considering are worn it may be worth taking them to a specialist to have them re-upholstered.

Interior trim panels like this can show signs of wear and neglect, although it may be possible to restore them using an upholstery cleaner. However, if the overall condition of the inside needs attention, the asking price should reflect this.

*The 1600E model, with its Lotus suspension and Cortina GT running gear,
has now become a sought-after classic. Look carefully at the front and
rear valance, inner and outer wing panels, door skins, sills and boot floors for
rot or badly made repairs when considering any sporting Ford; forget and it
could cost you money later.*

'fiddlers'. The adjustment of these Webers can affect the smooth running of the Twin Cam and affect its power output. Badly set up, the engine feels rough and down on power. Incidentally, the Webers are mounted on rubber 'O' rings which actually isolate the carbs from the hot manifold, thereby helping to reduce the likelihood of fuel frothing in the float chambers. The mounting bolts should be tightened such that there is a degree of free-play between the carbs themselves and the manifold; if there is none, someone has been over-zealous with a spanner!

On starting up, the unit should turn over easily with no clanks or mechanical protests. If there are, the starter drive may well be worn. The Lotus unit was never the quietest but anything more than a subdued ticking sound from the top end may indicate a worn tappet or camshaft lobe, while metallic noises from the bottom end which begin to diminish as the temperature increases could indicate worn bearings in the crankshaft.

As the engine warms up there should be no obvious rattles; look at the degree of adjustment left on the timing chain tension

Ford engines have always been known for their longevity. This cutaway drawing shows the 'crossflow' Kent bowl-in-crown unit which was introduced in 1967 in 1,300cc and 1,600cc sizes. It also formed the basis for the iron-blocked BDA engine. Listen for timing chain wear and check for low or fluctuating oil pressure and a smoking exhaust on over-run.

screw on the left-hand side of the timing case. Little or no adjustment clearly indicates that a new chain will be needed soon. Once warm, oil pressure should be around 38-40 psi, and idle as low as 20 psi. However, clouds of smoke issuing from the exhaust when the engine is revved indicates a major engine rebuild will be necessary.

Having convinced yourself that the engine starts happily (it's as well to start and then switch off a couple of times just to check the starter mechanism), the next step is a road test. Ideally, you should conduct at least part of this driving yourself since trying to judge wear and 'feel' while someone else is behind the wheel is almost impossible.

Under normal driving conditions with the engine running at its usual operating temperature, the oil pressure gauge should remain constant; a wavering needle could indicate worn big end or main bearings and even a worn pump. Using reasonable acceleration, there may be a slight oil mist but nothing more. A blue haze indicates worn

Maintenance Details – Escort RS2000

Sump: 6.6 pints, SAE 20W/40 (with filter)
Gearbox: 2.4 pints SAE 80 EP
Rear axle: 1.6 pints SAE 90 EP
Steering gear lubricant: SAE 90 EP
Cooling system capacity: 10.8 pints
Chassis lubrication: None
Ignition timing: 8 BTDC
Contact breaker gap: 0.025 (Motorcraft type)
Spark plugs: Champion NF7
Valve timing: Inlet open 24 BTDC and close 18 ATDC
Exhaust opens 70 BTDC and closes 18 ATDC
Tappet clearances (cold):   Inlet 0.00in
Exhaust 0.010in
Front wheel toe-in: 0.08–0.15in
Camber angle: 0 degrees 40 minutes
Castor angle: 1 degree 45 minutes
Tyre pressures: (front) 24lb
(rear) 22lb
Battery type and capacity: 12 volt 55 amp/hour

valve piston rings while if the same haze appears on over-run then quite likely it is the valve guides which have worn.

The water temperature gauge should remain constant throughout the test. Any rise and fall which corresponds with engine speed may well indicate a blown head gasket; the water system is being pressurized by the increased engine temperature with a resultant loss of coolant.

The clutch action should be smooth and jerk-free. Suspect any clutch which does not engage until almost at the limit of its travel. Very early Lotus Cortinas had a tall first gear, then came a revised set of ratios before the introduction of the 2000E gearbox from the Corsair saloon which continued into the Escort Twin Cam. Movements should be clean with no baulking, especially as you down-change from third to second. The gearbox should be quiet with no whines or 'sizzles' from the remote control. Indeed, the 2000E box was *the* unit by which other manufacturers' gearboxes were judged.

When stepping into a car like a Lotus Cortina or an Escort Twin Cam there is always the urge to make full use of the performance. For the purpose of your road test to assess the car's condition, this type of driving is to be avoided. The point of the exercise is to evaluate how the car handles and reacts. Does the car pull to one side when the brakes are applied? Does the steering self-centre? Are there any nasty crashing sounds as the suspension tries to cope with pot-holes? Does it roll badly on corners?

Both Graham and Tony agree that on the road the Lotus Cortina (and the Escort Twin Cam) give a hard ride by modern 'hot hatchback' standards. In fact, they say if the suspension is not firm and unforgiving over uneven surfaces the chances are the suspension is worn (faulty dampers, weary springs) or incorrect parts have been fitted. Classic cars do have their foibles, after all.

Turning now to Ford's ohv and ohc engines as fitted in the Mexico and RS2000 cars, these units also have a reputation for

Production Milestones and Chassis Identification Details
(Escort Twin Cam and RS)

Model			Series	Chassis No.
January 1968	:	Announcement of Escort Twin Cam	3026E	49G 01304
July 1969	:	Introduction of circular headlamps	3026E	49J 20645
January 1970	:	Announcement of RS1600	3026E	49K 22435
October 1970	:	Chassis series changed to		ATL
April 1971	:	Escort Twin Cam ceased		ATLC40214
October 1972	:	Introduction of alloy cylinder block on RS1600	ATL	ATM00112
November 1974	:	RS1600 ceased production	ATL	ATP00043
March 1975	:	Announcement of RS1800 using Mk II Escort body shell	ATS	GCATRDC23729
January 1976	:	RS1800 manufactured in Germany (as Mexico) and re-engined in Britain	ATS	GCATS . . . . . .
November 1970	:	Announcement of Mexico	ATL	ATK23624
October 1972	:	Modification to specification	ATL	ATM 00113
July 1973	:	Announcement of RS2000	ATL	BFATNC00066
January 1975	:	RS2000 and Mexico using Mk I bodies ceased at: Mexico	ATL	ATR 00442
		RS2000	ATL	ATR 00470
January 1976	:	Introduction of Mexico and RS2000, all cars built completely in Germany: RS Mexico	ATS	GCAT . . . . . .
		RS2000	ATS	GCAT . . . . . .
January 1977	:	New vehicle prefix	ATS	GXATT

longevity (say 100,000 miles if treated with respect) and reliability. Piston slap and tappet rattle are good indications of wear. Even so, the parts are readily available to give the engine new life. (However, as Tony astutely points out, there is little point in paying top price for the car if it requires work.) Another pointer to a worn engine is a thirst for oil caused by worn valve guides (the oil being burnt as the engine goes from over-run to acceleration, white smoke emerging from the exhaust). Sustained high revving is definitely something the ohv engine dislikes, causing valve train and camshaft wear.

Indications of wear in the ohc Pinto engine are very similar with the added cautionary note that high mileages can cause the familiar ticking sound from the camshaft or followers. In contrast to the ohv, the ohc engines are not afraid of sustained hard work, another very good reason why the Escort RS2000, especially in Mk II form, is so popular since it gives almost the same performance as the BDA with none of the headaches.

'Like the Lotus Cortina and Escort Twin Cam, the Escort RS models should be tight and taut on the road with no annoying squeaks and rattles,' said Tony. 'Certainly, the Mk I cars are noisier than their later relatives, with some resonance and booming through lack of adequate sound deadening, although the early RS2000 was about the quietest of the Mk I range.' The comments made over what to look for in the transmission fitted to the Twin Cam-engined cars also apply to these models of Escort.

With the road test finished, lift the bonnet to check for oil or water leaks. Even if the engine has been freshly cleaned with a degreasing agent, if there is a bad weep it will slow up after a reasonable run.

Inside, whether it be an early Lotus Cortina or one of the last Mk II Escort RS2000s, the condition of the seats, carpet and headlining can often reveal just how much of a hard life the car has led – and the respect its owners have shown it. As Tony commented, if the car is being sold for top money, the condition of the interior should reflect this. It is possible to repair or replace interior trim, the vinyl used in the earlier Lotus Cortinas and Escorts being that much easier to get than the fabrics used in the later cars.

In your final analysis, however, try to be objective. Estimate the total of approximately what it will cost to make good any repairs and relate that to the asking price. It is sometimes possible to negotiate a good deal when the cost of this work has been pointed out and taken into account.

RUNNING TIPS

Most experts agree (and my friends from the AVO Club reiterated these sentiments) that the reliability of the Lotus-based Twin Cam engine – fitted in either the Lotus Cortina or the Escort Twin Cam – is a direct result of attention to detail and careful reassembly when overhauling. Equally important is a regular maintenance programme which ensures that the correct type of oil is used and changed at the recommended intervals.

As for the attraction of fiddling with the engine, Graham Kent's view is that once the tappets have been shimmed correctly and the carburettors properly adjusted they should be left well alone.

For the Ford ohc and ohv engines to give of their best, the same approach to servicing should apply. Enthusiasts will tell you that it is better to have a regular servicing programme than to get stuck by the roadside during a fun day out, simply as a result of a lack of regular attention.

A weekly check under the bonnet will tell you if the oil, water and brake reservoir need to be topped up. Test that all important fan belt tension and look to see if the belt itself is showing any signs of decay. Also, look at the water hoses and check for cracks which could cause loss of coolant. (Do not forget that the radiator should be flushed through occasionally and refilled with the correct water/anti-freeze solution.)

A regular (say, every three months) clean with a degreasing agent will keep the mechanics clean and save you from getting dirty when carrying out these weekly inspections. As part of the same programme, regular checks of the wheel bearings, suspension bushes and brake pipes/hoses are well worth while. Look to see how the brake pads are wearing and make sure that the rear shoes still have some 'meat' left on them and that the mechanism is functioning correctly. A quick look under the car should reveal the state of the exhaust and its support brackets and whether there are any signs of oil leaks which will need attention.

Inside the car, vinyl trim can be cleaned using warm water, while the trim panels can be rejuvenated using a 'cockpit cleaner'. Fabrics can also be brought back to life by using a foam cleaner. It is quite surprising how often a car's interior gets overlooked and begins to look tired and grubby through lack of care and attention. Just a little time can add so much to the car's overall looks, resulting in a sporting Ford you will be proud to own.

7 Non-Starters

'Aerodynamics must be used, not only to keep the wheels glued to the road, but also to keep the body static relative to the ground,' said Len Bailey, highly respected stylist and development engineer whose name has long been linked with an impressive list of sports/racing cars: the GT40; the P68 and P69; the GT70 – to say nothing of important work in conjunction with Alan Mann and Ford's highly successful rally team which (as we have already seen) reigned supreme during the 1970s.

Len Bailey's career in the motor industry began with British Leyland. Then came time with BRM, Daimler, Rolls-Royce, Jaguar and Rover before he left England to join American Motors in Detroit. There he became involved with drawing up plans for an all-new AM V8 engine. Sadly, the project leader, Dave Potter, died and with him, so did the project. Bailey then left American Motors and joined Ford where he began work in their Chassis Design Department. (He had risen to become a Senior Designer when the job came up to re-engineer the Cobra's leaf-sprung chassis to take coil springs. Bailey says now that he was insulted by being given the task and delegated it to someone else.)

'With the parting of the ways when Ford decided to pull out of GT racing,' said Bailey, 'and Ford Advanced Vehicles, who had been responsible for the GT40 programme, was sold to ex-Aston Martin executive John Wyer, I moved to Alan Mann Racing where I became involved with turbocharged Escorts for tarmac racing.' In 1968 Bailey was commissioned by Ford to develop the F3L. Later renamed the P68 Sports Prototype, this was to form a research platform for the Cosworth

Unloading the Len Bailey-designed P68 prototype sports racing car from Alan Mann's 36ft (10.97m) long, two-deck transporter at Oulton Park. Bailey's notable career began with British Leyland, then came spells with BRM, Daimler, Rolls-Royce, Jaguar and Rover before moving to the US where he eventually joined Ford.

DFV 3-litre engine which went on to establish such an enviable reputation on the world's race tracks.

The green light for producing the P68 was given during an impromptu meeting between Bailey, the Director of Competitions; Walter Hayes, Team Manager; Alan Mann, Director of Engineering; Harley Copp, and Ford of Britain's Vice Chairman, Leonard Crossland. The programme was to bring together the expertise of Len Bailey, Castrol, Goodyear and the newly established Ford Research Centre at Dunton.

Bailey is insistent that, 'Aerodynamics must be used, not only to keep the wheels glued to the road, but also to keep the body static relative to the ground.' The P68 was just 35.3in (89.6cm) high and was one of the most aerodynamic prototypes ever constructed.

Without doubt, Bailey's handiwork created one of the prettiest shapes ever to grace the racing circuits. The centre section body/ chassis unit was formed from double-skinned alloy with detachable nose and rear engine covers, the beautifully curved wind-screen adding to the car's sleek lines. Just 35.5 in (901.7mm) high (4.5in (114.3mm) *lower* than the exciting GT40) and 166in (4,216mm)long (2in (50mm) shorter than the then-current Cortina), the P68 not only had a slippery silhouette but was a most compact design. Its 87in (220mm) wheelbase was some 10in (254mm) shorter than the

Formula 1 cars of the day. Width-wise, the P68 measured 70in (1,778mm) while at the rear the car featured a Ford-patented vortex-generating tail which helped to create the high downward loading which Bailey commented upon earlier.

Powered, of course, by the first generation of DFV Cosworth engine, drive was transmitted through a Hewland gearbox/differential unit with 11.5in (292mm) Girling disc brakes mounted some 3in (76mm) inboard to aid cooling from airflow. Raced in the Group 6 category, the P68 was entered in a number of important events during the 1968 series,

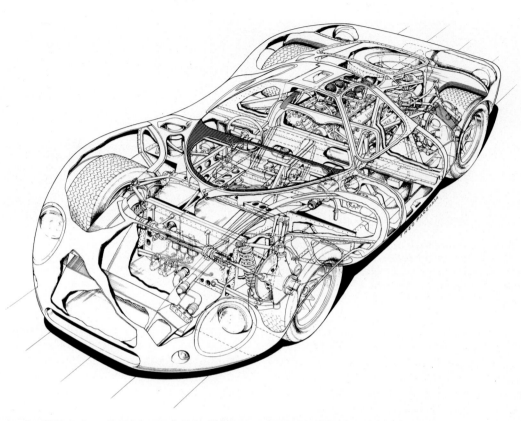

The P68 was built as a test platform for the new DFV 3 litre Cosworth engine.
Suspension utilized double wishbones fore and aft with trailing links on the
rear. The 11.5in (292mm) diameter Girling disc brakes are located 3in (76mm)
inboard of the hub carriers to allow greater cooling from the underbody airstream.

although reliability always seemed to be a problem. The following year, with a change in Group 6 regulations, came Bailey's next model, which was the open-topped P69. This was developed specifically to continue testing the Cosworth Formula 1 engine, as well as carrying out a study on the effect of aerofoils on race car bodies. The P69 was 5in (127mm) lower, 15in (381mm) shorter and 2.5in (63.5mm) wider than its predecessor but, again, it was an alloy body/chassis monocoque. To make room for the front aerofoil (which was located between the wheelarches), the radiator was moved to the rear. The rear aerofoil was located directly above the engine cover. Under test, these modifications appeared to produce a marked improvement on stability, although on the night before what was to have been its first race, the car was effectively outlawed by the other competitors. The P69 never ran and Alan Mann turned his attentions away from motor sport.

Like the P69, Bailey's next project for Ford – the GT70 – was also sadly short-lived. Rumour has it that the GT70 programme was hatched during a conversation between Roger Clark and Stuart Turner on their flight back from the 1970 Monte Carlo Rally early that year when the Ford team

The P69 sports prototype at speed during practice for the BOAC International at Brands Hatch in April 1969. Another Len Bailey design, the car was fitted with spoilers front and rear which gave a marked improvement on the car's stability, although the night before the race the car was effectively outlawed by its competitors and never ran; Alan Mann giving up racing for good.

had suffered a major disappointment. Of the four cars entered, two had failed to finish while a despondent Clark could only manage fifth slot with fellow team-mate Makinen two places back. 'Well,' said Clark, in effect, 'I drove as fast as I could but the car just couldn't keep up with the Porsches and Alpine-Renaults.'

The format for the new rally car began to emerge from this disenchanted chat. Clearly, it would need to be mid-engined with either a BDA or Weslake-tuned V6 engine driving a 5-speed GT40-type gearbox, the weight being almost directly over the driven rear wheels. With the basic concept agreed, Len Bailey was then involved with the brief that the car should be suitable for road events using a high proportion of production Ford parts. Under the strictest security blanket, work began and a first-cut prototype model was produced by AWR Components Ltd. of Hastings (who were well known in the racing world for their work with prototypes). A sleek silver-painted design with a rounded front and a graceful, tapering tail was then presented to Leonard Crossland, Ford's Chairman, for his approval.

In mid-1970 the first full-size body mock-up was sent to the Imperial College for wind tunnel evaluation, while Bailey was hard at work in his Byfleet workshops developing the chassis design. The car was to be put into limited production at FAVO, Averley, Ray Horrocks making all the necessary arrangements for production assembly. Within weeks a buck had been prepared which gave location points for seats, dashboard and main control functions. Apparently, it was at this stage that Stuart Turner came up with the name 'GT70' – the rally car for the 1970s!

Significantly, the GT70's body was to be made from fibreglass, an ideal material for the limited production levels envisaged. By October, the chassis and body were being brought together in the small Hastings workshops. Like everything else connected with the Competitions Department, time was limited and engineers from Ford descended upon AWR Components' limited accommodation to help finish the prototype. (It seems that Peter Ashcroft commented that the scene in the workshops looked like the Battle of Hastings, to which came the terse reply, 'Let's win this one, we lost last time.')

Towards the end of the 1960s the Escort began to be outstripped by strong opposition on international rallies, the GT70 programme being Stuart Turner's answer to the problem. The chassis and suspension configuration was also a Bailey design.

Looking a little dated from this rear view, the GT70 featured a perimeter frame chassis with a sheet steel floor pan. Sturdy roll-over hoops provided additional safety in the event of a crash, and locating points for the GRP body shell.

Looking like no other sporting Ford, under test at Boreham the GT70 proved to be significantly faster than the 4-wheel-drive rally-cross Capri used as a comparison. Engine options were to include the BDA, FVA, 1600 pushrod and 3-litre V6 with either a ZF or a Hewland transaxle.

In this cutaway drawing the GT70 is driven by a V6 unit although in competition the car was usually powered by a FVA or BDA unit. Tragically, the GT70 programme was halted when the Escort was given new life with the alloy-blocked BDA engine; a prolonged strike at Ford also took its toll.

The basis for the GT70 was a perimeter frame chassis assembled from 18 gauge tubing with a platform floorpan of 22 gauge steel sheet fitted to it. Sturdy steel roll-over hoops provided both integral safety and a suitable structure to which the fibreglass body could be bonded. In addition, the front roll bar was used to locate the dashboard and door hinges, while the rear hoop was used to locate the safety belts, the steel bulkhead between cockpit and engine compartment and the rear windows.

Initially, power was provided by a 2.6-litre V6 unit driving a ZF transaxle, although in his chassis design Bailey had catered for the installation of a number of engine options including the 3-litre V6, the 1,600cc pushrod Escort, the Ford-Cosworth FVA unit and the BDA engine. At the front, the steering, disc brakes and suspension components all came from the Cortina parts bin. The suspension itself utilized unequal-length, double wishbones with telescopic dampers and coil springs with the option of adding an anti-roll bar if required. The independent rear suspension set-up utilized single upper links and trailing arms with coil springs and telescopic dampers, the swinging-calliper disc brakes and hub bearings being Ford Zodiac parts.

An early modification made to the wheel-arch design on the first prototype produced more interior and boot space. Meanwhile, a second prototype was being hurriedly assembled in readiness for launching to the public at the Brussels Show in January 1971. Under test, with such masters as Roger Clark at the wheel, GT70/01 proved to be very fast indeed – markedly quicker, apparently, than the four-wheel-drive rally-cross Capri which was tested around the same track at Boreham. Behind the scenes,

GT70 prototypes 3 and 4 were well on their way towards completion.

For the Ronde Cevenole in 1972 the Ford V6 unit was replaced by an all-alloy RS 1.8-litre engine in order to see how the car would perform in a French tarmac rally. Sadly, it failed to finish. As a result of this, Len Bailey and Gerry Birrell were then asked to make some fundamental changes to the GT70's design, paying particular attention to the strength of the suspension and the overall handling. The car was stripped down and a new floorpan was fitted with box-section strengthening and a roll-over bar fitted to the cockpit. The ZF transaxle was replaced by a Hewland DG400 unit and the engine mountings were lowered by 4in (101mm) to reduce the car's centre of gravity and to ensure that the drive through the rubber driveshaft couplings was almost level. However, the light yet powerful alloy block RS engine had proved the wisdom of replacing the much heavier V6 unit. In the event, a 1,977cc unit with Lucas fuel injection (which produced a creditable 240bhp at 8,000 rpm), sufficient to give the 1,756lb (796.5kg) car a top speed of around 140 mph (225kph), was fitted. To handle this kind of performance, Bailey and Birrell opted for 10in (254mm) ventilated discs at the front and 10in (254mm) solid disc brakes at the rear.

The opportunity to test this redesign work came in April 1973 with the chance to enter the Criterium Touraine Rally in France. A ten lap event of 22.3miles (36km) each lap, the GT70 succeeded in returning a quite impressive performance and, against the Simca CG Spyder, it managed lap times within 4 seconds of this ultra-lightweight car before retiring with a broken driveshaft.

But, despite the GT70's undisputed

Dieter Hahne

Dieter Hahne was born in Germany in 1942 and was educated at Braunschweign University where he graduated with an MSc in Mechanical Engineering.

In 1970 Dieter joined Ford Europe as a graduate trainee and two years later was appointed to the post of Vehicle Systems Engineer in Ford's Product Development area where, apart from a short period in Parts Operations, he has spent the major part of his career with the company.

Dieter has held a number of key positions including Manager, Driveline Engineering. Later, he was appointed Manager for Medium Car Programmes where he was responsible for vehicle testing and development.

With the appointment of Rod Mansfield as Director of Engineering at Aston Martin, Dieter Hahne was made Manager, Special Vehicle Engineering and Vehicle Component Engineering at Ford's Research Centre at Dunton, Essex.

Dieter Hahne is married with three sons. His interests include sport and unusual cars.

Dieter Hahne.

performance potential and the enthusiasm put into the programme by people such as Len Bailey, Gerry Birrell and John Griffiths (the man in charge of engine development at Boreham), this sleek, mid-engined car was never to reach the limited production level of which everyone had dreamed. To begin with, a prolonged strike at Ford placed considerable financial constraints on the company's operations. Equally important were the manufacturing arrangements necessary to produce the 400-odd cars which would have made the programme viable. But perhaps by far the most significant factor in the GT70's downfall was that Brian Hart's alloy block completely transformed the Escort into a world-beater. Indeed, many Ford rally stars actually preferred the Escort's 'chuckability', its handling being more suited to a rough-surface rally. In the background, Ford Detroit were not impressed either because they saw the GT70 cutting directly across their Pantera programme. A very directly worded telegram landed on a desk at Dagenham saying, in effect, 'bury it'.

Another of the might-have-beens was the RS1700T. This exciting rally car dates back to 1977 when Peter Ashcroft and his team in the Competitions Department began looking around seriously for a replacement for the Escort RS1800. Most observers agree that the RS1700T went the furthest towards production (thereby costing the most in development) than perhaps any other still-born Ford.

The origins of this fascinating car go back to the time when plans were being drawn up for a high-performance version of Ford's new baby car, the Fiesta. The programme involved two prototypes: one, built by the 'Boreham Boys', which would feature a Ford-Cosworth BDA engine, fitted 'north-south' in the Fiesta engine bay, driving the rear wheels via a much-modified Hewland

The 'Erika' parentage is clearly visible in this view of the short-lived RS1700T. With its turbocharged 1.78-litre front engine/rear-wheel-drive layout, this car came close to production before being abandoned, its lack of all-wheel-drive being significant in Turner's decision to stop the programme.

Formula 1 transaxle. The other, developed by Len Bailey, was fitted with a BDA engine located behind the front seats and mounted 'east-west' across the car, again driving the rear wheels. Indeed, the emphasis on rear-wheel-drive lay chiefly in the fact that rigorous tests continued to indicate the benefit of this layout for rallying over front-wheel-drive.

Meanwhile, the team at Boreham were still busy maintaining their current (if ageing) group of Mk II RS Escorts in top condition for world rallies, so development on the next generation of rally car was temporarily halted.

After winning the coveted Lombard-RAC Rally, Ford decided to close down its Motor Sport Department and all but one Escort RS were sold off, this one car, WTW 569S, being kept for comparison performance purposes. In the summer of 1980 a series of shakedown tests were carried out in Wales between a front-engined, rear-wheel-drive, BDA-engined Fiesta and the old stager, WTW569S. Taking the wheel was the experienced Stig Blomqvist who proved, once and for all, just how effective the old car still was. As a result, the idea of a Fiesta rally car was dropped.

It was at about this time that rumours began to circulate of a four-wheel-drive car being developed by Audi. Some sceptics even questioned the bonus of FWD. Nevertheless, it galvanized the Boreham team into action.

In a short time a proposal for an all-new rally car had been put together by ex-Porsche engineer, John Wheeler, for approval by the Ford Board. The outline was for a front-engined/rear-wheel-drive car based on the Mk III Escort body shell and driven by a 2.5-litre engine producing some 350 bhp, the homologation rules calling for 200 cars to be built. The Board gave its approval for such a programme to be financed.

With the green light, more detailed discussion took place and the decision was made to transmit the power via a torque tube (which encased the propeller shaft) to a rear-mounted gearbox/final drive unit, specially commissioned by Ford from Hewland. However, while Group B regulations imposed specific engine weight limits for given capacities, (making the 2.5-litre engine seem ideal for the body size) the hurdle was the 200 unit production figure: the Hart 420R engine and the Ford-based Pinto engine with special 16-valve cylinder heads both presented manufacturing difficulties. The alternative was the BDT unit, a turbocharged 1.78-litre Ford-Cosworth engine which, using the turbocharger multiplication factor of 1.4:1, gave an acceptable capacity within the regulations.

While there were considerable marketing and publicity benefits to be gained from the similarity between the rally cars and the showroom Mk III Escort, it soon became obvious that the Boreham-built cars would share few body panels with their mass-produced brother. A wider track back and front dictated that the wheelarches be flared to cover the big rally wheels and tyres, while the original floorpan was almost entirely different in order to clear the torque tube drive. Then, in an effort to reduce weight, many of the original GRP body panels were replaced by panels fabricated from Kevlar. Air scoops were moulded into the bonnet, stylish sills were added beneath the doors and a large rear spoiler attached. It looked like a Mk III Escort, just!

In mid-1981 work on the prototypes was stepped up with the first two cars being used to finalize body styling and drive train installation details. The first running car was fitted with a 2-litre BDA engine driving through a Porsche transaxle, while another – a non-runner – was shown to the Press in July that year and was officially named 'RS1700T'. A further two cars – destined to become the first test vehicles – were also 'in build', one fitted with a Hart 420 engine, the other with a BDT unit, both driving much-modified Hewland FGB400 transaxles. At

GT70, RS1700T and RS200 Date Profile

January 1970	:	Concept of GT70 conceived by Stuart Turner and Roger Clark on return from Monte Carlo rally where Ford's Escort was no match for latest Alpine-Renault and Porsche.
February 1970	:	Walter Hayes gives his approval for scale model prototype to be designed by Len Bailey.
April/May 1970	:	Model presented to Sir Leonard Crossland for his approval.
June 1970	:	Work started at AWR Components of Hastings on full-size model and scale model produced to be sent to Imperial College for wind tunnel aerodynamics assessment.
July 1970	:	Seating 'buck' ready for rally drivers to evaluate driving position. Stuart Turner christens the project, 'GT70'.
August 1970	:	Engineering drawings of chassis now completed by Len Bailey and work begins on first chassis structure at AWR Components at Hastings.
September 1970	:	First full-size body mock-up almost complete.
October 1970	:	First GT70 body shell removed from its mould ready for mounting on its chassis. Prototype then completed for presentation to Sir Leonard Crossland and then first test drive by Roger Clark at Boreham.
December 1970	:	Testing continues on first prototype. Proves to be quicker than 3-litre FWD rallycross Capri. Work on second prototype almost finished.
January 1971	:	Second prototype exhibited at Brussels Motor Show. Originally designed to take the German V6 2,600cc engine but could be adapted to take British 3 litre V6; Ford-Cosworth FVA or 1,601cc BDA engine. Work begins on two more prototypes.
January 1971 – January 1972	:	Testing with 1.8-litre BDA engine with entries in selected French tarmac rallies.
January 1972 – April 1972	:	Chassis, suspension and engine location re-engineered to increase strength, roadholding and handling. ZF gearbox replaced by Hewland DG400 unit.
1972	:	Project cancelled due to introduction of 2-litre Hart BDA engine making Escort competitive and lack of funds and facilities to make sufficient GT70s for homologation.
April/May 1977	:	Work begins on two Fiesta rally prototypes: one with front-mounted engine, rear-mounted gearbox; the second with mid-mounted engine, both with BDA engines.
1978/79	:	Development of BDA-powered front-wheel-drive Fiesta rally prototypes.
Mid 1980	:	Len Bailey-designed mid-engined car dropped in favour of front-engine/rear-wheel-drive Fiesta.
October/ November 1980	:	Proposal to Ford Directors of front-engine/rear-drive rally car based on latest FWD Escort body shell.
1981	:	Work progresses with 10 prototypes; P7 with Hart engine and P10 with BDT unit, cars in full rally spec.

July 1981	:	P5 shown to Press as RS1700T. Ford say car will be competing by mid-1982 with 200 homologation cars built at Saarlouis.
Spring 1982	:	Test begins with P7 and P10. Ari Vatanen crashes P7.
Mid 1982	:	Launch date of RS1700T missed as car is still not ready for production.
1982/83	:	Cosworth build 200 BDT engines; Hewland assemble 200 transaxles and Abbey Panels produce body panels for modification of 200 body shells.
March 1983	:	New production start date with homologation planned for 1 April. First event to be Tour de Corse in May.
14 March 1983	:	Stuart Turner cancels RS1700T programme.
March – September 1983	:	Planning proposals for new mid-engined rally car. Vehicle concept and chassis design by Tony Southgate and John Wheeler; styling by Ghia with input from Ford, Dunton.
September 1983	:	Turner has top-level meeting with Executive Vice President, Bob Lutz, over RS200 Programme. Result is agreement for construction of one prototype.
March 1984	:	First prototype finished and presented to Ford senior management at Balderton Street. Agreement for the construction of a further five prototypes. Engineer John Wheeler spends time on detail design to aid 'serviceability'.
November 1984	:	RS200 is launched at Turin Motor Show. Specification for RS1700T engine to be used in RS200 indicated power output as 240bhp at 6,000rpm in road tune and 380bhp for rallying.
December 1984	:	Testing of prototype cars well in hand. Turner presents fully costed World Rally Championship project using RS200 to Bob Lutz. Lutz agrees to the construction of a further 194 cars, which are to be built by Reliant at Shenstone.
September 1985	:	Eight prototype cars now completed. Malcolm Wilson wins Lindisfarne Rally in RS200's debut rally.
December 1985	:	Reliant begin series production.
14 January 1986	:	Turner advises press of completion of first 60 cars.
30 January 1986	:	Completion of scheduled 200 RS200s.
January 1986	:	Stig Blomqvist finishes second in Norway Rally.
February 1986	:	Boreham prepare to contest first World Championship rally since 1979 with 420bhp powered RS200s. Kalle Grundel finishes third overall in Swedish Rally, in its first homologation event.
Mid 1986	:	FISA react to fatalities among rally competitors and spectators by shortening remaining 1986 events and announcing that 1987 World Rally series would be for Group A cars (of which 5000 a year had to be built).
July 1986	:	Turner announces that Ford will continue to compete in 1987 World Rally Championship using XR4×4 and Sierra Cosworth. 120 RS200s would be sold off, others would be used as spares.

the time, the American space shuttle was being given considerable publicity and the name 'Columbia' was chosen for the RS1700T rally car programme.

At its launch, Ford's publicity men spoke confidently of the RS1700T being entered in its first rally the following year with the necessary 200 units for homologation being programmed into the production line at Ford's Saarlouis plant in Germany. But there was still a lot of work to be done by both the Boreham Boys and Special Vehicle Operations before the design could be finalized; arrangements had to be made for the manufacturing of the special body panels (a job which would bring in Ford's design team in Cologne), as well as Type Approval, which would make the car 'road legal'.

Meanwhile, the rally test cars were beginning to be put through their paces by such star drivers as Markku Alen, Penti Airikkala, Hannu Mikkola and Malcolm Wilson. Under similar conditions, the RS1700T was shown to be markedly faster than the older Mk II Escort RS. The worry, however, was that the four-wheel-drive sceptics were being proven wrong. The exciting Audi Quattro was gaining a reputation as being the car to beat, the Quattro going on to win the World Rally Championship for Makes in 1982. Unfortunately, 'Columbia' was not four-wheel-drive.

Trouble with the project really began to emerge as dates set for Saarlouis to begin body production came and went. In early 1983 a production 'window' was set aside for the RS1700T to be assembled, before the factory was scheduled to begin manufacture of the new four-door Escort (the Orion). Meanwhile, Cosworth and JQF Ltd. of Towcester, Northamptonshire were on target with engine production, as were Hewland regarding delivery of the special rear-mounted gearbox/final drive units.

However, in the background Ford's hierarchy were becoming increasingly concerned that the RS1700T's specification did not include all-wheel-drive. Worried Ford personnel were talking about homologation of the two-wheel-drive cars with a further run of 200 four-wheel-drive versions by late 1984. In a desperate attempt to push the programme through, Lotus, Reliant and Aston Martin were all asked to quote for completing 186 cars (by this time some 14 prototypes had been built). The same companies, plus FF Developments of Coventry (who were involved with the Jensen FF in the mid-1960s), were also asked to consider undertaking the development work necessary to make the RS1700T into FWD. Sadly, it was all in vain. Stuart Turner, back in the slot as Director of European Motor Sport (replacing Karl Ludvigsen), issued a short note to the effect that Project 'Columbia' (i.e. the RS1700T) was cancelled and that all work was to stop immediately.

Turner had quickly realized that Ford's Motor Sport Department was pursuing a wrong route with the RS1700T. After all, he could not fail to be aware of the success being enjoyed by Audi with their FWD rally cars. Lancia, on the other hand, were achieving the same result but with a purpose-built rally car. Other manufacturers, too, were known to have similar FWD projects on their drawing boards. Between 1983 (when the RS1700T had been brought to a sudden halt) and 1986, Turner instigated and implemented a whole new project the purpose of which was to enter in rallies under Group B homologation regulations, the necessary 200 units being completed – just – by 1 February 1986.

Like the RS1700T, Turner's new rally tool was to be fully Type Approved so that complete cars could be sold for road use in Europe, even though they would carry a hefty price tag of around £50,000 each. However, unlike its predecessor, this car – called the RS200, simply because 200 would need to be built for homologation – would share very little with other production vehicles in Ford's range. Turner's prerequisites

*Prerequisites in the design of the RS200 were that it should be safe, fast enough
to win and be ageless in its design. Almost ten years on the styling has stood the
test of time well. (Inset left) The special light 'pod' added to the standard bonnet
panel. Motor noters from the press were given the chance to try out the RS200 in
Sardinia during the spring of 1985 where the car's performance was considered
most impressive. (Inset right) Built by Aston Martin Tickford, the interior of the
production RS200 looks business-like rather than opulent with manual window
lifts and Ford steering column controls. On competition cars an additional stick
was produced to switch out of 4WD.*

for this car were that it should be safe, be fast
enough to win and be ageless in its design so
that, from a sales aspect, it would not quickly
go out of style.

From March to September 1983, Turner
consulted many specialists in the field of
motorsport design (Turner, apparently,
recalls with some candour talking with
Brabham's F1 expert, Gordon Murray, realiz-
ing immediately the man's genius as an
engineer/designer) before putting together a
package suitable for placing before Ford's
hierarchy. Early on, Turner was enamoured
with the notion of using Ghia of Turin to style
the car's coachwork. In the event, even this

was not to be without its traumas! The first
proposals from Ghia were met with little
enthusiasm at Ford, so Mike Moreton (who
was later to become Project Manager for the
RS200) went back to Turin armed with some
styling suggestions drawn up in the UK. The
Italians were not amused but at least it fired
them with enough enthusiasm to get on with
the job – and quickly! (It seems that one of the
suggestions was that, to give the RS200 a
Ford 'family' look, it should utilize cut-down
doors from the Sierra saloon.)

The basic concept for the RS200 was set
down by Ford Motor Sport's Chief Engineer,
John Wheeler (who would be responsible for

the car's overall mechanical design and development). The project was then put out to a number of freelance designers who were commissioned to produce drawings of how the car would be built. After much deliberation by Turner and his team – with helpful advice from well-respected engineers such as Keith Duckworth – the winning proposal was that put forward by Tony Southgate (whose reputation went back to the GT40 days when Southgate worked for Lola as Eric Broadley's assistant designer, subsequently joining the teams of Lotus and BRM).

Power would be provided by an 1,803cc version of the BDT engine located 'north-south' ahead of the rear wheels. A key issue in the design of the transmission configuration was Wheeler's desire to position the driveshaft line, linking the front and rear differentials, centrally down the car. By so doing, all four half-shafts would be of equal length, while CV joint angles would be kept within reasonable limits. To accommodate this, the clutch housing was fitted with a transfer box which allowed the engine to be located to one side of the car's centre line.

From the engine transfer box, drive was then taken forward to a 5-speed gearbox (with Hewland ratios) by a short drive shaft. To provide the choice of torque split between the front and rear wheels, a VC (viscous coupling) was inserted on the front end of the gearbox giving three choices of drive: all the drive going to the rear wheels; only 37 per cent to the front wheels (the usual four-wheel-drive torque split arrangement); and 50 per cent front and back; the selection being controlled by an extra cabin-mounted gearstick. There was also a power-take-off point feeding the rear wheel differential driveshaft. Adhesion was further improved by the addition of VC-type limited slip differentials in both front and rear axles, each VC being similar in design to the one used in the Escort RS Turbo.

The suspension would feature alloy uprights

With its 1.78-litre BDT engine, power was rated at 250bhp at 6,500rpm giving a 0–60mph (0–100kph) time of 6.1 seconds and a maximum speed of 140mph (225kph). The pipes running up from the Ford-Bosch electronic fuel injection system either side of the rear window connect with the roof-mounted intercooler. Just 200 cars were built, making the RS200 nowadays a rare collector's car.

supporting adjustable double wishbones linked to double coil spring damper units located either side of each drive shaft. Brakes would be 11.5in (292mm) ventilated-type with 16 × 8in (40.6 × 20.3cm) Speedline alloy road wheels shod with Pirelli P700 225/50 VR16s. Two spare wheels would be carried, one at each end of the car.

For road use, the 1,803cc BDA engine was tuned to produce some 250bhp at 6,500rpm, while the rally versions were considerably more powerful, developing some 420bhp (a 2,137cc version developed by Brian Hart would have given around 506bhp at 7,500rpm had the RS200 programme not been prematurely killed off), making the car very competitive indeed against the other Group B supercars.

The chassis was to comprise a centre platform of stressed alloy honeycomb with a tough front bulkhead structure. The front suspension and transaxle, and the engine and rear suspension, were to be mounted on a mild steel box-section fabrication. Wheeler placed considerable importance on the ease with which repairs could be carried out in mid-rally, catering for the competition staff's preference for removing parts out through the top of the car rather than working underneath the car, as would be the case on Escort rally cars. To provide total access to the front and rear sections of the car, the nose and engine-cover body panels were single sections made to hinge outwards, tipping away from the centre section of the car. On paper the RS200 looked set to be the most exciting project Stuart Turner had instigated, well able to give the competition a very good run for its money.

As a package, it represented state-of-the-art design for a world-beating rally car but, from Turner down, everyone was aware of the grave scepticism with which Ford's hierarchy would greet the proposal: it would be costly to finance, while people could still remember the RS1700T (to say nothing of the GT70). Could Ford's top brass be persuaded?

Perhaps it was just one of those quirks of timing, who can say. But it seems that the very day before he was due to make his presentation to Bob Lutz (Executive Vice President, Ford International Automotive Operations) in September 1983, Turner had been contacted by a job agency. Turner has since admitted that the effect of this was to give him a more cavalier approach to his presentation. No matter, he was given the green light, despite words of caution from others at the meeting (particularly regarding the safety of those spectating at a rally).

With the agreement in the bag, John Thompson's pressings business, TC Prototypes/AFT of Northampton, were commissioned to take on the work. Within six months, in early March 1984, the first RS200 was finished and being presented to Bob Lutz and his team at Balderton Street (Ford's headquarters for their import/export dealership). It was to be a telling time but, again, the green light was given, this time for more cars to be built. These would be used for road development, Type Approval (which would involve a full crash test programme handled by Aston Martin Tickford) and rally specification analysis. A low volume cost appraisal was calculated, which involved Reliant at Shenstone, to build the remaining 194 vehicles which were necessary to comply with the homologation rules. By the year's end Turner was able to report back to Lutz with a clear budget requirement for Ford to return to world class rallying. Agreement was given there and then.

Some four weeks earlier, Stuart Turner had taken the opportunity formally to announce the RS200 to an expectant Press, thereby quashing rumours of what Ford were up to behind the scenes. Premature or not, despite predictions of cars taking up the rally gauntlet during 1985, assembly at Reliant's Shenstone factory did not actually begin until some twelve months after Lutz had signed the historic piece of paper giving low volume manufacture the green light.

Indeed, putting this exciting and highly technically advanced FWD sporting Ford into manufacture was to demand considerable management and co-ordination for it involved around 2,000 parts, of which just under half were special to the RS200. It was not until December 1985 that cars began to come off Reliant's production line. However, assembly quickly gathered momentum, with all 194 finished by 30 January the following year.

Driven by Malcolm Wilson the RS200 realized its first rally win in the Marlboro

Lindisfarne in September 1985 while the first event to be contested in the World Rally Championship for 1986 was the Swedish, where Ford entered a pair of RS200s driven by Swedes Blomqvist and Kalle Grundel, Blomqvist retiring from third place with engine problems and Grundel finishing in third position overall. Thereafter, bad luck was to hinder the team and of 67 starts the team managed 19 wins, finishing in the top three places on 32 occasions. However, 1986 was to be notable for the number of rally accidents and fatalities with even some spectators being killed. The international authority, FISA, acted swiftly and decreed that the World Series for 1987 would be contested with less spectacular Group A cars, homologation rules dictating the manufacture of at least 5,000 units. For

Ford, this meant a radical change in policy and, despite the RS200's rumoured £10 million investment, sadly the programme was dropped in favour of the Sierra RS Cosworth and Sierra 4×4. Of the 200 RS200 built, Turner decided that some 120 would be sold off, lucky customers paying around £50,000 for a car in road trim. Others were held back to be broken down and used as spares.

Today, the RS200 is the ultimate Ford collector's item, representing state-of-the-art design and manufacture, in a sleek, timeless body with power to match. For those involved with the project, the RS200 programme was an interlude which was both demanding yet rewarding – and one which, almost certainly, will never be repeated.

Index